The Films of Luis Buñuel

Subjectivity and Desire

PETER WILLIAM EVANS

CLARENDON PRESS · OXFORD

1995

Oxford University Press, Walton Street, Oxford OX2 6DP

Oxford New York
Athens Auckland Bangkok Bombay
Calcutta Cape Town Dar es Salaam Delhi
Florence Hong Kong Istanbul Karachi
Kuala Lumpur Madras Madrid Melbourne
Mexico City Nairobi Paris Singapore
Taipei Tokyo Toronto
and associated companies in
Berlin Ibadan

Oxford is a trade mark of Oxford University Press

Published in the United States
by Oxford University Press Inc., New York

British Library Cataloguing in Publication Data
Data available

Library of Congress Cataloging in Publication Data
The films of Luis Buñuel : subjectivity and desire / Peter William
Evans.
(Oxford Hispanic studies)
Includes bibliographical references and index.
1. Buñuel, Luis, 1900- —Criticism and interpretation.
I. Evans, Peter William. II. Series.
√ PN1998.3.B86F55 1995
791.43'0233'092—dc20 94–29626
ISBN 0 19 815193 4
ISBN 0 19 815906 4 (Pbk)

1 3 5 7 9 10 8 6 4 2

Typeset by Graphicraft Typesetters Ltd., Hong Kong
Printed in Great Britain
on acid-free paper by Bookcraft Ltd.,
Midsomer Norton, Bath

For Isabel

Oxford Hispanic Studies

General Editor: Paul Julian Smith

The last twenty years have seen a revolution in the humanities. On the one hand, there has been a massive influence on literary studies of other disciplines: philosophy, psychoanalysis, and anthropology. On the other, there has been a displacement of the boundaries of literary studies, an opening out on to other forms of expression: cinema, popular culture, and historical documentation.

The new *Oxford Hispanic Studies* series reflects the fact that Hispanic studies are particularly well placed to take advantage of this revolution. Unlike those working in French or English studies, Hispanists have little reason to genuflect to a canon of European culture which has tended to exclude them. Historically, moreover, Hispanic societies tend to exhibit plurality and difference: thus Medieval Spain was the product of the three cultures of Jew, Moslem, and Christian; modern Spain is a federation of discrete autonomous regions; and Spanish America is a continent in which cultural identity must always be brought into question, can never be taken for granted.

The incursion of new models of critical theory into Spanish-speaking countries has been uneven. And while cultural studies in other language areas have moved through post-structuralism (Lacan, Derrida, Foucault) to create new disciplines focusing on gender, ethnicity, and homosexuality, it is only recently that Hispanists have contributed to the latest fields of enquiry. Now, however, there is an upsurge of exciting new work in both Europe and the Americas. *Oxford Hispanic Studies* is intended to provide a medium for writing engaged in and taking account of these developments. It will serve both as a vehicle and a stimulus for innovative and challenging work in an important and rapidly changing field. The series aims to facilitate both the development of new approaches in Hispanic studies and the awareness of Hispanic studies in other subject areas. It will embrace discussions of literary and non-literary cultural forms, and focus on the publication of illuminating original research and theory.

Acknowledgements

THE seeds of this book were sown in the early summer of 1982 when I had the great honour and pleasure of meeting Luis Buñuel and his wife Jeanne at their house in the Cerrada de Félix Cuevas in Mexico City. Their hospitality and cordiality, as well as Don Luis's cheerful patience in answering my questions, have remained with me ever since. For all their help in leading up to my visit I am indebted to my friends the late George Cheyne and Agustín Sánchez Vidal, and the British Academy who awarded me a grant, without whom the visit would not have been possible. For their companionship, conversation, and support of my work on Buñuel I would like to thank Katie Rutherford, Salvador Bacarisse, Pamela Bacarisse, David McGrath, Michael Wood, Christopher Stone, María Delgado, Nuria Triana, Stephen Roberts, Mª José Martínez Jurico, Xon de Ros, Manucha Lisboa, Jo Labanyi, Marianne Guillon, Christopher Cordess, and Ron Guariento. I have also received help in various ways related to the writing of this book from José Luis Santaolalla, Miguel Angel Ramón, Celestino Deleyto, Leandro Martínez (Departamento de Difusión y Exhibición, Filmoteca Municipal de Zaragoza), Carmen Solano (Departamento de Cultura, Ayuntamiento de Zaragoza), the British Film Institute Stills Library, the Robinson Library at the University of Newcastle upon Tyne, Hilaria Loyo, John Hopewell, and Phil Powrie. My special thanks to Paul Julian Smith for kindly inviting me to write this volume for the Oxford Hispanic Studies series. I would also like to thank the University of Newcastle upon Tyne for granting me leave of absence to complete this work; my colleagues for covering for me during that period; and students in Combined Honours, in the Department of Spanish, Portuguese, and Latin American Studies of the School of Modern Languages, in European Film Studies, and in the Department of Adult Education who attended various courses with which I was involved and in which they contributed so much to discussions on Buñuel. My special thanks to José Luis Borau (for sending me, hot off the press, a copy of Jeanne Rucar de Buñuel's autobiography); to my *compadre* Robin Fiddian for many years of friendship and various involvements in matters related to Spanish film; to Bruce Babington for over twenty years of friendship, stimulating discussion, and collaboration which have helped shape so much of my thinking about film; to Tom and Jenny for tolerating my absences and seemingly endless hours at the word-processor when we might have been watching another film together, or swimming at the club; and to Isabel who in many senses made it all possible.

P.W.E.

Contents

List of Plates

Introduction

'Dangerous woman into what an abyss of misery have you plunged me!'

Matthew Lewis, *The Monk*

RECENT writing on film, especially on the Hollywood cinema and on issues related to authorship, has begun to recover some of the ground lost in the explosion of structuralist and post-structuralist approaches to cultural theory. In discussions of literature the notion of the deconstruction of the author has its origins above all in Nietzsche, Freud, Marx, and their influence over a whole generation of cultural theorists, including, most prominently, Lacan, Althusser, Derrida, Barthes, and Foucault, whose radically new perspectives led to a more rigorous contextualization of cultural production and an inevitable erosion of the previously largely undisputed notion of exclusive authorial hegemony. These trends were very quickly assimilated by film theory and criticism, and death-of-the-author approaches—given their most extreme promotion in Seventies' issues of *Screen*—resulted in writing on film often giving the impression that, since they would inevitably be compromised by bourgeois notions of subjectivity, discussions of authorship had no real place in serious analysis. More recently, though, the author has made something of a comeback. A more balanced approach, acknowledging authorship but giving it a text-based definition that does not dislodge it from historical frameworks and awareness, seems to offer greater scope for theorizing the complex relations between the text and its reception by its various audiences. Models of subjectivity developed by Lacan and Althusser have been enormously important in subverting the idea of the constituting subject as creator of the self, developing instead the notion of a subjectivity produced by psycho-social processes lying outside the individual's control and leading to misrecognition of his or her subjectivity, or to what Althusser calls an 'Imaginary relationship of individuals to their real conditions of existence' (1977: 152). On the other hand, to be too seduced by theories of misrecognition and interpellation (extremely important as it is not to lose sight of them) is to be in danger of leaving virtually no room for resistance, something that recent trends in feminist theory have been keen to address.[1]

As a result, acknowledging and assimilating the force of theoretical and critical developments of the last twenty years or so, more recent work—say, Tania Modleski's on Hitchcock (1988)—has started to question approaches concentrating exclusively on the unconscious as distinct from the conscious determinants and choices underlying any text. Work on Buñuel, however, has largely been free of the de-authorizing tendencies to which most Hollywood or British directors have been subjected, the great majority of discussions of his films taking place within narrowly auteurist frames of reference.[2] Accordingly, while the ultimate priorities of this book are film-centred, prompted by recognition and analysis of the materiality of the text through exploration of the complexities of choices made as well as avoided, the focus will also sometimes ignore the claims of authorship or auteurism, grounding discussion in awareness of the contexts of history and culture and, above all, since sexuality and the relations between the sexes represent perhaps the most significant area of Buñuel's work, of sexual theory.

The perspective is double-focused: from one angle recognizing the stature of one of the great directors of film history, recognizing his relative autonomy in many films, and attempting to explore his work through the range of his many familiar, complex, and iconoclastic obsessions; from another, refusing to be overawed by that authorial presence, arguing that even a director like Buñuel, and not just in those films he referred to as his Mexican 'películas alimenticias' ('bread-and-butter films'), is a construct of culture and history, someone whose exercise of autonomy as a film director was inevitably compromised not only by contributions from other creative personnel or producers involved in the films, but also by historically or culturally determined conscious and unconscious allegiances to aesthetics and ideology.

Of course, wherever he worked, whether in Spain, Mexico, or

---

[1] For a summary of the Althusserian/Lacanian approach to the constitution of subjectivity, see Terry Lovell (1980: esp. 39–46). For a clear summary of feminist arguments and counter-arguments on these issues, see Jackie Byars (1991) and Christine Gledhill (1988).

[2] For a definition of auteurism, see Pam Cook (ed.) (1985: 114–206).

France, whoever his collaborators (screenwriters like Julio Alejandro or Jean-Claude Carrière, directors of cinematography like Gabriel Figueroa or Sacha Vierney), and whatever the sources of inspiration (novels by Galdós, Emily Brontë, and Defoe), Buñuel's films—quarrying disparate texts for material suitable for use in narratives about chance, freedom, constraint, corruption, subjectivity, and desire—retain their characteristically witty subversiveness and their lucid exposure of hypocrisy no matter how unpromising the original material from which he worked. In even his most minor film Buñuel's signature as the great scourge of the bourgeoisie is unmistakable. But these films are also in another sense not simply Buñuel's. They are, additionally, the site for mediation of the multi-textured historical voices of the cultures by which he was formed.

With one or two exceptions (e.g. Linda Williams 1992), writing on subjectivity and desire in Buñuel's films has virtually ignored discussions of these questions through reference to sexual theory. Traditional writing on Buñuel routinely acknowledges Surrealism's debts to psychoanalysis but, beyond either referring in general terms to Oedipality or itemizing the films' 'Freudian symbols', little effort has been made to look more carefully at the links between mainstream psychoanalysis and post-Freudian gender theory of the last twenty years or so, a neglect that has meant lost opportunities in drawing these films and their radical Surrealistic potential for opening up questions related to perception into, for instance, recent film-studies debates about looking and pleasure.

In the chapters that follow, the project of considering Buñuel's films from distant as well as from near perspectives derives its greatest force from linking questions of subjectivity and relations between the sexes with developments in sexual theory, or desire, relying mainly on Freud (especially key works like *The Interpretation of Dreams, Jokes and their Relation to the Unconscious*, papers on paranoia, masochism, narcissism, and femininity) as well as on writing by Melanie Klein, Karen Horney, and more recent psychoanalytically inspired feminist writers, especially Linda Williams, Jessica Benjamin, and Nancy Chodorow. Subjectivity and desire ('desire' used here in a restricted but crucially unifying sexual sense) provide the main focus for discussion because these issues are not only more than usually fascinating in Buñuel, but also keys to many other areas of interest. As the approach is film-centred there is no attempt to fit Buñuel into preconceived theoretical frameworks.

Aware of Buñuel's objectives, the focus is simultaneously alert to the contradictions and inconsistencies of the films, problematizing them and, through critical detachment, exploring their preconceptions and convictions, measuring their truths against their own and alternative constructions of meaning. The discussion of these questions has additionally sought to account for the different stages of Buñuel's work, covering the later sophisticated comedies but also reclaiming some of the lesser-known and insufficiently discussed commercial, as well as more auteuristic, Mexican melodramas. The opportunity is thus taken to explore the creative tensions between the natural instincts of the European art-cinema director and the demands of a box-office-led commercial Mexican cinema. It has also seemed appropriate to structure discussion of these questions around analysis of individual films, although in each case a general preliminary part opens up the specific areas chosen for survey in each film. The book begins with *Le Charme discret de la bourgeoisie*, a film drawing together so many of the threads of Buñuel's work, both as regards content—confusions of identity, Oedipality, exile, sexual desire, and much more—and as regards form, above all the seamless elisions and disturbing, shifting levels of reality in what is perhaps his most brilliant dream narrative. Chapter 2 considers— in the context of commercial (*Susana, Una mujer sin amor*) as well as more personal films (*Los olvidados*)—the family melodrama, allegiances and indifference to generic traditions, and the use of Mexican stars and mediated contemporary Mexican realities. Chapter 3 highlights three films, two Mexican (*Ensayo de un crimen* and *El*) and one, his very last, French (*Cet obscur objet du désir*), that most obviously focus on questions of masculinity and its various discontents. Chapter 4 reverses the process, looking at Buñuel's attempts in *Le Journal d'une femme de chambre* and *Belle de jour* to see things from the woman's point of view.

Devoting the main section of a chapter to analysis of an individual film means that discussion can be detailed, focusing attention on the text itself rather than becoming an excuse for abstract theory, but it also means that there are bound to be many unfortunate omissions. Nevertheless, although much greater attention has been paid here to those films on which Buñuel's reputation has traditionally rested—*Los olvidados, El, Ensayo de un crimen*, *Le Journal d'une femme de chambre*, *Belle de jour*, *Le Charme discret de la bourgeoisie*, *Cet obscur objet du désir*—others, usually either ignored or dismissed as hack work undertaken for purely economic reasons, are given extensive mention, whether in detailed analysis (*Susana*, *Una mujer sin amor*) or at appropriate points throughout the book. Concentration on these films has meant denying more than cursory reference to extraordinarily interesting ones like *The Young One* (1960), *Robinson Crusoe* (1952), *Viridiana* (1961), *Tristana* (1970), *La Voie lactée* (1969), and *Le Fantôme de la liberté* (1974). But, while allusion to these films in the discussion of those that have been chosen does them no real justice, the selection of the latter has been made on the basis of their coverage of the main areas of aesthetic, thematic, historical, or cultural significance in Buñuel's films as a whole.

Underlying them all is a profound sense of exile, a theme characteristic of almost all Buñuel's work, sometimes indirectly, as in *The Young One*'s narrative of racial prejudice against a black musician accused of rape, and sometimes directly, as in the representation of Latin America in the 'European' narrative *Le Charme discret de la bourgeoisie*.[3] At the most obvious level, Buñuel's necessary departure from Spain at the end of the Civil War in view of his Republican sympathies—after producing (as distinct from directing) four films at Filmófono, Spain's more liberal studio in the 1930s—moving first to the USA and then to Mexico, meant that he was to remain (until it was too late to take advantage of changed political circumstances after Franco's death) a wanderer, his material home in foreign parts, his memories and desires locked in the Spain of his childhood and youth. In one way this led, from the point of view of engagement with Mexican realities, to an outsider's impartial scrutinies, a perspective remaining largely free of the pressures to which his Mexican contemporaries (in the cinema, above all, Emilio 'El Indio' Fernández) were more usually subject. Buñuel was thus better placed to observe and comment on the difficulties and failures, as well as the achievements, of Mexican society, but his efforts were not always appreciated, with Mexican intellectuals and others failing sometimes to concur with the view, aptly expressed by Raymond Durgnat, that 'any attempt to escape a culture

[3] On exile and other matters related to Buñuel, see the excellent very recent book by Marsha Kinder (1993).

needs help from outside that culture if it is to succeed' (Durgnat 1968: 95). Indirect criticism through the ironies of commercial films like *Susana* managed to escape the condemnation of Buñuel's new compatriots, whereas, when it came unalloyed and direct, as in *Los olvidados*, it provoked a huge national outcry. But, of course, Buñuel's place in Mexican culture and society could only ever be equivocal because, at another level, it is arguable that, in some senses and in some ways, all of the films he made there retained, to a greater or lesser extent, their Spanish perspective.

Buñuel's formative years in Spain—so thoroughly and expertly described by Agustín Sánchez Vidal (1988)—left an imprint never to be completely erased throughout the remainder of his long career in exile.[4] Though admittedly not bereft, like other exiles, of his own language, he was nevertheless severed from roots and customs, habits of mind and pleasures, making films in which the recurrent and related motifs of journeys and various forms of confinement express the inner loneliness of someone destined for many years to play out in his mind the memories of what eventually becomes a fantasy homeland. Exile, of course, has its many advantages, through distance creating awareness of the realities not only of one's adopted homeland, but also of the country left behind.

Born with the century, Buñuel soon disappointed his parents not only by abandoning prospects of a career in engineering, but also by going into films, a calling so shameful it provoked his mother to tears. Yet for all the traumatic cultural influences of his childhood, like the ambivalent effects of a Catholic upbringing, he was also exposed in early years to more creative cultural influences, including of course the work of fellow Aragonese figures like Goya and Gracián, whose shadows hang over his work so much.[5] Buñuel actually wrote a script for a Goya biopic,[6] reproduced his paintings (in *Cela s'appelle l'aurore*, 1955, and *Le Fantôme de la liberté*), and was inspired by his portrait of Saturn devouring his offspring to add characteristically witty and subversive touches to *Tristana*. These are obvious links, but Goya's macabre humour repeatedly finds room for expression throughout

---

[4] See also, for the early years of Buñuel's career, C. B. Morris (1980).

[5] On Buñuel's indebtedness to Gracián, see Carlos Saura (1993).

[6] The film script, with an introduction by Gonzalo M. Borrás Gualis, has recently been published (Buñuel 1992). The script of *Là-bas* has also recently been published for the first time in the same series (Buñuel 1990).

the full range of Buñuel's films. Gracián's presence is also very noticeable, his cynical, world-weary attitudes of *desengaño* ('disillusionment') *vis-à-vis* all human aspiration and achievement, including love, providing Buñuel with a necessary antidote to the French Surrealists' more lyrical celebrations of *amour fou* to which he was also strongly drawn.[7] From the Spanish tradition, too, experiments in narrative and deviant psychology can also be traced to the picaresque novel, to Valle-Inclán and to Galdós—*Los olvidados*, *Nazarín* (1958), and *Tristana* are all in various ways indebted to these earlier writers and texts—while Buñuel's fascination with mystery is at least partly inspired by Spain's Romantics, especially Zorilla, whose Don Juan Tenorio is a recurrent motif in Buñuel's life and art, and Bécquer, one of whose stories provides the starting-point for a narrative segment in *Le Fantôme de la liberté*.

Perhaps it is the *agreste* landscape of Aragón ('wild', though inadequate, is the closest that English comes to the Spanish word) that drew Buñuel to the *other*, not just as regards questions of sexuality, but also of setting. Bécquer in Spain, but also the other Gothic novelists—Lewis, Maturin, and so on—inspired Buñuel to introduce Gothic elements into his own work. *Los olvidados*, *Le Charme discret*, and *Abismos de pasión*—the latter based on *Wuthering Heights*, a text so special to the Surrealists because of its eulogy of *amour fou*—are only three films that recreate the Poe-like atmosphere of deranged reverie and the uncanny in the most unexpected places: dream sequences in *Los olvidados* and *Le Charme discret* not only replay, through their rhetoric of horror, Freudian primal scenes, but also redefine the Gothic in terms of more contemporary *mise-en-scènes* and narratives; the Yorkshire moors of *Wuthering Heights* become an arid Mexican landscape in *Abismos de pasión*.

Linking all these strands together is Buñuel's interest in Sade,

---

[7] On the links between love and death, see Pérez Turrent and de la Colina (1993: 115): 'Para mí, la fornicación tiene algo de terrible. La cópula, considerada objetivamente, me parece risible y a la vez trágica. Es lo más parecido a la muerte: los ojos en blanco, los espasmos, la baba. Y la fornicación es diabólica: siempre veo al diablo en ella.' ('For me, fornication has something terrible about it. Coupling, considered objectively, seems ludicrous to me, and also tragic. It resembles dying: eyes blank, spasms, dribbling. And fornication is diabolical. I always see the devil in it.') The description finds its perfect visual equivalents in *Un chien andalou*, where the young man at one point looks like Buñuel's description of the lover here, and in *Susana*, where the anti-heroine is regularly described as the devil.

a figure of endless fascination to him, not just because of his Gargantuan sexual appetites and experiments but also because of what Buñuel regarded as his admirable desire for total, unconditional freedom.[8] Yet, of course, when Buñuel refers to Sade's liberating force on his own work—'La imaginación es libre; el hombre no' (in Pérez Turrent and de la Colina 1993: 32) ('The imagination is free, man is not')—the work of deconstruction begins, for, however potent the ideal, the reality surely escapes few of the constraints of ordinary human thought and behaviour. The pursuit of freedom, the desire to transgress the constricting norms of his provincial middle-class upbringing, led to an interest in Freud and Surrealism, something which coincided with his friendship with Lorca at the Residencia de Estudiantes in Madrid, Spain's own mini Oxbridge, a period in which Buñuel also came to know, among others, Dalí, Gómez de la Serna (both of whom had a profound influence on him)[9] and Giménez Caballero, by whom he was appointed film critic on the *Gaceta literaria*, a post that fuelled his already growing interest in the cinema and led to articles on Abel Gance, Fritz Lang, Theodor Dreyer and, elsewhere, on the silent comic stars.[10] Buñuel's knowledge of Freud (and also Jung) was extensive. Having read *The Interpretation of Dreams* as a student, he was also very familiar—from the evidence of films like *El*, *Ensayo de un crimen*, and *Belle de jour*—with many other key texts, including those on paranoia and femininity. His interest in Freud (later somewhat ironized through remarks by largely comic characters like the ambassador of Miranda in *Le Charme discret*) paralleled Breton's many flattering references in the *Manifeste du surréalisme* (Breton 1988) and elsewhere. Buñuel's narratives, either in their entirety, as in *Un Chien andalou*, *Belle de jour*, *La Voie lactée*, or *Le*

---

[8] On Robert Desnos's introduction of Buñuel to Sade, see Pérez Turrent and de la Colina (1993: 29): 'En Sade descubrí un mundo de subversión extraordinario, en el que entra todo: desde los insectos a las costumbres de la sociedad humana, el sexo, la teología.' ('In Sade I discovered an extraordinary subversive world, which covers everything: from insects to human customs, sex and theology.') For the Sade-related idea that only in the imagination is it possible to be truly free, see Pérez Turrent and de la Colina (1993: 32).

[9] For Buñuel's admiring references to Gómez de la Serna, see Buñuel (1982*a*: 70–2) and Monegal (1993: 25–38).

[10] On Buñuel's fondness for the silent comic stars, see Pérez Turrent and de la Colina (1993: 19). In this respect it is interesting that Buñuel liked reading Benjamin Péret the Surrealist, chiefly because of his humour (Pérez Turrent and de la Colina 1993: 21).

Fantôme de la liberté, or at various points, as in, say, *Los olvidados*, *Tristana*, or *Viridiana*, rely on dreams. Flippant remarks by Buñuel himself about slipping in a dream to fill up space need not detract from recognition of the Surrealistic origins of his interest in Freudian dream theory and its potential for an exploration of the mystery and cryptic, opaque poetry of the unconscious, a fascination acquiring its most intricate treatment in *Le Charme discret de la bourgeoisie*.

As these films are often dependent not just on dream or reverie imagery but also on comedy, it has often proved useful to theorize the comic mode of Buñuel's narratives through what is probably the most brilliant analysis of comedy, Freud's *Jokes and their Relation to the Unconscious*. Buñuel's films are usually devoid of the kinds of verbal joke that Freud analyses in the first part of this work, but Freud's essay on comedy and his remarks about humour, especially, are highly relevant to a discussion of Buñuel's comedy of desire (in particular, *Le Charme discret* and *Cet obscur objet*).

Buñuel's interest in Freudian theory is always complemented by social and political awareness.[11] Flirting with Communism, he never joined the party but was always ready to dramatize the social and political causes of various kinds of disturbance, dreams and comedy providing the disruptive mechanisms to expose the inhibitions of the psyche. Off-screen, Buñuel himself draws attention to these perspectives:

El surrealismo me ha hecho comprender que la libertad y la justicia no existen, pero me ha aportado también una moral. Una moral sobre la solidaridad humana cuya importancia para mí había sido comprendida por Eluard y Breton cuando me llamaban con humor 'el director de conciencia'. (Buñuel 1985*a*: 34)

(Surrealism has made me understand that liberty and justice do not exist, but it has also given me a sense of morality. A morality about human solidarity whose importance for me had been understood by Eluard and Breton when they used to call me, jokingly, the 'director of conscience'.)

The documentary *Las Hurdes*, and then his first international success in Mexico, *Los olvidados*, are among the cinema's most vivid exposures of the social determinants of tragedy. Both films

---

[11] This is something also acknowledged by Víctor Fuentes, who considers that Buñuel is always interested in 'la realidad social, . . . la problemática de la persona en relación con las demás personas' (Fuentes 1993: 32) ('social reality, . . . questions about the individual and his or her relations with others').

were made with relative autonomy, offered to Buñuel as a sort of reward for the box-office success of *El gran calavera* (1949). With traces of De Sica's *Sciuscia* (1946) and Hollywood delinquent films like *Boys' Town* (1938) or *Angels with Dirty Faces* (1938), *Los olvidados* is a modern horror story of the Mexican slums, a narrative of neglect unambiguously pinning the blame for delinquency on a politics of indifference.

Yet Buñuel was as much a director of commercial as of art-house films and simply to ignore the mass-audience-orientated melodramas, comedies, and musicals as economically motivated aberrations leads only to a distortion of his overall achievement. At the very least, these films are interesting in terms of their challenges and compromises for a director whose instincts were largely ill at ease with the aesthetic and ideological commonplaces with which they were identified. But, equally interestingly, made with a mixture of respect and—through irony, humour, and sex—mild subversion, they are also significant texts, testimony to Buñuel's interest in popular forms and in their hold over audiences, raising important questions about identity and sexuality. The section on family melodrama considers the collisions between Mexican and European traditions: the films are firmly contextualized in the popular generic forms of Mexican melodrama but attention is also paid to European elements of narrative (*Una mujer sin amor* is based on a Maupassant story), psychology (*Susana* seems very much indebted to Freud's early daughter's seduction theory), and neo-realism (*Los olvidados* is in some ways in dialogue with, for instance, *Roma, città aperta*, 1945).[12] All of them, auteurist or popular, are fascinating examples of culture's mediations of the vicissitudes of desire and family life. It is even arguable that the enforced aesthetic and ideological constraints of the popular films reflect more unambiguously through their mechanisms of displacement what is both for Buñuel—significantly described by Fernando Rey as someone more often drawing back from than yielding to excess (in Aub 1985: 461)—and for dominant elements of the cultures for whom he speaks, both approvingly and subversively, the inseparability of sexuality and sin, something retaining its force even after the loss of religious faith. In conversation with Max Aub he confesses: 'Para mí, toda la vida, el coito y el pecado han

---

[12] Buñuel claims he hated the film (1982a: 278).

sido una misma cosa. Aun cuando perdí la fe. Es curioso, pierde uno la fe, pero no el sentimiento del pecado' (Aub 1985: 160). ('For me, throughout my life, coitus and sin have been the same thing. Even when I lost my faith. It's strange, one loses one's faith but not the feeling of sin.') Buñuel's popular Mexican melodramas are an indispensable source of information both for the history of the Mexican cinema—in that they simultaneously extend, respect, and provide critical commentary on some of its forms—and for their exposure from different perspectives of his own enduring preoccupations.

One of the most disappointing aspects of Buñuel's career as a director was his failure, despite all his efforts to the contrary while in America, to have more than the negligible impact on the Hollywod cinema of a nevertheless characteristic scene in Florey's *The Beast with Five Fingers* (1946). *Robinson Crusoe* and *The Young One*, both in English, are not Hollywood but they do show what might have been possible. Each in its own way, like his Mexican *El río y la muerte* (1954)—as Raymond Durgnat (1968) rightly argues, a sort of Mexican Western—borrows from and reshapes Hollywood adventure and melodramatic genres. The popular films, in which he used the various resources of the commercial cinema (including stars like Jorge Negrete, Pedro Armendáriz, and Katy Jurado), placed him under the same sorts of pressure and constraint as those endured by his great *émigré* contemporaries in Hollywood: Sirk, Lang, and Hitchcock, among others. On his own admission, the Hollywood cinema was capable of the finest films made anywhere in the world: although detesting militaristic films like *From Here to Eternity* (1953), he adored others like *The Portrait of Jennie* (1948) and *The Treasure of the Sierra Madre* (1947).[13] But perhaps if Buñuel had made his mark in Hollywood, he might never have gone on to make the great films of his maturity, largely free of production constraints, marvellous experiments in form, even though by then they had become more ambivalent and more tolerant of the eccentricities and failings of human behaviour.[14]

---

[13] See Buñuel (1982a: 277–8).

[14] Víctor Fuentes argues that there is a difference between Buñuelian and Hollywood characters in that for Buñuel there is a 'fracaso de los héroes de la voluntad, quienes, por el contrario, suelen salir triunfadores en el cine de Hollywood' (Fuentes 1993: 98) ('will-governed heroes thrive in Hollywood films, while in Buñuel's they are destroyed'). For further reference to Buñuel's time in Hollywood, see Rubio (1992).

The last two sections of the book, looking at male and female subjectivity and desire, explore the extent to which Buñuel's approach is directed towards mixing the ruthless, implacable exposure of extreme situations, which takes the audience to the very edge of experience, with a rhetoric of compassion and tolerance. Some films are governed almost relentlessly by an atmosphere of darkness and despair: *Los olvidados, Abismos de pasión, Tristana*, and *El bruto* (1952) come into this category. In most of the other films, especially the very late ones, darkness is lightened above all through humour and gestures of humanity, bearing out a conviction that providential coincidences, aleatory laws of destiny, the constraints of social and family structures, and cultural determinants largely shape our chaotic desires. For this reason there are very few irredeemable, thoroughgoing villains in Buñuel: 'En mis películas nadie es fatalmente malo ni enteramente bueno. No soy... ¿cómo se dice ahora?... no soy maniqueo' (Pérez Turrent and de la Colina 1993: 52). ('In my films no one is fatally evil or entirely good. I am not... how does one put it nowadays?... I am not Manichean.') Fernando Rey's perhaps initially somewhat surprising references to Buñuel's tenderness and to what he considers to be the dominant theme of his films— 'el ser humano tratado con terrible injusticia por la Naturaleza y por las estructuras creadas a su alrededor' (Aub 1985: 464) ('humans treated with terrible injustice by Nature and by the structures created all around them')—seem apt as an introduction to any preliminary understanding of his characters' struggles for access to grace and fulfilment, pursuing the phantoms of love and liberty through the interminable labyrinths of subjectivity and desire.[15]

---

[15] Joan Mellen has a slightly different focus on this: 'Hope is kept alive in these dark films of Buñuel, where the rule of the bourgeoisie seems interminable, by the director's faith in his enemy's historical demise' (1978: 11).

Roads to and from the Abyss:
Le Charme discret de la bourgeoisie and the Comedy of Desire

'¿Qué pasión hay, dime por tu vida, Fortuna amiga, que no se ciegue?'

Baltasar Gracián, *El Criticón*

('Tell me, friend Fortune, which passion is not blind?')

PLOT SYNOPSIS: In Paris, a group of bourgeois friends—the Ambassador of Miranda, M. and Mme Sénéchal, M. and Mme Thévenot, and Florence, Mme Thévenot's sister—constantly invite one another to dinner. The Ambassador and Mme Thévenot are lovers. Eventually the group is joined by a bishop who begins work as a gardener *chez* M. and Mme Sénéchal. The frequent rendezvous of the friends are interrupted by five dreams or reveries (their own or those of other characters) and, even more mysteriously, by shots throughout the narrative of the group, but not including the bishop, walking down a country road. Again with the exception of the bishop, the men in the group are involved in drug-trafficking. Although they are eventually arrested, a high-ranking government minister orders their release.

Like the Sade of the poem 'El prisionero' (1949) by Octavio Paz (Buñuel-admirer and fellow Mexican Surrealist), the sextet of friends in *Le Charme discret de la bourgeoisie* are both liberated and trapped: liberated by Sadean appeals to self-gratifying desires and by economic and social privilege, trapped by *le hasard* and by culture—their brisk stroll along an anonymous country road suggesting urgent flight from rational urbanity. Though this image often acts as a sort of counterpoint to the atmosphere of claustrophobia elsewhere built up in the film, the road seems to be leading the friends nowhere, and we are never allowed to see their journey's end. The open road remains an interminable blind alley, its phantom travellers' destination, like *Pedro Páramo*'s Comala, only the dream of a vanished world (Rulfo 1973).

This tension between strivings for liberty and various forms of frustration and entrapment is characteristic of many Buñuel films. The narratives of *La Voie lactée*, *Nazarín*, and *Le Fantôme de la liberté*, for instance, are all driven by the idea of a journey or quest, mainly spiritual in the first two, mainly psychological and social in the third; *Robinson Crusoe*, *The Young One*, *El ángel exterminador*, and *La Fièvre monte à El Pao* reverse the process, imprisoning their characters physically and inwardly, ridiculing initiatives seeking lasting freedoms. In *Nazarín* the narrative follows a pattern of endless on-the-road humiliations and entrapment, in which Nazarín himself, to whose quixotic mind all life is a sort of journey in the footsteps of Christ, and his companions witness the confinement of individuals, sometimes in literal, sometimes in mental and emotional forms of cul-de-sac or imprisonment, whose realistic hopes of finding liberation are dashed on the very roads they choose to freedom. Slightly more positively, in *La Fièvre monte à El Pao* what for its hero Vázquez begins as a world of rigid authoritarian control and tyranny eventually becomes one in which he finds temporary release through restored ideals of self-sacrifice and idealism, the physical boundaries of the island setting (as in *Robinson Crusoe*, *The Young One*, and *Cela s'appelle l'aurore*) being transcended inwardly, even if only momentarily, through the triumph of morality over corruption.

While in some films—*Los olvidados*, *Abismos de pasión*, *Tristana*— the processes of discovery and liberation, of quests for lost selves and desires struggling for expression through the repressions of the super-ego are darkly pessimistic, in *Le Charme discret* the fumbling search for freedom, for ill-defined instincts of what Bakhtin has termed 'festivity' (1968), for epiphanies of love and self-knowledge, is mediated through a gentler rhetoric, through comic rather than through satirical treatment of the aspirations and practices of the bourgeoisie. Buñuel himself declares that the film avoids the cutting edge of satire, preferring the softer, more indulgent tone of comedy: 'No es una sátira, y mucho menos feroz. Creo que es la película que he hecho con un espíritu de humor más amable' ('It's not a satire, let alone a fierce one. I think it's my most gently humorous film'). For this, of course, he has been rebuked by more socially orientated critics, disappointed to find the old Surrealist's powder no longer dry.

Perhaps the late films do reflect a more comfortable accommodation with the class whose tics and tyrannies he had been more eager to denounce in his youth, but, for all its corrupt

tolerance, *Le Charme* is a film turning on a whole range of structural devices that locate the expression of desire within the framework of traditional mechanisms of humour, jokes, and comedy,
as vibrant here, almost at the end of his career, as at the very
beginning of it. Like most other areas of Buñuel's work, his
comedy is more indebted to Freud than he has cared to admit.
In some ways his most consistently comic film, *Le Charme* is also
perhaps Buñuel's most complex and most relentlessly oneiric
work.[1] Both comedy and dream-work exemplify Freud's explorations of the unconscious.

Like the overall comic mode through which the dreams and
dream-like memories (these are the young cavalry lieutenant's,
which because of their oneiric structure I shall henceforward
include among the film's authentic dreams), as well as all the
other narrative segments, are transmitted, the dreams themselves
carry mainly sexual and Oedipal meanings. Although the five
dreams cover at manifest levels a wide range of obsessions and
anxieties they are also all in some ways at latent levels either
directly or indirectly Oedipal.[2] Like the dreams, the comedy is
also ultimately related, whatever its manifest form, to latent
Oedipal/sexual subtexts.

At manifest levels, Buñuel's films defy classification under
unified theories of the comic. While earlier films, say, *Gran Casino*
(1946), focus on the absurdities of Mexican *ranchero* genres or,
as in *Nazarín* or *Simón del desierto* (1965), on religious oddities or
hallucinations, *Le Charme discret* scrutinizes the idiosyncrasies of
language, dress, dinner-engagement or cocktail-party etiquette
of late Sixties' and Seventies' bourgeois French society. Here
Buñuel's comedy seems to bear out Freud's remarks on humour
(in the last section of the analysis of the relations between jokes
and the comic), where, in distinguishing humour from comedy
and jokes, he reflects on mechanisms giving pleasure through
normally distressing affects:

Now humour is a means of obtaining pleasure in spite of the distressing
affects that interfere with it; it acts as a substitute for the generation of
these affects, it puts itself in their place. The conditions for its appearance

---

[1] For Agustín Sánchez Vidal (1984: 353) the film's form 'trata de mostrar muy
sutilmente la inseguridad de un orden basado en convencionalismos sumamente
frágiles' ('tries to show very carefully the insecurity of an order based on conventions
that are extremely fragile').

[2] For the distinction between manifest and latent levels of dream work, see Freud
(1982: 381).

are given if there is a situation in which, according to our usual habits, we should be tempted to release a distressing affect and if motives then operate upon us which suppress that affect *in statu nascendi* . . . The pleasure of humour, if this is so, comes about—we cannot say otherwise —at the cost of a release of affect that does not occur; it arises from an economy in the expenditure of affect. (Freud 1983: 293)

Don Quixote is one of Freud's examples of a humorous character, one who starts out as purely comic, a 'big child', but who through gradual acquisition of wisdom and noble purpose becomes a symbol of idealism, taking seriously its aims and duties, the humour of his situation deriving precisely from his seriousness. So, in Buñuel's films, Nazarín is ultimately a humorous figure, his mishaps and humiliations allowing us to draw pleasure from his serious but ultimately futile commitment to Christian ideals. This kind of humour is also available in *Le Charme discret* through the figure of Don Raphael, the ambassador to France of the fictitious Latin American Republic of Miranda, towards whom, as with Sir John Falstaff, our response originates in 'an economy in contempt and indignation' (Freud 1983: 296–7). A self-seeker and drug-trafficker, adulterer and fascist, he is ultimately given a more redemptive aura through wit, elegance, and charm—all qualities relayed through the overwhelmingly favourable rhetoric of Fernando Rey's star meanings, often in Buñuel's films given loosely autobiographical significance.[3]

These links have even been stressed in interview by Rey himself, but the matter is complex. In various ways, radical differences distance more than unite the pair. On the grounds of look, age, and background, at the very least, difference exceeds similarity.[4] But Rey's narrative function in the four films he made with Buñuel often opens up questions of autobiography, allowing Buñuel opportunities for either rediscovering and exploring his Spanish roots (as in *Viridiana* and *Tristana*) or reflecting his outsider status as the eternal *émigré*, whether in Mexico or Europe (as in *Le Charme discret* and *Cet obscur objet*). On the one hand both Rey's background—Galician by birth, Madrilenian by upbringing—and his early career in the Francoist Cifesa melodramas —e.g. *La princesa de los Ursinos* (1947), *Don Quijote de la Mancha* (1948), *Locura de amor* (1948), *Agustina de Aragón* (1950)—set him

[3] Virginia Higginbotham (1979: 167) rightly notes that the comedy is not centred on one person, but rather, as in a Mack Sennett film, on a group of characters.
[4] In 'The Life and Times of Don Luis Buñuel', *Arena*, BBC, 11 Feb. 1984.

apart from Buñuel, whose Surrealist, neo-Marxist sympathies and
Aragonese origins so conspicuously define his on- and off-screen
persona. On the other, though, they were united by Republican
sympathies: Rey's father was a Republican army officer, and he
himself fought in the Civil War on the Republican side. In due
course Rey's conservative roles began to give way to the more
subversive roles he played in the 'New' Spanish Cinema: *Esa
pareja feliz* (1951) (*That Happy Couple*), *Bienvenido, Míster Marshall*
(1952), (*Welcome, Mr Marshall*), and others. For a Hispanic audience Rey's appearances as Jaime in *Viridiana* or Lope in *Tristana*
suggest all sorts of localized meanings, among them that the
professed liberal's deep-rooted conservatism originates in identifications with the conventional, sometimes authoritarian, roles
of his Cifesa period. Denied access to such knowledge, the international audience relies much more heavily on the sign-systems
in operation in the films themselves, and on the intertextual
resonances shared with other international films, for example
The Adventurers (1970) or *The French Connection* (1972). Rey's meanings, whether formulated through knowledge of the Cifesa or
'New' Cinema roles or exclusively on the basis of his international appearances, evolve from identifications with a contradictory mixture of convention and transgression. In all four Buñuel
roles he represents authority. His status as landowner (*Viridiana*),
guardian (*Tristana*), ambassador (*Le Charme discret*), or idle wealthy
bourgeois *(Cet obscur objet)* emphasizes his identifications with
tradition and privilege. The Cifesa films, where he usually plays
a patriot of some sort or other, similarly emphasize these tendencies. In Buñuel his conservatism is projected not only through
narrative function but also through speech and dress. In *Le Charme
discret* the sentiment of Don Raphael's polite but vacuous or
patronizing linguistic mannerisms is perfectly suited to Rey's
calm, fluent delivery in a Hispanicized pronunciation of a patrician form of French. Furthermore, in keeping with the patterns
of dominant class dress described by Bourdieu (1984: 200–1),
Rey's clothes, resisting working-class preference for a function-
alist style, prioritizing the impact of form and a concern to introduce formality into all levels of daily life, provide more clues
to his bourgeois affiliations. In the two earlier films, *Viridiana*
and *Tristana*, the Rey character has fallen on hard times, but
when, in the latter, fortune eventually smiles, little time is lost
in restocking a wardrobe with essential items of bourgeois chic.

The Rey look of discreetly 'conspicuous consumption'—Thorstein Veblen's key description of bourgeois display (1970)—reaches its most complete form in *Cet obscur objet*. Here the bourgeoisie's dapper diplomat, the club-class man about international lounges strolls through the narrative in perfectly styled designer suits and casual clothes leaping off the pages of glossy fashion magazines. Yet always, beneath the veneer of middle-class semiotics of speech, gesture, and dress, glimmers of subversion ever threaten to compromise the image of conformist urbanity. The order of the perfectly trimmed beard and moustache is undermined by unmistakable signs of carnal surrender, like the slightly overfed cheeks and the amused, ironized air of a man perhaps ultimately aware of the absurdities of elegant, formalized language and the repressive behaviour of which they are merely the outward expression.

Even in *Le Charme discret*, Don Raphael's most sinister remarks or acts are surrounded by disarming compensations. When, for instance, he describes Miranda's need to rid itself of dissident elements, his casual, amusingly non-plussed analogy with the swatting of flies and his characteristically visual and verbal *savoirfaire* undermine outrage at the ruthless cruelties of many authentic Latin American regimes whose spirit at one level he plainly represents.

In his dealings, too, with the female terrorist, at first shooting her mechanical toys outside the embassy gates with an airgun, later fondling her breasts and nether regions while checking to see whether she is armed, and then urging her to use her body not for the political but for the sexual gratification of her country's heroes, the suaveness and self-contained unflappability of the character soften the grotesque political and sexual/political prejudices of the degenerate bourgeois.

In Raphael's transgressions against decent standards of moral or political behaviour may be glimpsed the Sadean terrorism of a Surrealist once more momentarily declaring war on all norms and standards, not just those that most people normally find objectionable. In this respect the Almodóvar of his day, Buñuel sometimes looks for humour in even its most unrepentantly unfeminist forms. Refusing to be denied access to normally taboo areas, Buñuel suffers few anxieties (in a film made against the background of late-Sixties' and early-Seventies' explosions of interest in feminism—at first, of course, in the USA, and later in France and elsewhere in Europe) about the inclusion of a

scene partially deriving its humour from the sexual humiliation
of a woman. There is nothing here of the edginess or hesitation
of his contemporary, Woody Allen, another comic analyst of desire
whose Annie Halls and other heroines normally escape comic
victimization of this type. But scenes like these are balanced in
Buñuel's work by others, as here in *Le Charme*, for instance, where
Bulle Ogier's Florence displays in her rebelliousness and transgressions against various bourgeois forms of etiquette—taking
back flowers from the hosts of a postponed dinner party, flouting
middle-class rationality through interest in a significantly irrational science like astrology, or drinking excessively and vomit-
ing out of the window of the Cadillac that eternally transports
the group to their various dinner rendezvous—an embryonic
feminism striking at specifically male as well as generally bourgeois standards of behaviour. In the last film, too, *Cet obscur objet
du désir*, Conchita's attack on Mateo expresses the rage and
frustrations of the Seventies' New Woman against not only the
eccentric individuality of her would-be ageing lover, but also all
his outmoded, latent, and overt antifeminism. Bulle Ogier's
gestures of defiance against the bourgeois order belong to the
film's patterns of Oedipal transgression. The film approves of
such defiance, at one moment, when the diners converge on the
Sénéchal home for the first of their interrupted dinner parties,
allowing her to move in close-up (rare in Buñuel) towards the
centre of the frame, in a way that eventually blots out the hud-
dled group in the drawing-room background, her face of ennui
and detachment providing a mute but resonant commentary on
the trivialities of bourgeois pursuits and conversations taking
place elsewhere in the room.

In the same scene the comedy of bourgeois manners adopts
a double focus through the humiliation of Raphael's chauffeur
Maurice. François Thévenot's exposure of the social failings of
the proletariat also carries Buñuel's exemplification of the bourgeois sense of humour. In so far as the comic humiliation of the
unfortunate Maurice takes the form of an experiment on proletarian drinking etiquette—correct and incorrect ways of drinking
dry martinis—the joke also has an autobiographical dimension,
through which Buñuel at once addresses that coterie of five or
six friends for whom he says he made his films and admits complicity in the formulation of laws of taste and prejudice to which
outsiders and unsophisticates fall victim. Buñuel's thoughts,

amounting to a mini-treatise on the preparation, serving, and consumption of the dry martini, his favourite aperitif, are wittily recorded in *Mon dernier soupir*: 'Un bon dry-martini, disait-on à une certaine époque en Amérique, doit ressembler à la conception de la Vierge. On sait en effet que selon saint Thomas d'Aquin le pouvoir générateur du Saint-Esprit traversa l'hymen de la Vierge "comme un rayon de soleil passe à travers une vitre, sans la briser". De même pour le Noilly-Prat, disait-on. Mais cela me semble un peu excessif' (Buñuel 1982*a*: 54). ('A good dry Martini, one used to say at one time in America, should resemble the Virgin birth. One knows in fact that according to St Thomas Aquinas the creative power of the Holy Spirit penetrated the hymen of the Virgin "as a ray of sunshine passes through glass, without breaking it". You could say the same for a Noilly-Prat. But that may be going too far.')

As Thévenot is something of an old bore, Buñuel implicitly ridicules his own wearisome eccentricities. Nevertheless, Thévenot's dry-martini metaphysics lack no admirers among his bourgeois audience, Maurice becoming the naïve butt of what really amounts to Freud's definition, referring specifically to verbal jokes, of tendentious comedy. The relativity of comedy is again stressed in this scene. What is uncontroversial and practical for the chauffeur—knocking the Martini back in one gulp—is to the bourgeois, offended as much by the crudity of the gesture as by ignorance of what the film ultimately knows to be merely arbitrary codes of etiquette, the operation of a comic law. Maurice is the embodiment of Freud's 'naïve', whose remarks and actions disregard inhibition because it is not something by which he is affected. Freud goes on to argue (1983: 241) that the 'naïve occurs far the most often in children, and is then carried over to uneducated adults, whom we may regard as childish so far as their intellectual development is concerned'. For the film, though, the comedy derives not so much from the wretched Maurice's *naïveté* and ignorance of the bourgeois arts of cocktail-taking as more precisely from the exposure of the arbitrariness of those norms, and from what Bergson would have termed the mechanization of those who make of them the measure of their lives.[5]

Thévenot's patronizing reaction towards Maurice's social

---

[5] Carlos Barbáchano (1986: 187) refers to Buñuel's satire of empty bourgeois rituals.

blunder is prohibited expression in front of Maurice himself by the protocols of bourgeois orthodoxy. These are inhibitions shared by most of Buñuel's bourgeois characters: 'no dejes nada por cortesía' ('don't leave anything out of politeness'), a female guest remarks in *El ángel exterminador*, 'cortesía' here invoked as the better part of discretion. As bourgeois truths are often denied direct expression, Thévenot waits for Maurice's withdrawal before subjecting him to ridicule. Frequently, though, where there are initiatives challenging the imperatives of the bourgeois order they are often significantly taken by women, more often in Buñuel's films the victims than the agents of the patriarchal law and, as such therefore, potentially its most willing saboteurs. At the restaurant whose owner lies dead in a room adjacent to the one in which the diners are examining the menu, the sobbing of family members of the deceased standing around the corpse leads the women to leave the table as a group, curiosity triumphing over manners, to earn the disapproval of their male companions, one of whom remarks 'vous allez être indiscrètes' ('you are going to be indiscreet').

The tensions between discretion and indiscretion, exemplified by boundaries of class distinction involving an event as simple as the consumption of an aperitif, are related to the film's more elaborate comic structures concerning food and drink. In the contrast between Maurice's awkwardness and Thévenot's sophistication the film seems aware that the working man's hurried consumption and the bourgeois's leisurely delectation turn on sociological questions. These are defined by Bourdieu (1984) *vis-à-vis* a more general discussion of social habits and customs in contemporary France. For the working man, eating or drinking habits develop from a desire for solidarity with others and from opportunistic enjoyment of pleasures normally denied, something motivated by experience of hardships and the unpredictable availability of basic commodities. For the bourgeois, by contrast, they are determined by the free-flowing provision of all types of consumer goods, abundance allowing for a less hurried consumption of items whose supply is never expected to run dry:

It becomes clearer why the practical materialism which is particularly manifested in the relation to food is one of the most fundamental components of the popular ethos and even the popular ethic. The being-in-the-present which is affirmed in the readiness to take advantage of the good times and take time as it comes is, in itself, an affirmation of solidarity with others (who are often the only present guarantee against the threat of the future), in as much as this temporal immanentism is a recognition of the limits which define the condition. (1984: 183)

The upper-class bourgeois's search for distinction in all matters concerning the body finds its most elaborate expression in the film's attention to rituals of food preparation and consumption. As Bourdieu later adds, taste in food, its enjoyment, display, and ritualistic provision in social gatherings, depends on each class's notions of its effects on the body, especially as regards strength, health, and beauty. Concentrating here on the upper bourgeoisie, the film makes its statements about class distinction by refraining, for instance, from highlighting working-class preference for stomach-filling, cheap, and nutritious food, focusing instead on, say, Mme Sénéchal's gigots or vol-au-vents, or at the dead man's restaurant on its menu of filet of sole, fried whiting, skate, pike, and trout, food emphasizing taste, health, and expensiveness. The film's interest in food-based class distinctions follows a consistent pattern in its dependence on actresses— Stéphane Audran, Delphine Seyrig, Bulle Ogier—whose slim-line forms vindicate the light, non-fattening, and expensive diets of the upper-middle classes, while the trio of bourgeois men, deprived of the proletarian male's muscle-building, meat-based diet for the brutal duties of daily working life, are a composite image of culinary ideals of refinement. None has the look of Pedro Armendáriz's proletarian slaughterhouse anti-hero, the dead-end bully raised on protein-giving, man-sized plates of beef. Of the three, Thévenot and the ambassador are slightly overweight, their surplus kilos no sign of physical power, more of self-indulgence in the stuffy indoor milieux of their unnatural urban habitat from which their periodic post-prandial country walks seem destined never to bring them release. The round of dinner engagements to which they seem eternally condemned resembles more a materialistic purgatory—reminiscent of some of the work of the great muralist Diego Rivera—than a festive ritual through which, however temporarily, to escape the duties and responsibilities of ordinary daily life.

Neither here nor in *El ángel exterminador* does food become an occasion for the sort of festive release defined by Bakhtin in his work on Rabelaisian comedy. Like those at the brothel in *Belle de jour*, the dining scenes in *Le Charme discret* reinforce more than challenge the social law. The meals' disruptions are themselves proof of the efficient operation of the mechanisms of repression, inhibiting instinct and desire.[6] The death of the restaurant owner, the unavailability of even the most basic beverages at a café, the confusion over dinner dates at the Sénéchals, and the interruptions by, first, an army on manœuvres, and then by terrorists, whether in the conscious or unconscious lives of the diners, are all reflections of the failure by the victims of ideology to find release in the potentially liberating festive world of food. Nothing here, then, of what Octavio Paz, writing in *El laberinto de soledad* about Mexican culture, saw as the *fiesta*'s abdications of reason, temporal cares, and responsibilities: 'A través de la Fiesta la sociedad se libera de las normas que se ha impuesto. Se burla de sus dioses, de sus principios y de sus leyes: se niega a sí misma' (1991: 59). ('Through *fiesta*, society frees itself from the norms it has established. It ridicules its gods, its principles, and its laws: it denies its own self.')

The meals which offer the diners an escape from selfhood, a discharge of pent-up emotions, a saturnalian assault on the monsters of reason, become instead the lifeless reproductions of normal life, in their frozen patterns becoming the film equivalents of Rivera's *Wall Street Banquet* (1926), in which humourless plutocrats feast off not some Gargantuan *fiesta* of the palate but a gold-coloured ticker-tape update of the latest Dow Jones prices. At Mme Sénéchal's, Buñuel's plutocrats are served not with ticker-tape but with a gigot, though the meal is invested so heavily with bourgeois etiquette as to make corporeal, instinctual release virtually impossible. Only in the ambassador's dream, last in the sequence of five, in which the dinner party is interrupted by the terrorists, is there some awareness of the extent to which instinct has been compromised by reason. The ambassador dreams that, moments after accepting another slice of gigot (though on his own admission he prefers fish, an astrological identification with the Piscean Buñuel with whom he shares the day and month of birth), terrorists burst into the Sénéchal dining-room, line up the hosts and guests against the wall, before machine-gunning them all, save the ambassador, to death. The ambassador has sought refuge under the dining-table, thus

---

[6] For Durgnat, '[d]istraction, rather than prohibition, is the conspicuous mode of modern repression'. (1978: 375).

avoiding the fate of his friends, but greed overcomes the instinct for self-preservation, and as he reaches for that extra slice of mutton from underneath the table he is spotted by the terrorists, who prepare to consign him to the same oblivion as his fellow diners.

Freud's thoughts on the operations of the laws of humour as something in which the normal expenditure of affect is somewhat compromised are relevant here. In medium shot, the ambassador's humiliating posture, cowering under the table, a large medium-rare slice of gigot hanging from his lips, releases humour through distress. From one point of view, the dream as manifest expression of a latent wish reveals the ambassador's hostility towards his friends. Perhaps finally peeved by their prejudices against Miranda—symbol here of European misconceptions of the kind described by Edward Said (1987) *vis-à-vis* Western 'Orientalist' misrepresentations of Islam—and even perhaps by now intolerant of their various superficialities of character and behaviour, Raphael dreams of their violent destruction. Nevertheless, the force of the attack on the bourgeoisie is somewhat softened through Raphael's acknowledgement of his own complicity in its laws and practices, the dream representing his own attitudes and actions far more humiliatingly and critically than his friends'.

Edging towards satire, the film draws back towards softer, more tolerant modes of comedy prompted by Raphael's self-awareness, even if this remains at unconscious levels and even if, his consciousness restored, his first act, untroubled by the more profound truths of his nightmare, is to raid the fridge for a midnight snack. Here the comedy flows not only from the unmasking of the self through dream mechanisms, but also from a process of identification. In the dream, Raphael's gross, cowardly behaviour corresponds to the exaggerations of physical appearance or gesture associated with the clown. Freud's descriptions of excess leading to comedy provide a helpful perspective: 'Staring eyes, a hooked nose hanging down to the mouth, ears sticking out, a humpback—all such things probably only produce a comic effect in so far as movements are imagined which would be necessary to bring about these features' (1983: 250).

Raphael's defects are exaggerated in the dream, the under-the-table shot with the meat dangling from his teeth exposing the brutish scavenger beneath the cultured diplomat, but, in

laughing at this image of excessive egocentricity and materialism, we are simultaneously drawn to him not only through the
introspection presenting him so unflatteringly to our view, but
also through the perfectly normal impulse of an individual's
attempts to soften the effects of a nightmare through the consolations of a midnight feast. The result is that audience reaction
towards Raphael is less likely to be of the superior, 'sudden
glory' Hobbesian sort than of the Freudian type, stressing processes not of distance but of identification, in which the 'feeling
of superiority bears no essential relation to comic pleasure' (Freud
1983: 256).

Nevertheless, however sympathetically the film views the failings or lapses of the bourgeoisie, the ultimate source of comedy,
whether of the 'humorous' Freudian variety or not, derives from
its critique of the norms and practices of a repressive order.[7]
Comedy here, exemplifying Freud's all-embracing theory, is a
mode of the unconscious, its effects achieved through processes
of Oedipal transgression and pre-Oedipal memory. In its specific contexts, much of the comedy of this film is motivated by
infantile patterns of behaviour and exposure of the absurdity of
socialized Oedipal adult conduct. At the most trivial levels this
involves scenes of almost slapstick dimensions in which figures
of authority are caught behaving in transgressive or infantile
ways. So, army colonels smoke marijuana at dinner parties; a
bishop, as if fulfilling a normal pastoral duty, calmly shoots
a dying man as postscript to the administering of final rites; a
female dinner guest interrupts civilized conversation with vulgar
disquisitions on astrology. More sophisticatedly, the hollowness
of bourgeois norms of language is elsewhere the comic target, as
when virtually throughout the film the ruling class's discursive
idiosyncrasies are exposed to various forms of ridicule. What
Bourdieu calls the highly censored language of the bourgeoisie
(1984: 176) perhaps achieves its greatest comic impact through
the verbal trivialization of complex issues and through the hollow
modes of greeting, like the formulaic 'je suis ravi de vous revoir'
('how marvellous to see you again') delivered by characters whose
constant rendezvous with one another undermine the force of
the courtesy. These modes of address stress the bourgeoisie's

---

[7] Gwynne Edwards notes the 'stylisation of quite ordinary aspects of bourgeois
activity' (1982: 253).

subjectivity to the operations of discourse and act as a sort of preface of triviality to all subsequent remarks and dialogue. The effect is double-edged: from one point of view, the bourgeoisie's detachment from profound, thoughtfully pondered realities, its 'censoring' of complexity (to use Bourdieu's argument), comes once more under attack; but, from another, the empty formulaic phrases and trivializations seem playful, unreal, their emptiness signs, also, of ill-defined transgressive disillusionment with the more serious processes of linguistic attempts to make sense of human realities. In these circumstances, linguistic patterns of this sort are given further perspectives of comedy when, for instance, the proletarian woman promises to speak plainly, or free of censorship, about her dislike of Jesus Christ. Herself undaunted by the consequences of so extreme a transgression, she is nevertheless—in a comic gesture by Buñuel—censored by the text itself, which is deliberately silenced, prohibited from opening itself up to so direct a challenge to its own repressive mechanisms and procedures.

Elsewhere when the bourgeoisie itself seeks refuge from the oppressions of its own discourse, a nonsense word is invented to symbolize the unspeakable realities of urgent desires. When Raphael refers mysteriously to 'sursiks' we are left to wonder whether even if the proletarian woman had been free to explain her animosity towards Jesus Christ, her repressed, ideologized discourse would have been equal to the task. As it is, Raphael's nonsense word 'sursiks', invented in the heat of the moment as the impromptu arrival of Mme Thévenot's husband threatens to frustrate an afternoon of Sadean lubricity (are the marks on her flesh the signs of a harmless rash, or scars, like those on the wrists of M. Husson's mistress in *Belle de jour*, sustained in the course of energetic love-play?), functions simultaneously as subterfuge and commentary on the bankruptcy of the normal discourse of desire. Yet even here, the word 'sursiks', at once expressing through verbal hieroglyph Raphael's playfulness and obedience to decorum, reflects the strategies of bourgeois discourse. M. Thévenot realizes the word is the ambassador's tactic for delaying his wife, a move only possible because of all participants' respect for the laws of discretion, something eventually triumphing even over Mme Thévenot's sexual urges, forcing her to compound her own and Raphael's frustrations by remaining behind only long enough after her husband's departure to inform him of her respect for the higher law of discretion.[8]

The film overflows with scenes like this that play out the comedy of transgressive sexual desires. While François Thévenot's role identifies him as someone almost wholly lost to materialism, virtually devoid of any libidinal drive, the ambassador—more playful, less ideologized—carries some of the film's more sanctioned, less purely ludicrous forms of transgression. The comedy surrounding Thévenot springs from his inner desiccation. At home, sleeping in a single bed—as much, we infer, out of indifference to sex as in conformity with fashionable organization of the *habitus* and life-style of bourgeois space—he only ever infringes his overpowering sublimations in dreams. Yet even there defence mechanisms protect him from the severest damage to a psyche bruised by knowledge of his wife's affair with the ambassador.

Dreams, of course, are the open arena, above all, of sexuality's relatively free expression, and here they merge with Buñuel's all-embracing mode of comedy to provide an ambience of Oedipal transgression mediated through ridicule. The prelude to Thévenot's mazy dream is provided by two mini-narratives, one a dream, the other a dream-like memory in which the Oedipal framework is alluded to more directly. In the latter a young cavalry lieutenant approaches the female threesome, unable to contain an impulse to describe the horrors of his childhood. His audacious approach, itself a sign of transgression, may be motivated partly by a desire to strike up a flirtatious relationship with one of them—though no overt declaration is ever made during the course of their meeting—and also partly by the intuition that among these women he may find a mother-surrogate willing to listen sympathetically to his tale of childhood misfortune. As the scene progresses the music played by the Palm Court musicians in the background is significantly Schubert's 'Ave Maria'. The content of his tragic narrative is pure horror. He describes in gory detail the severity of a life of military discipline imposed on him by the man who turns out not to be his natural father. His real father and mother have perished, the former in a duel with his mother's husband, the latter replaced

---

[8] For Aranda, irony (not aggression), a characteristic of the rebel classes, is a bourgeois strategy (1975: 247). For further discussion of Buñuel's social criticism, see Marie-Claude Taranger (1990: 199–218).

in his life by an extremely severe-looking, raven-haired, prison-warder-dressed governess. The boy sees his mother's ghost calling to him, writing her name on his bedroom mirror, instructing him to poison his stepfather. He becomes, we assume, despite his implausible remark about the 'vie passionante' of his attendance at military school, eternally mother-fixated seeking to find her not only in memories but also in the women he approaches in ordinary daily life.

This Oedipal framework is maintained in the sergeant's dream, narrated at the Sénéchal dinner party gatecrashed by the army. In this dream the young man walks down a dark street. A church bell tolls, and indecipherable background noises are heard. The young man meets a friend, Ramírez, who suddenly disappears; he then meets another friend, who informs him that Ramírez died six years ago. Later he meets a young woman referred to simply as 'toi' ('you'), too young to be his mother, yet after whom, once she disappears, he cries out: 'Où es tu, mère? Je te cherche parmi les ombres' ('Where are you, mother? I seek you in the shadows'). While she is still there he refers to their last meeting, when she had turned her back on him as she faced the sand. These surreal references recall the burial in the sand of the couple at the end of *Un chien andalou* (1928) and look ahead to the seduction of the aunt in *Le Fantôme de la liberté*, where the nephew sees his elderly aunt's naked body as the lissom form of a nubile maiden. Here the dream *mise-en-scène* relies on the atmosphere of death, burial, and loss from the Gothic novels so admired by Buñuel, especially perhaps Poe's, whose *The Fall of the House of Usher* he worked on in Paris with Jean Epstein. Poe's opium-dream perspectives are paralleled by a late Sixties' and early Seventies' preference for marijuana-induced hallucinations. The lugubrious *mise-en-scène* is reminiscent also, as the sergeant wanders down the gloomy streets, of the ghostly opening of *Pedro Páramo* (1955), written by another of Buñuel's favourite reverie-obsessed Latin American writers, Juan Rulfo. As the sergeant calls after the girlfriend/mother his words simultaneously recall Poe's necrophiliac passion for entombed Oedipal beauties and Rulfo's narrative experiments and thematic explorations of memory. In looking ahead to the nephew–aunt episode in *Le Fantôme de la liberté* the film confirms Freudian views both about the Oedipal models on which all sexual relationships between adults are ultimately based, and about romantic fantasies involving one's mother, in which 'one is never concerned with her as she is in the present but with her youthful mnemonic image carried over from one's childhood' (Freud 1982: 232–3).

The sergeant here, like the nephew in *Le Fantôme*, is locked in a two-way process imposing equivocal Oedipal fantasies of youth and beauty on his own mother and mother-surrogates. Both here and in the later sequence—not a dream, but nevertheless given an oneiric setting at the inn where the furtive couple are putting up for the night—the narrative explores the sexual transgressions of the unconscious, speaking the censored truths of desire, challenging the norms and practices of the Oedipal order. The dreams here, defining the conflicts of their waking lives, have none of the liberating force of that film so admired by Breton and other Surrealists, *Peter Ibbetson* (1935). Regarded by Breton in *L'Amour fou* (1977: 113) as the equal of *L'Âge d'or*, *Peter Ibbetson* narrates the story of the flight by two lovers from the material confinements and tyrannies to which their bodies have been subjected. This is achieved by communication with each other through dreams. But no comparable forms of release are available to the dreamers in *Le Charme discret*. Yet these moments of regression, potentially destructive to the dreamer, instead become through contextualization sources of comedy accommodated in an ultimately tolerant narrative where infringements of social laws need not lead only to disaster but also, even though the characters themselves seem incapable of taking any advantage, to potential enlightenment.

In the scene of the lieutenant's dream narrative, the comic effects of the waiter's constant frustrations of the elegant ladies' orders and Florence's irreverent allusion to Freud, claiming that as a child she suffered not from an Oedipus but from a Euclid complex, at once reflect Buñuel's own Surrealistic obsessions with the themes of frustration and Oedipality, modify the potential for trauma through the softening mechanisms of comedy, and act as playful guides to the Oedipal perspectives of these dreams. The traumatic material of the sergeant's dream is also mollified by the comic frame of narration, while the regressive indiscipline of officers smoking marijuana and interrupting their military exercises to listen to a dream recalls the desire of little children to hear bedtime stories from parents before dropping off to sleep.

These dreams lead up to the most complex comic and

Oedipally focused dream (reminiscent of Éluard's poem 'Mon amour', which ends with the line 'Je rêve que je dors, je rêve que je rêve'), in which François Thévenot dreams that his friend Henri Sénéchal dreams that the group of friends are invited to dine at the colonel's house, where eventually Raphael himself and the Republic of Miranda are both insulted, an incident that provokes Raphael into shooting the colonel. The dream is in two parts: the first appears to be a dream by Sénéchal, in which the group of friends, now including the bishop, believing they have been sitting at the colonel's dining-table waiting for their meal to be served, actually turn out to be on stage, just before the curtain goes up for a performance of Zorrilla's *Don Juan Tenorio* (1844). The sequence leading up to the curtain's opening is full of witty detail: first, Sénéchal, trying on what is described as the hat worn by Napoleon at the battle of Wagram, insists that it does not fit his head and places it instead on the bishop's, which it fits perfectly. This is entirely compatible with the film's convictions about the perfect match between Church and Army, both in thrall to laws and discipline of various kinds, both socially oppressive. The sight of the hat on the bishop's head provokes Alice, Sénéchal's wife, to uncontrolled laughter, something that identifies both her and her husband with 'mauvais goût' ('bad taste') and, to Thévenot's sober dreaming mind, with prankish, childish behaviour. Transferring his feelings onto another character in the dream, Thévenot actually forces the bishop to call Sénéchal a child: 'un grand enfant vous faîtes' ('you are behaving like a child').

The dream formulates processes of bourgeois repression and release, since Sénéchal's irreverent attitudes towards both State and religion are at first regarded by his wife as 'mauvais goût', momentarily still constrained by codes of dress, food, manners, and so on, before finally capitulating to the comedy of ecclesiastical and nationalistic subversion. But the comedy of Oedipal transgression also continues to spin further patterns of complexity as Florence is portrayed in the dream as a violent person, possibly also sexually aggressive, the camera following her movements towards a shield hanging on a wall, in medium-shot capturing her approving, gentle caress of a collection of unmistakably phallic swords fixed to the shield.

The sexual thematics of the first stage of Thévenot's dream are expanded in the complex allusions to Don Juan, but not before the dream has also found an opportunity for targeting the colonel's and, through him, the bourgeoisie's social veneer of polite etiquette covering a seething mass of spiteful complexes, all in some way connected with the exigencies and repercussions of the theatricality and superficialities of the patriarchal law. So, the colonel's food and drink, commodities normally vital to the bourgeois's sense of distinction, are ridiculed as tasting like rubber and coca cola. The targets here are the patriarchal law represented by the colonel and a rival in love. This is the core of the dream. Significantly, at the table, Thévenot sits apart from his wife, who is placed beside the ambassador. As the guests realize they are actors on a public stage, the camera, from the back, shows the curtains opening to reveal a packed theatre auditorium, with a prompt positioned at the front of the stage ready to help the actors remember their lines. Realizing they are not at the colonel's after all, but on stage, some of the guests begin to leave, and as they do so, again significantly, Simone Thévenot and the ambassador are seen surreptitiously touching each other's arms and waist. François Thévenot, at the other end of the table, remains isolated, a stock figure of comedy, the cuckolded husband.

The Oedipal comedy of subversion, springing from cuckoldry of one of the film's bourgeois patriarchs, is paralleled by related processes directed against the Church, ultimate symbol of patriarchy. Here the comedy is sparked off by the bishop's attempts, helped by the prompter, as all the other guests begin to leave, to say the lines of the play, his reflex-action willingness to repeat the lines being an indication of the Church's complementary obedience to authority and contempt for independent thought. It seems entirely natural that a man who as a worker-bishop insists on being paid according to union rules should here once more be seen preparing to subject himself to an alien but authoritative discourse.

Zorrilla's play is referred to here partly in memory of Buñuel's student days in Madrid, but also partly because of his continuing affection for it, especially its protagonist, as may be judged by his involvement in a production not only in 1920 at the Residencia de Estudiantes but also again in Mexico, as his wife Jeanne's autobiography records (Rucar de Buñuel 1991). In general terms, the play seems to have attracted Buñuel because of what he saw as its many surreal elements (Moix 1983: 14).

More specifically, though, the reference to the play arises naturally from the dreamer's anxieties about his wife's relations with the ambassador, in the process raising questions about male desire. When the dinner guests are expected to start speaking the lines of the play, the scene has fast-forwarded to the moment when the *Comendador*'s ghost has been invited to dinner by Don Juan. The scene is of course highly appropriate as a dark reference-point for a group of friends endlessly inviting one another to dinner. More than this, though, the references to the play and to this scene in particular, in which, though ultimately saved by his beloved, Don Juan is about to be dragged off to hell, stem from a need unconsciously expressed by the dreamer to cause the destruction of his hated rival. Additionally, Thévenot's identification of the ambassador with Don Juan simultaneously clarifies his own perception of the ambassador, while reactivating the Oedipal mechanisms of the dream.

Significantly, of the original group of friends (only later including the bishop, employed as gardener by the Sénéchals), only Raphael is unmarried. Alienated from the others by his Latin American nationality, he is also in some ways a stranger to the ideology of the couple, a Don Juan figure, more than the others a rebel of desire. Don Juan has been the subject, of course, of much psychoanalytical attention, with Otto Rank, Karen Horney, and Melanie Klein all developing lively theories from Freud's initial meditations. According to Horney, a woman's interest in the Don Juan type is prompted by an 'overvaluation of love' originating in childhood experiences of rejection that lead to a wish constantly to prove desirability to an endless number of men, something more possible if the objects of her desire are Don Juans, by definition not satisfied with one woman (1967: 208).

On the other hand, as regards male approximations to the type, Melanie Klein's slightly differently focused argument from Rank's thoughts on latent homosexuality seems especially interesting in view of the Oedipal thematics of this film. Following on from her point about the typical Don Juan's dread of the death of the women he loves, she elaborates a theory about his behaviour defining his need for a succession of women in terms of a defence mechanism:

By means of this he is proving to himself over and over again that his *one* greatly loved object (originally his mother, whose death he dreaded because he felt his love for her to be greedy and destructive), is not after all indispensable since he can always find another woman to whom he has passionate but shallow feelings. . . . By deserting and rejecting some women he unconsciously turns away from his mother, saves her from his dangerous desires and frees himself from his painful dependence on her, and by turning to other women and giving them pleasure and love he is in his unconscious mind retaining the loved mother or re-creating her. (Klein 1964: 86)

It must be remembered that all these Don Juan comparisons and definitions are imposed on Raphael by Thévenot, someone in the routine exchanges of conscious daily life repressing desires to humiliate and expose his cuckolder. For the dreamer, the Don Juan associations are predominantly negative. At this level of the dream's dual structure, the text wittily acknowledges Freud's analysis of the dream mechanisms of condensation, transference, and so on. The dream is ultimately one, moreover, in which Thévenot's own defence mechanisms ensure that the guilt and aggression released by desires for revenge against the ambassador are transferred onto someone else, Sénéchal here becoming the scapegoat for antisocial impulses. This pattern of self-protectiveness continues into the second part of the dream, in which aggression against the ambassador is now directed through the various guests at the colonel's house (no longer now a theatre) and, above all, at the colonel himself.

Among the various forms of humiliation heaped on Raphael is his enforced opinion that Napoleon's hat, not a stage prop any longer but an item of antique value at the colonel's house, is rather effeminate. Whatever subversive feelings Thévenot may himself harbour against Napoleon's representation of macho masculinity, his projection onto Raphael of anti-establishment criticism through scepticism about Napoleon's sexuality gestures towards Rank's descriptions of Don Juanism as a form of latent homosexuality, in which this Don Juan's (Raphael's) latent homosexuality with which Thévenot's avenging mind insultingly associates him is transferred onto Napoleon.

Raphael's humiliation is therefore double-edged: social condemnation by his peers for questioning the virility of a national hero; suspicion of his sexual prowess through transference onto another individual of a socially unacceptable latent homosexuality. The latter is prompted by parody of the Latin American cult of machismo. Latin America is, after all, the Mecca of machismo (see Paz 1991: 97–100), where no greater insult to the conventional male can be delivered than through suspicions about the potency or authenticity of his heterosexuality. As Thévenot's dreaming mind takes its revenge on the ambassador of Miranda, the film exposes the processes of the colonizing mentality, in which Buñuel becomes momentarily not the Spaniard in exile in Mexico, but the marginalized Mexican in Europe, twice over an outsider, his uprootedness finding its complex formulation in the endless brisk walks of the group of friends, at once a geographical and a metaphysical condition, also acquiring anti-colonial significance.

The remainder of the dream, in which successive guests, followed eventually by the colonel himself, deliver a volley of discreet insults to Raphael and Miranda, to the point where he is finally goaded into shooting the colonel, is merely the fine detail in a strategy of wish-fulfilment mechanisms that have already partially fulfilled their duty in exacting revenge on the ambassador. The dramatic incidents of Thévenot's dream have no equivalents in his conscious life, where even after the dream normal life resumes, and the round of dinners and meetings with the group of friends, including Raphael, continues.

But if through Thévenot the film focuses perhaps a little more on the negative, room is found elsewhere for accentuating the positive. There are characters who, however compromised in other ways, are able to find time for instinct and, like the female revolutionary (even though she is seized by the ambassador's henchmen), are free enough to strike blows for justice. For instance, among the group of corrupt friends, the Sénéchals— whatever their other failings—are prepared to risk transgressions of social form, delaying the welcome of their guests in the first dinner-party scene by escaping out of the window of their house to satisfy in their garden more urgent sexual needs. Even a police inspector, in the fourth of the film's five dreams, dreams his prisoners have miraculously escaped, his unconscious if not his conscious mind revealing a desire to be liberated from various laws.[9] Equivocally, and without the more lyrical rhetoric of other Surrealists like, say, Breton, the film manages to celebrate the pleasures of desire. Especially in moments like the Sénéchals'

---

[9] For an earlier treatment of some of these dream-related questions, see Babington and Evans (1985: 5–20).

priapic garden rituals, the comedy of repression and blocked exits, of Oedipal trauma and frustration, is balanced by a comedy of momentarily liberating desire. Even if ultimately no permanent escape is possible from the abyss, those walks down a country lane probably only leading to more frustration and disappointment, the film belongs to a slightly more amusingly tolerant, if not actually ever optimistic, tendency in Buñuel's work, affirming as far as heaven allows the rewards as well as the pitfalls of desire.[10]

---

[10] For Buñuel's equivocal attitudes towards the bourgeoisie, see Pérez Turrent and de la Colina: 'He conocido burgueses encantadores y discretos. ¿Ustedes creen que todo lo que ha aportado la burguesía es malo? No. Algo habría que conservar de ella' (1993: 161). ('I've known discreet and enchanting members of the bourgeoisie. Do you think that everything bourgeois is bad? No. One should retain some of the bourgeoisie's achievements.')

2
Family Romances:
Buñuel's Mexican Melodramas

'Can't you see how happy we'd be together?'

Douglas Sirk, *Imitation of Life*

BUÑUEL's Mexican films fall into two categories: those like *Gran Casino*, *El gran calavera* (1949), *Susana*, *La hija del engaño* (1951), *Subida al cielo* (1951), *El bruto*, *Abismos de pasión*, and *La ilusión viaja en tranvía* (1953) belonging to a *cine de consumo* largely obeying the generic laws of the popular *ranchera*, musical, or melodramatic films of the commercial Mexican cinema; others, like *Los olvidados*, *El*, *Ensayo de un crimen*, *Nazarín*, breaking free of commercial constraints, reflecting the more personal interests and obsessions of the Surrealist auteur. Yet the two Buñuels, commercial and auteurist, cannot be so simplistically polarized, their schizophrenia not so much, like Borges's relationship with his other self, a genuine paradox of artistic or personal identity, as a categorization forced upon his work by viewers and critics (Borges 1979). Admittedly, Buñuel has himself often encouraged this schizophrenia, sometimes even dismissing whole films as unworthy of anyone's serious attention. Yet on other occasions, in accordance with the drives and prejudices of a persona of massive contradictions, he claims these 'películas alimenticias' ('bread-and-butter films') have been made not only with respect for the conventions of their genres, producers, and audiences, but also with a care for the intelligence and gratification of friends. In a discussion of *Susana*, Buñuel remarks:

esas películas las he hecho sintiendo la responsabilidad de cumplir con el productor y no las 'boicoteo' deliberadamente. Aparte de eso, puedo querer divertirme un poco y meter algunas cosas que hagan gracia a los amigos. No son 'guiños', porque detesto al cineasta que parece decir 'Miren qué listo soy.' Digamos que meto recuerdos compartidos con algunas personas, 'claves' inocentes. Si en *Susana* hay bromas, habré

tenido buen cuidado de que la película entera no resultara una burla.
(Pérez Turrent and de la Colina 1993: 60)

(I've made these films with a sense of responsibility towards the producers, and I don't boycott them deliberately. Apart from that, I can
amuse myself by putting in a few things that might divert my friends.
They're not 'winks', because I detest directors who seem to be saying
'Look how clever I am.' Let's say that I insert memories shared with
a few people, innocent clues. If there are jokes in *Susana*, I will have
made sure the whole film hasn't been turned into a joke).

On Buñuel's own admission, a point often repeated and developed by critics looking for rationales of these supposedly
unauteuristic aberrations, the commercial films operate at various
levels in which covert strategies of 'gracia' ('amusement', but
here also, by extension, characteristically Buñuelian humour and
wit) often ironize the sometimes banal determinants of generic
laws. In this respect Buñuel's accommodations with the popular
Mexican cinema bear a close resemblance to the strategies
of directors like Douglas Sirk, working within the constraints of
the Hollywood film industry. Even if they had wished to do so,
neither Sirk nor Buñuel would have survived on outright subversion. Both seem rather to have relished the challenge of making
films that, while remaining true to their commercial and generic
laws, nevertheless manage to offer alternative perspectives largely
through various modes of irony.[1]

While discussion of Buñuel has so far been largely untouched
by post-auteurist, neo-Marxian, and feminist questions and debate, it is as well here to summarize their impact on the Hollywood melodrama in order to clarify the theoretical approach of
the following section on both the commercial (*Susana*, *Una mujer
sin amor*) and auteurist (*Los olvidados*) melodramas. Early post-
structuralist approaches to Hollywood melodrama questioned
notions of authorial coherence, insisting on the contradictions
of the genre itself, highlighting these as the true site of textual
meaning in terms of the return of the repressed, and identifying
coherence with bourgeois closure, incoherence with resistance. A
more radical neo-Marxist approach viewed even incoherence
as a distortion of the reality of social relations. Feminist readings
have ranged from exposure of the misogyny of Hollywood melodrama to more recent, less monolithic responses in which the

---

[1] On irony in Sirk, see Babington and Evans (1990: 48–58).

woman's place is seen as problematic, often questioning the workings of patriarchy both on- and off-screen. Even though theories reducing almost to invisibility the organizing presence of the author have lost some of their provocative force, their virtual absence from discussion of Buñuel has meant that, while undue attention has focused on the auteur's overall control of the text, insufficient space has been left for consideration of mechanisms operating beyond it.

Nevertheless, even in the commercial melodramas it is important not to lose sight of authorial control, however narrowly defined its limits, looking for meaning in the interstices and tensions of commercial, generic, and authorial demands and preferences. Looked at like this, the connections between the commercial and auteurist films are not as starkly incompatible as might initially seem to be the case. The auteurist films are of course themselves the result of various forms of compromise (the imposition, say, on Buñuel of Catherine Deneuve as the star for *Belle de jour*), their coherence fragmented by all sorts of unconscious as well as conscious processes. On the other hand, the commercial films, especially through form, sexuality, humour and, perhaps above all, irony, reworking the auteurist thematics through the patterns and drives of the popular cinema, can appeal as much to the minority audience of 'friends' as to the box-office majority.

Among the most striking features of the commercial films' thematics is a preoccupation with issues concerning the family. These involve generational questions, relations between the sexes, adultery, women's independence, and reviews of dominant forms of masculinity, often in the process seeming to bear out Eli Zaretsky's view that 'the bourgeois familial ideal obscured two contradictions that emerged in the course of capitalist development: the oppression of women and the family's subordination to class relations' (1976: 44). All are part of the staple diet of the commercial Mexican melodrama of the Forties and Fifties, not problematized as in Buñuel, but used in a straighter, more direct, and more ideologized form by leading directors of the day like Emilio Fernández, Julio Bracho, Juan Oro, and many others. Raiding not only the genres and thematics of the commercial cinema, but also its stars—e.g. Pedro Armendáriz (*El bruto*), Jorge Negrete (*Gran Casino*), María Félix (*La Fièvre monte à El Pao*), Ernesto Alonso (*Ensayo de un crimen*), Miguel Inclán (*Los olvidados*)—Buñuel's commercial melodramas are the underside of popular Mexican cinema of the Forties and Fifties, respecting and embodying as well as exposing its aims, achievements, and failures. This process, necessarily muted in these films, acquires its most sardonic, ferocious character in others like *El, Ensayo de un crimen* and, above all, *Los olvidados*, managing to free themselves from the severest commercial and artistic constraints.

Projecting, as Carl J. Mora argues (1989), the largely conservative values of its middle-class audiences, Mexican films of the Forties and Fifties can be grouped under three main headings: family melodramas, *comedias rancheras*, and comedies. Not even under the more liberal government of Lázaro Cárdenas (1934–40)—his surname significantly identical to the murdered political reformer in *La Fièvre monte à El Pao*—could the Mexican cinema be described as adopting a more progressive politics or tone, though even here one should be careful not to dismiss all films of this period as being too compromised ideologically to deserve much attention.[2] The celebration of traditional values, as in family-centred melodramas starring Fernando Soler (also a patriarch in some of Buñuel's commercial melodramas: *El gran calavera*, *La hija del engaño*, and *Susana*) or in *ranchera* comedies starring Jorge Negrete, was occasionally placed under restrained threat in films like *Distinto amanecer* (1943), the Film Noir equivalents of criminal or menacing ambience, violence, flashing neon-lit urban night scenes undermining the more usual ethos of sunny optimism and *fiesta* of other films. Negrete's persona and identification with bouncy *boleros* are ironized directly in *Gran Casino*, and indirectly in *Susana*, their macho connotations gently undermined through settings, costumes, and compositions only marginally more kitschy than the originals. Elsewhere, the city *mise-en-scène* of films, not only *Distinto amanecer* but also, say, *Crepúsculo* (1944) and many others, places in question the more lyricized rural settings of films like *María Candelaria* and *Flor silvestre* (both 1943), with their celebratory, stylized photography by Gabriel Figueroa (Buñuel's cameraman on *Los olvidados*, *El*, *Nazarín*, *La Fièvre monte à El Pao*, *La joven*, *El ángel exterminador*, and *Simón del desierto*) designed to represent the idealized essence of Mexico and its natural, Mother-Earth-related harmonies reflected in the social order and its various institutions. These

---

[2] For a general survey of Latin American cinema, see John King (1990).

include perhaps above all the family, set up, like the *patria* and religion, by Buñuel as one of his principal targets of abuse (Pérez Turrent and de la Colina 1993: 29). The popular comedies starring Cantinflas and 'Tin Tan', the former a *pelado* proletarian, the latter a more hip *pachuco*—the 'upwardly mobile huckster', to use Mora's phrase (1989: 82)—also brought a vitality and corrosive humour to a genre often content to reflect dominant norms and preconceptions. These films and, later, the more openly sexual *cabaretera* films, with their stress on Afro-Cuban music and more self-assertive cabaret or bar girls, also sometimes managed to question dominant practice. Here their sexuality is at least channelled by the women characters into use as an instrument of power, not simply commodified and crudely exposed as in, say, a more straightforwardly exploitative melodrama like *Medias de seda* (1955), where the main actress Rosario Durcal seems to fulfil no other purpose than at most available opportunities to expose her stockingless legs and prodigious bosom.

In keeping with the tendencies of some of the more thoughtful popular melodramas, Buñuel's films, even his most routine ones, while respecting the constraints of generic laws, comment through hyperbole, humour, or contradiction on prevalent attitudes towards sexuality, social structures and, perhaps above all, on generational relationships and conflicts.[3] The liberation of the individual from parental authority, described by Freud in the essay 'Family Romances' as one 'of the most necessary though one of the most painful results brought about by the course of development' (1981*a*: 221), informs the action of many films. More commercially, films like *Susana*, *El gran calavera*, *Una mujer sin amor*, and *La hija del engaño* concentrate at some point or other on this issue, often highlighting the neurosis of individuals failing to negotiate their liberation (*Una mujer sin amor*, *La hija del engaño*) or ironizing what seem to be more successful rites of passage (*El gran calavera*, *Susana*). These questions also provide the thematic force for the defiantly uncommercial melodrama, *Los olvidados*, but even later on, once Buñuel had largely severed his official links with the Mexican cinema (effectively from 1965,

---

[3] Humour as a means of subverting popular melodramatic form is mentioned by Daniel Díaz Torres and Enrique Colina (1972: 158). They make the further interesting point that, while the conflict between erotic drives and social laws is for Buñuel a potential source of liberation, for the commercial melodrama it is a confirmation of alienation (ibid. 162).

after *Simón del desierto*), fathers are still looking for their daughters, sons for their fathers, and sons, daughters, mothers, and fathers for one another, as in, say, *Tristana* or *Le Fantôme de la liberté*.

The most comic version of this process occurs in *Le Fantôme*, where the pseudo-Cervantine joke of a couple's search for their daughter who is actually there, though unseen by them, relates to a familiar Buñuel obsession with failures of perception, though here it is connected with questions about family conflict. The most tragic variant of this process, in some ways less reminiscent of Cervantes than of Quevedo, whose anti-hero Pablos in *El Buscón* (1626) is also said to be at one point in the narrative figuratively 'buscando mi padre' ('looking for my father'), appears in *Los olvidados*. Inspired as much by Freud as by any other literary or cinematic prototype, *Los olvidados* is structured around events involving a group of delinquents, all in some way seeking liberation as well as acknowledgement from their parents or parent subsitutes.

Among the more poignant of these figures in *Los olvidados* is Jaibo, abandoned as an infant, yet still despite the bitterness and resentment towards the mother he never knew, recasting her in his imagination while planning the seduction of his friend Pedro's mother as an idealized Oedipal Virgin-Mary-equivalent, a process extremely reminiscent of Freud's remarks at the end of the essay on 'Family Romances':

If we examine in detail the commonest of these imaginative romances, the replacement of both parents or of the father alone by grander people, we find that these new and aristocratic parents are equipped with attributes that are derived entirely from real recollections of the actual and humble ones; so that in fact the child is not getting rid of his father but exalting him. Indeed the whole effort at replacing the real father by a superior one is only an expression of the child's longing for the happy, vanished days when his father seemed to him the noblest and strongest of men and his mother the dearest and loveliest of women. (1981*a*: 224–5)

As Jaibo has known neither mother nor father, the fantasy of noble, ideal parents is all the stronger. The comparison with the Virgin Mary, a ubiquitous presence in Buñuel narratives (her picture hanging in the unlikeliest of places, as at the slaughterhouse in *El bruto*), resonates with equivocal meanings. A source of Oedipal fantasy, she is also a figure of purity, as Julio

Alejandro, Buñuel's scriptwriter on *Abismos de pasión, Nazarín, Viridiana, Simón del desierto*, and *Tristana*, makes clear:

Hay algo que le emociona profundamente: el dogma de la Inmaculada Concepción. No como dogma, sino como inclinación y sentimiento hacia la pureza. Para él la pureza es algo muy importante. Entonces, en el misterio de la Inmaculada Concepción ve, simple y llanamente, una exteriorización de este sentimiento. (1980: 44)

(There is something that moves him profoundly: the dogma of the Immaculate Conception. Not as dogma, but as a leaning towards or feeling for purity. For him, purity is something very important. Then, in the mystery of the Immaculate Conception he sees, simply and plainly, an outward expression of this feeling.)

Even *Simón del desierto*, a film imbued with asceticism and mysticism, revolves around Oedipal questions, seeming to recognize the marvellous even in mother–son relationships, at one moment exchanging the mortifications of visionary experience for playful Oedipal rituals as, in a fantasy, Simón imagines himself having momentarily descended from his saintly pillar to run around the arid countryside, friskily chasing his mother, dancing, laying his head in her lap in a vulgar New World version of Renaissance madonna and child poses. Elsewhere, though, Mexican melodrama's inveterate orientation towards explorations of power relations in the family leads Buñuel to focus on the clash between Good and Bad fathers, the place of women in the social order, and the negotiations or rejections of that order. In *La hija del engaño, El bruto*, and *Una mujer sin amor* the Bad father causes the break-up of the family in the former, and his wife's adultery, though not a breakup of their marriage, in the latter two. In all three films the *mise-en-scène* of closed spaces, especially in *El bruto*, accentuates psychological and social forms of entrapment.

In keeping with the traditions of the genre, especially its Hollywood variants, Buñuel's melodramas are characterized by a mode of excess. Melodramatic form is synonymous with verbal and visual hyperbole. Emotions, for instance, are given, in Peter Brooks's description of the 'Melodramatic Imagination', a 'full acting-out, a full representation before our eyes.' (Brooks 1984: 41). In its dramatization of the explosive return of the repressed, it parallels the mechanisms and procedures of the unconscious, of dream-worlds, something of clear appeal to a Surrealist auteur seeking to shock his audience into awareness, however wearisome the constraints at other levels of the mode's often necessary allegiances to the drives and rhetoric of the commercial cinema. An example of how, working against the auteur's more restrained instincts, these practices actually help clarify the darkest corners of the unconscious involves the use of music.

Buñuel himself undervalues *Abismos de pasión* for this reason (Pérez Turrent and de la Colina 1993: 85). But the excess of music here, as in Sirk or Minnelli, for instance, in the Hollywood melodrama, heightens the emotionality of the narrative, the repetitive 'Tristan und Isolde' motifs providing an aural complement to the overblown visual style of thunder, lightning, and howling winds, especially in the scenes after Catalina's death, leading up to Alejandro's own demise by her tomb in a climax of necrophiliac *amour fou*. Constrained by the poetics of a commercial genre, Buñuel has no control over the film's final cut or sound, but in films like *Abismos, Susana, Una mujer sin amor,* or *El bruto* the auteur's restraint benefits from other priorities taking the films beyond the personal control of their director and into a wider domain. Buñuel's known prejudices against what he saw as film music's detraction in non-musical genres from the visual and verbal impact of the narrative are here overruled by other considerations.

But if Buñuel's unavoidable capitulation to the genre's musical traditions seems complete in *Abismos*, his surrender to the usually happy-ending format of melodrama seems less unconditional. With the exception of *El bruto, Abismos,* and *Los olvidados,* all of which end tragically, Buñuel's melodramas end happily, but in ways vitiated with irony. Although melodramatic characters, usually imaged as uncomprehending victims of an enigmatic world, willingly resume their places in the social order, their embrace of that order's values is often so exaggerated or humorous as to suggest covert irony, a strategy casting doubt not on the characters' embrace of that order, but on the premises on which it is so firmly based.

For the majority audience no resistance to the text and its reflection of ideology has been made. For the minority audience, Buñuel's 'friends' and their equivalents in cinemas or in front of video screens throughout the world, resistance, more mute, more cautious, is as much in evidence here as in the uninhibited auteurist films on which his critical reputation has traditionally rested.

2.1. *Susana*: The Daughter's Seduction

'Primeramente pues, hija mía, considera que tú tienes a
Dios por padre y por esposo a Cristo tienes, por madre y
hermana a la Virgen y Madre suya.'

Juan Luis Vives, *Instrucción de la mujer cristiana*

('First then, daughter, consider that God is your father,
Christ your husband, and his Virgin Mother your
mother and sister.')

Three of Buñuel's commercial Mexican melodramas—*Susana*,
El gran calavera, and *La hija del engaño*—highlight relationships
between fathers and daughters (the pattern is maintained in
the more personal, English-language film *The Young One*). *El gran
calavera* and *La hija del engaño* explore the natural bonds between
fathers and daughters, *Susana* an involvement between a father
and daughter-surrogate. In all three films the father is played
by Fernando Soler, an actor of some popularity and influence
before Buñuel's arrival in Mexico, someone who in various
respects was a kind of less ironic version of Fernando Rey, his
patriarchal equivalent in Buñuel's later films. In *El gran calavera*—
a remake of *Don Quintín el amargao*, a film produced by him during
his Filmófono days in Spain (1935–6)—Fernando Soler's benevolent, indulgent father enjoys a relationship with his daughter
full of sweetness and light, idealized to the point of fantasy. Here,
somewhat in contrast to her role in *Una mujer sin amor* (1951),
made only two years earlier, Rosario Granados' Virginia, the
symbolically named patrician daughter and girlfriend of the
proletarian Pablo, exudes demureness and charm, devotion and
loyalty, a symbol of purity but also, as Agustín Sánchez Vidal
points out (1984: 115), of true love, the Virginie to her sweet-
heart Pablo's Paul. As regards the film's interest in class, she is
the character above all identified with transgressions against
social norms. As regards her relationship with her father, she is
the family member closest to him, his staunchest and most win-
some ally.

As always, Buñuel's irony veils banalities of psychology and
narrative (the script is based on a comedy by Adolfo Torrado).
Virginie will have her Paul, but for a patrician *petite fille*, will life
with a proletarian hero whose profession involves driving around
in a beaten-up old van publicizing a range of tacky goods through

a loudspeaker in the downtown areas of Mexico city not eventually pall? Another of Buñuel's dream-texts, though not in the formal Surrealist sense of, say, *Belle de jour* or *Un chien andalou*, where the entire narrative seems to be driven by dream mechanisms, *El gran calavera* reflects more the patterns of a Preston Sturges comic melodrama, subverting its thematics of love's fulfilment through humour and irony. As in many plays, too, by Shakespeare, Tirso, and Calderón, *El gran calavera* relies on a unifying spatial dream metaphor in its middle part, where the main characters undergo a process of transformation from which they emerge renewed to take up their lawful place in the social order. The reversals of the proletarian world parallel the confusions of the wood near Athens in *A Midsummer Night's Dream*, or the Duke's palace in *El pretendiente al revés*, but Buñuel's rhetoric, like Shakespeare's and Tirso's, undermines the upbeat tone through questions about the durability of the dream-world's lessons, about the social order's unchallenged structures to which the characters return, and about incompatibilities of class and temperament which the text hints at but, for undoubtedly ideologically determined commercial reasons, refuses directly to develop.

While *El gran calavera* prefers a lighter touch, *La hija del engaño* projects a more consistently negative image of human behaviour, reserving its more positive moments for the very last sequence. In contrast to *El gran calavera*, where the father–daughter relationship is one of several family ties explored by the film, *La hija del engaño* restricts itself, once relations with his wife have in practical terms come to an end, to the father's search—literal, emotional, ideological—for the daughter. The human condition, especially as regards family relations, is again in a Buñuel film given an infernal definition. Having returned one night to find his wife sharing their bed with a lover, Quintín throws her out onto the street, dumps his toddler daughter—whose paternity his wife now falsely claims is illegitimate—at the door of a working-class house, and becomes the owner of a nightclub that he later christens 'El Infierno' ('Hell'). Abandoning the security of a life of subservience to the bourgeois order, Quintín becomes the film's unlikely social rebel, outraged by the unjust rewards of a trusted system, determined to replace the sacrifices and denials demanded by that system with despairing forms of self-indulgence exemplifying the guiltless man's desire to be hanged for a sheep as for a lamb. In this family melodrama, Quintín is a secular, more comic variant of Tirso's despairing ascetic Paulo in *El condenado por desconfiado* (1635), apparently rewarded for ten years' service to God in the desert with damnation and driven, like Quintín, by a desire to make the punishment fit the crime. Quintín's self-imposed punishment, decreed as marginalization from conventional society, aversion to sexual and family relations, and condemnation to the sleazy world of rough-trade nightclubs, is eventually overturned through the deathbed confession from his wife that her daughter Marta really is his after all. From that point on, the father's pursuit of his long-lost daughter becomes in its melodramatic trajectory—through the suspense and pathos of the search, eventual discovery, and final loving embrace—a narrative whose thematics, no longer concerned with displaced adult sexual hostilities, address questions about an idealized daughter's substitution for the unforgiven, wicked mother in the deepest affections of the father.

Remaining true to the *deus ex machina* closures of melodrama, the film's ending is deliberately facile. Incredibly, in a city of several million inhabitants, two characters who after twenty years of separation and who by now belong to wholly different worlds are united again through a miracle of fate. In addition to satisfying the Surrealist's enduring fondness for *le hasard,* chance here acts as confirmation not only of melodrama's operation of an arbitrary law but also of its fondness for heightened states of emotion caused by the spectacle of reappearing long-lost friends, relatives, or lovers. The arbitrary happy ending of *La hija del engaño* mirrors the patterns of Hollywood melodramas of the Forties and Fifties made by Ophuls, Stevenson, Sirk, Minnelli, and others, by avoiding a downbeat closure in obedience to the laws of a largely conservative popular genre. Yet like its illustrious Hollywood equivalents—not the hack work, but those films made by directors who did manage to stamp their personality on the unpromising material often forced on them by their studios—and through its resistant strategies of excess, irony, humour, and sexuality, *La hija del engaño* manages to conform to the genre's naturalizing rhetoric while simultaneously exposing the principle of arbitrariness motivating its own procedures. To an uncritical mind the ending conforms to the genre's familiar and predominant patterns of restored order. But no critical mind, especially not one possessing a knowledge of Buñuel's earlier history of film-making in Europe, seeing these films at the time of their first release, could have failed to be sceptical—especially in view of their many earlier signs of gentle subversion—about the significance of its unnatural conservative ending. In Sirk's *Written on the Wind* (1956), for instance, the ending—with its final union between Rock Hudson's Mitch and Lauren Bacall's demure adventuress Lucy, who has spectacularly failed earlier to become interested in her ardent but conformist suitor—raises as many questions as it answers. In *La hija del engaño* the reconciliation of father and daughter, years after misanthropy has taken root in the father, and moments after he has been trying to kill the man he fails to recognize as his daughter's husband, seems so farcical as to undermine radically the neatness of the ending and, at a superficial level, the naturally gratifying sight of a father's recovery of his lost daughter.

The daughter bears the scars of separation from her natural parents and victimization by her adoptive family (especially the Bad surrogate father), and remains as yet unaware of her natural father's act of cruelty leading to her abandonment at the door of strangers. In the mean time, too, Quintín has become *amargao* ('bitter'), a deranged misogynist whose attitude towards women ranges from contempt to cruelty, failing to be moved by his dying wife's pleas to be informed of the whereabouts of the daughter she lost all those years ago, using a cliché dear to misogynists everywhere to advise a female stranger in the street (who turns out to be his own daughter) to avoid meddling in men's affairs by going indoors to mend socks. The place of the father in the daughter's inner life has been filled by a husband, in a process through which paternal absence once more leaves its deleterious effect on a child whose hidden traumas help perpetuate the cycle of imbalances in adult sexual relations.

Recognizing the incompatibilities of far-reaching questions like these and the simplifications of the conventional happy ending, the text forces Quintín to break the frame of the narrative, to step out and address the audience directly: '¿Oyen Uds? Nada me sale bien' ('Do you hear? Nothing ever works out for me'). He is referring to his frustration at not yet being able to meet his grandson—since Marta, his daughter, has yet to give birth—but, through him, and through his failure to respect the laws of realism, the audience is warned that the characteristically happy resolutions of melodrama are not to be trusted as anything more

than devices for gratifying all too human desires for reconciliation and order. His comic licence in transgressing an aesthetic
law carries a message more profound than the one he himself
delivers about his own destiny ever to be *amargao*.

*

PLOT SYNOPSIS: Susana escapes from a reformatory. Pretending to
be a destitute orphan, she seeks shelter in a ranch where the three
men, the ranch owner (Guadalupe), his son (Alberto), and the
foreman (Jesús), are all attracted by her flamboyant sexuality. As
Guadalupe eventually orders his wife Carmen out of the house so
that Susana can take her place as his mistress, the police finally
catch up with her, reveal her true identity, and return her to
captivity. Ranch life returns to what passes for normality.

Arbitrary closure continues to be a feature of what is perhaps
Buñuel's most provocative father–daughter narrative, *Susana*.
Jesús G. Requena has referred to it as 'eminentemente subversivo,
animado por un gesto de violencia sobre el propio género en el
que se inscribe' (1980: 16) ('highly subversive, motivated by a
violent impulse against the very genre to which it belongs').
Here the daughter-surrogate, not a real daughter, is a far more
disruptive, sexualized figure over whom not only the father but
also the rest of the household must triumph as a prerequisite for
the restoration of family order. For Buñuel, sex is a threat to
order, overcoming all barriers:

Dans une société organisée et hierarchisée le sexe, qui ne respecte
aucune barrière, aucune loi, peut à chaque instant devenir un facteur
de désordre et un véritable danger. (Buñuel 1982 *a*: 21)

(In an organized and hierarchical society, sex, which respects no barrier,
no law, can at any moment become a force for disorder and a real danger.)

These remarks appear in a general discussion about the Church's
hostility to sexuality, and they are highly relevant to the narrative of a devil-woman of desire, a wild girl on the run from a
reformatory, bursting into the lives of a pious Catholic household, leaving havoc everywhere in her trail while she remains an
undetected fugitive from the law of sexual discretion as well as
of criminal justice.[4] But as freedom is only available to Buñuel

---

[4] The maid, who constantly associates Susana with the Devil, seems to be a
throw-back to another age. Asunción Larvin, writing about sexuality in colonial
Mexico, remarks: 'In the seventeenth century it was still believed that the devil
could assume the shape of an animal or even a person to tempt humans' (1989: 51).

in the realm of the imagination, this exterminating angel of desire finds only temporary release from various constraints, her final removal to the reformatory from which she had escaped leaving the way open for the family's reaffirmation of their sanctimonious way of life.

The rancher household, comprising Guadalupe the father, Carmen his wife, Alberto his son, Felisa the maid, Jesús the foreman, and various other anonymous servants and ranch hands, epitomizes through its claustrophobic *mise-en-scène* the extent and influence of the bourgeois order. The ranch house itself and the various outhouses and barns attached to it contrast sharply with the surrounding wilderness. The buildings represent order and constraint, the irony of the names 'Guadalupe', 'Carmen', and 'Jesús' reinforcing their suggestion of authority, while the wilderness projects a *mise-en-scène* of desire, sometimes of irresistible turbulence symbolized by the characteristically melodramatic atmosphere of thunder, lightning, and rain periodically disturbing the peace of the countryside. Sexual desire is additionally expressed in complementary ways, above all through activities related to the care or hunting of animals. As in Buñuel's friend Lorca's 'Romance sonámbulo' (1928), the wilderness here is a place of danger of various types, including male tests of endurance, while the home is a realm of security, of stasis sometimes and death. In the 'Romance sonámbulo' the unnamed hero finds manly fulfilment outside the home in his various escapades on sea and land, but significantly these are identified with criminality, something contradictorily given a temporary authorization, but from which eventually the hero must free himself before returning to the domesticated, female-related order of the house. The *casa*, the private space to which he returns, is a symbol simultaneously of order, legitimating and giving sense to his life of action in the wilderness, and of death. There his beloved has died, and there he returns only when he is himself at the point of death.

Something of that dichotomy characteristic of his friend's poetry spreads over Buñuel's films, especially here, where all three principal male characters are trapped in seemingly conflicting drives concerning domestic, family responsibilities and liberty-seeking, wilderness-identified activities testing their mettle as full-blooded males. Of the three, Guadalupe and his foreman Jesús seem most relaxed about such conflicts, managing to reconcile their domestication with commitment to the virile pursuits of the wilderness. Jesús, on whom Guadalupe depends for the smooth running of the ranch, is a sort of natural heir, more in sympathy through temperament and capability for the work of the ranch than the son, Alberto, a boy some way short of exemplifying the macho ideals of his father, lost in a world of unmanly scholarship, drawn more to the theory than to the practice of agronomy.

Jesús's ambience is a rough world of barns and stables, Alberto's the quiet seclusion of a book-lined study. Jesús stands tall and firm, resolutely confident in his masculinity, his dandified look of huge sombrero, dark clothes, bandanna, and other sartorial flourishes the sign not of a wavering sexuality but of a masculinity so self-assured and relaxed as to permit a certain visual ostentation through baroque, self-preening forms of dress. Owing nothing here to the deep-lying hesitations of sexual orientation associated with fussily dressed Hollywood Westerners, such as Lash Larue, Roy Rogers, Gene Autry, the Lone Ranger, or the Cisco Kid, Jesús parades his macho self-confidence like a peacock spreading his plumes. He represents the more serious version of the *charro*, the Mexican cowboy, appearing only slightly less tongue-in-cheek through Buñuel's use of Jorge Negrete, the doyen of all *charros*, in *Gran Casino* and caricatured by Walt Disney through the sombrero-clad, pistol-packin' Mexican *charro*-bird Panchito in *The Three Caballeros* (1945), a film designed to help the Good Neighbour Policy with the USA. Set beside Jesús, Alberto looks drab, undistinguished by narcissistic dress, with a physique and physiognomy the envy of no self-respecting *charro*.

Equally unprepossessing in appearance is Guadalupe, the ageing, heavy-featured *hacendado* ('ranch owner'), who, though lacking Jesús's posturing dandyism, never gives the impression of a wavering patriarchal authority, since he too, like Jesús and unlike Alberto, is identified with animals and hunting. His first appearance in the film sees him fretting over the birth of a colt; later scenes show him out hunting. But however relaxed Guadalupe and Jesús seem to be over the rival claims of home and wilderness, the film stresses the contradictions of a system in which the demands of one are not necessarily any guide to suitable behaviour for the other. So it proves when the order of the home is disrupted by a creature emerging from the wilderness, whose radical force is described by some as infernal, but left by the text for the viewer to read as an explosive return of the repressed, the exposure of the bourgeois order's many contradictions.

Susana is another of Buñuel's outsider figures, an ideological saboteur attempting to tear off the mask of a socially constructed femininity, confronting the audience with its complicity. In appearance and behaviour she epitomizes melodramatic excess, her disruptive presence in the narrative a self-conscious expression of realism's subversion. While elsewhere, for instance, dreams or comedy are the text's methods of questioning its own mechanisms and framework of intelligibility, here the same is achieved above all through excess of characterization in Susana's overblown, relentless sexuality.[5]

In a discussion of Hollywood melodrama Geoffrey Nowell-Smith refers to the process through which pent-up emotions often constrained by the narrative are sometimes released through music or *mise-en-scène*, which act as substitutes for the body of the patient:

The undischarged emotion which cannot be accommodated within the action, subordinated as it is to the demands of family/lineage/inheritance, is traditionally expressed in the music and, in the case of film, in certain elements of the *mise-en-scène*. That is to say, music and *mise-en-scène* do not just heighten the emotionality of an element of the action: to some extent they substitute for it. The mechanism here is strikingly similar to that of the psychopathology of hysteria. In hysteria the energy attached to an idea that has been repressed returns converted into a bodily symptom. The 'return of the repressed' takes place, not in conscious discourse, but displaced on to the body of the patient. In the melodrama, where there is always material which cannot be expressed in discourse or in the actions of the characters furthering the designs of the plot, a conversion can take place in the body of the text. (1987: 73–4)

Excess, the explosive release of unfulfilled desires, takes place in *Susana* through the use of Raúl Lavista's highly-charged romantic Tchaikovsky- and Brahms-inspired musical score, through a tempestuous natural *mise-en-scène* and, above all, through the body, especially the voice, gestures, dress, and exaggerated acting style—what in a general discussion of melodramatic acting

[5] Víctor Fuentes (1993: 58) refers to the thematics of guilt runnning through the film.

Peter Brooks has called a 'plastic figurability of emotion' (1984: 47)—of Susana herself. All of this contributes towards the externalization of feeling, here the rage and frustration at the social order's constraints on female subjectivity, symbolized by the film's beginning and closure, both of which see her imprisoned in the reformatory. As elsewhere in melodrama, in the Mexican—e.g. *Naná* (1943), *María Candelaria* (1943), *Doña Bárbara* (1943), *La trepadora* (1944)—as well as in the Spanish traditions—e.g. Cifesa films like *Agustina de Aragón* (1950) or *La Leona de Castilla* (1951)— the centrality of the female in the narrative at least ensures that some space is reserved for women-related questions.

Throughout the film Susana's body represents a complex, highly eroticized formulation of the return of the repressed. Her first appearance, clothes almost slipping off her buxom shape, contrasts markedly with the mummified look of her captors, the nuns of an unspecified charitable order. The nuns' denial of their own bodies is paralleled by the attitudes of the women in the Guadalupe household towards themselves and Susana. There, both Carmen the wife and Felisa the maid dress with characteristic sobriety, their repressed sexuality further stressed through Felisa's constant stream of 'Ave María Purísima's' to exorcise all manner of carnal dangers. Into this prim world a libido-dominated angel falls, her semi-naked thighs, muddied by the storm-tossed wilderness, becoming not just a voyeuristic site for the delectation of the sex-starved household males, but also an eruption of the feminine, of the female body, into a world tyrannized by decorum. Less a psychologically plausible character than a recasting in secular terms of a figure from one of the great *autos*, Susana represents self-conscious female sexuality, desired and feared, pursued and banished, both by the text and by the social order from which that text emerges and for whose consumption it has been designed.

In recognition of the ultimately doomed project for the reclamation of female space, Susana strives constantly to impose her vibrant sexuality on her environment. Her characteristic gesture of lowering her already extravagant *decolleté*, represents as well as exhibitionism a form of ideologically provocative disruption. From her earliest appearance, imprisoned with only rats and a tarantula, her *alter egos*, for company, she lives up to the crudest forms of negative stereotyping associated with the melodramatic figure of the *femme fatale*, the *mujer devoradora*, in the Mexican

cinema best exemplified by María Félix in *Doña Bárbara* (1943).[6]
Not only flaunting her body, Susana reverses gender roles, taking the initiative whenever possible or necessary. In an early
scene, hoping to ensnare Alberto, she passes by his room, looks
in from the outside through the open window and provokes him
into making various overtures towards her. The shot is composed in a way reversing the usual patterns of screen courtship
(boy outdoors, girl indoors). Here, Alberto is inside, separated
from his female wooer through the bedroom window bars. His
poetic eulogy identifies Susana with the outdoors, a process also
stressing her communion with the wilderness and with a place
of definition already established in the film as masculine: 'Eres
como una hierba del campo, Susana. No se sabe cuándo ni
cómo crece, hasta que uno se fija en ella.' ('You're like a grass
growing in the countryside. No one knows when or how it grows
until one looks at it carefully.') Susana's identification with nature makes her neither a Guadalupe nor a Chingada, but a
demotic earth-monster, a Coatlicue or Cihuacoatl, the woman-
serpent of indigenous mythology, the insatiable goddess who
eats men.

The ambivalence of the image, of women's *rapport* with nature, free and yet constrained, finds its equivalent inside the
house. At one point, Guadalupe, the hunter, returns home from
the wilderness and approaches Susana, who is completing a
domestic chore. The shot is framed with Susana standing slightly
higher than Guadalupe, to the left of the frame, on a raised
platform inside the house, cleaning the window-panes of a glass
door, while Guadalupe stands to the right of the frame cleaning
his rifle. Susana has her characteristically vampish but also
mocking look of a Virginia Mayo from the other side of the
tracks. Her luxuriant hair cascading in bouncy coils onto bare
shoulders, her face applied with enough cosmetics to earn a
'severa represión de las pinturas, afeites y arreboles de la cara'
(Vives 1944: 54) ('reprimand for using cosmetics and make-up')
from even the mildest patriarch, Susana is after big game now,
stalking the great white hunter, Guadalupe himself. Resisting all
calls to be the chaste extreme of the virgin/whore dichotomy, she
has no intention of living up to the significance of her biblical

---

[6] María Félix seems to have been too much of a *mujer devoradora* for Gérard Philippe,
who complained to Buñuel about her over-enthusiastic kisses during the love-scenes
of *La Fièvre monte à El Pao* (Rucar de Buñuel 1991: 88).

name explained to her by Alberto, preferring instead the challenge and potentially more fulfilling rewards of the fallen woman.

The ambiguities of social constructions of female subjectivity are economically expressed here in visual form through Susana's identification with cleansing and transparency. The woman here is imaged as both subservient and insubstantial, a fantasy of male desire as the submissive, unclean slave of passion whose essence, as Ortega remarks via a metaphor from Cervantes, is wholly diaphanous, reflecting only the substance of the male:

La esencia del cristal consiste en servir de tránsito a otros objetos: su ser es precisamente no ser él, sino ser las otras cosas. ¡Extraña misión de humildad, de negación de sí mismos, adscrita a ciertos seres! La mujer que es, según Cervantes, 'un cristal transparente de hermosura' parece también condenada a 'ser lo otro que ella': en lo corporal, como en lo espiritual, parece destinada a ser un aromado tránsito de otros seres, a dejarse penetrar del amante, del hijo. (1976: 131–2)

(The essence of glass lies in serving as a place of transit for other objects: its essence is specifically not to be itself, but other things. A strange mission of humility, of self-negation, decreed for certain beings. Woman, who is, according to Cervantes, a 'transparent glass of beauty' also seems condemned to be 'something different': in material as in spiritual things, she seems destined to be a fragrant place of transit for other beings, allowing her to be penetrated by her lover or child.)

As Susana stands by the door polishing the glass panels, her eroticization and effect on her admiring employer are further stressed by his pose and action. The phallic significance of his rifle becomes even clearer as soon as he lifts up and begins to caress the barrel. Transparent, subservient, unclean, Susana's only recourse is to retaliate by making use of these negative associations. In the long run the forces against her prove too powerful, but before eventually surrendering—kicking, fighting, screaming to the last—she plays along with the fantasy of greatest appeal to her patriarchal guardian, by living up to his image of her as an eroticized daughter-surrogate, the nymphet he will seduce as her father.

Throughout the early part of the film, following her admission to the house and the offer of refuge from the storm and—accepting her version of her mysterious past—from abandonment by a faithless lover, Susana is often referred to as a 'niña' ('little girl'), 'muchacha' ('girl'), or 'hija' ('daughter'), encouraged to address her benefactors as her parents. From the start (though late in the film the policeman reveals her age as 20), her child-ishness is stressed, as when Carmen remarks: 'Eres muy joven, una niña casi. Tú eres como mi hija. Desde este momento te protegeremos.' ('You're very young, still a child. You are like my daughter. From this moment on we will protect you.') Else-where Guadalupe asks his wife: '¿Qué piensas hacer con esta muchacha?' ('What do you intend to do with this girl?') And Susana herself, colluding mischievously in her own oppression, encourages these parent–daughter relations by remarking: 'Para mí es usted más que mi madre, a quien no conocí, Señora.' ('You are more a mother to me than my own, whom I never knew, madam.')

Susana belongs to a tradition of sexually precocious daughter figures of varying ages: in Hollywood, Shirley Temple, Carroll Baker, Sue Lyon, and others, and, in the Spanish cinema, Marisol or Rocío Durcal. The configuration of these daughter figures all benefit from a reading through descriptions by Freud and some post-Freudians (like Juliet Mitchell, Jessica Benjamin, and Karen Horney) of the various processes through which a daughter for-mulates her relations with her father and mother. The daugh-ter's belief in the mother's castration leads her at first to turn to the father, replacing a wish for the penis with one for a baby, before submitting herself to the socializing process of the Oedi-pal complex, eventually confirming, according to Juliet Mitchell, 'her pre-Oedipal identification (as opposed to attachment) with the mother, and instead of taking on qualities of aggression and control, she acquires the art of love and conciliation. Not being heir to the law of culture, her task is to see that mankind repro-duces itself within the circularity of the supposedly natural family' (1982: 405). This is the route through which, in Freud's terms, the daughter submits to the socializing process. Freud's revisions of the theory of the daughter's seduction—in which he came to believe that his female patients' confessions of seduction by their fathers were more fantasy than reality—seem to provide the film with much of its complex theoretical background. In *Susana*, as in *Tristana*, Buñuel introduces the figure of the rebel daughter attempting to overthrow the social order in which she has grown up, ultimately overpowered by a resistant ideology, Tristana becoming a hyperbolized monstrous 'other', incorpor-ating all the nightmare fantasies of the castrating woman, Susana returning to the cell from which she managed only temporary liberation. Her seduction of the father, paying the patriarch in kind, reflects a desire to attack the mother, not necessarily here because, following classic Freudian theory, she blames her for not having a penis, but partly because Carmen is a woman seemingly content to endure and therefore help sustain a victimizing ideology. Even though there is no mention of Susana's relations with her real mother, her involvement with mother figures (the nuns at the reformatory, Guadalupe's wife Carmen) suggests that there is still some scope for following Estela Welldon's argument *vis-à-vis* a general discussion of relations between mothers and daughters where promiscuity in daughters (Susana flirts with the three men on the ranch) is explained as 'looking in men for what she missed in her contact with her mother' (1992: 48). But Susana also partly attacks her, in line with Jessica Benjamin's wider discussion of female desire, because of a wish to identify herself with the father and his involvement with the outside world (1990: 114–23). If Carmen is the symbol of disempowerment, the object of Susana's sadistic fantasies, the woman whose place she willingly tries to usurp, Guadalupe represents the outside world, the public space beyond the cell of her socially constructed femininity, the male-dominated realm of power. This is the essence of Susana's desire, and her strategy for achieving it is the daughter's seduction, at once hyperbolizing her own femininity and infantility, a process that leads her to question, and ultimately to be punished for questioning, the passivity of the female.

For Guadalupe, on the other hand, the Lolita syndrome, the seduction of a daughter-surrogate, entails not only, as in Lope's passion for Tristana, desire for the defloration of a girl uncontaminated by the 'memory of sexual relations with another' (Freud 1981*d*: 265), but also a search for someone as yet untutored by experience, still callow enough to submit unquestioningly to the authority of the father, through whom he can indulge his immortality fantasy. Too long in thrall, as his name suggests, to the Virgin of Guadalupe[7] he is the Elder who now seeks a more secular virgin in Susana. Like Tristana, Séverine—the 'collégienne précoce' ('precocious schoolgirl')—in *Belle de jour*,

---

[7] Octavio Paz (1991: 101–3) points out the importance for Catholicism in Mexico of the figures of the Virgin of Guadalupe (Our Lady of Guadalupe was declared the patroness of New Spain by Pope Benedict XIV in 1756) and of the 'Chingada', who is the violated Mother.

Evie in *The Young One,* and others, Susana is a daughter fantasy, offering herself to the father as an obedient child of desire. While Jesús—closer to her in age and background, and under no illusions about her daughter masquerade—treats her roughly, and while Alberto is too pubertal to see any reality beyond an adolescent obsession, Guadalupe cloaks his baser appetites with the gestures and rhetoric of the caring father, creating his own masquerade for a desire ultimately to subject and abuse her. Karen Horney's remarks about the masculine tendency to lower women's self-respect through identifying women with infantility as well as emotionality (1967: 146) seem to find their perfect formulation in Guadalupe's attitude towards Susana. The male's hostility towards his mother (Carmen here cast as mother figure for Guadalupe as well as for the children) originates in his real mother's prohibitions of instinctive activities, something which leads to sadistic impulses on the part of the child towards the mother's body. Furthermore, while for the girl anxiety is caused by the feeling that her genitals are too small for her father's penis, the boy's fears that the size of his penis is too small for his mother's genitals lead him to dread them and inspire in him feelings of inadequacy, rejection, and derision. As a result the male turns to infantile, non-maternal, and hysterical daughter figures. In this film Susana is the non-maternal, hysterical daughter figure of melodramatic excess, through her presence at once exposing the limitations of realism and the root causes of daughter-obsessed male sexuality.

The focus on the other two women is directly on their representation as matriarchs. Felisa the servant represents an ideological colonization so extreme as to make impossible discourse unmotivated by the platitudes of religious superstition. Anything mysterious or slightly disturbing (a favourite word of Buñuel's in this context is *inquietante*) is considered the work of the Devil, any blessing the act of divine providence.[8] Marginally less pious, and continuing the tradition of the mother figure of a stream of Mexican melodramas often starring the rather formidable matriarch Sara García (e.g. *Cuando los hijos se van,* 1941), Carmen verges on parody as the prototype Christian mother, her individuality

---

[8] As Wallace Fowlie points out, *inquiétude* was a characteristically Surrealistic motif: 'man in the twentieth century is forced to live in a period of threatened warfare or literal wars of such increasing cosmic magnitude that his state of mind is anything but peaceful' (1963: 17–21).

willingly forfeited in the cause of devotion to husband and son. Her function is double-edged: sometimes highlighted as a 'perfecta casada' ('perfect wife') and mother,[9] at other times exploring her interiority and introjected values of the social order to which she belongs. The traditional image of mother as nurturer, supervising the moral and physical welfare of her family, is represented in a predominantly positive way here, although three scenes in particular dramatically expose not only the frustrations of a life of self-denial, but also the bitterness arising out of recognition that love and attention so selflessly and willingly lavished on others have been received with such fragile, almost contemptuous gratitude.

On all three occasions Susana is the cause of the mother's frustration and anger. First, Carmen responds to her son's curt remarks by exclaiming: 'Tú tan bueno, tan cariñoso siempre.' ('You, so good, always so affectionate!') Secondly, she chides her husband, also by now crazed through lust for Susana, with an '¡Ay! ¡Qué hombres!' ('Men!'), following his own '¡Ay! ¡Qué mujeres!' ('Women!'), a phrase, paralleling his son's earlier abrupt way of addressing his mother, that seeks to preserve a distance from what both regard as the interference of a woman in the affairs of men. Even though at one level the film's rhetoric ultimately presents Susana sympathetically, the ingratitude dealt to the mother by the beneficiaries of her life-long personal and career self-denials exposes the shortcomings of a social order in which injustices like these are occupational hazards. From one point of view, the film acknowledges and appreciates the mother's sacrifices, recognizing her contribution to the stability of the home, with Buñuel showing elsewhere, especially in *Los olvidados* and *La hija del engaño*, the disastrous consequences for a family devoid of the love and care here taken for granted. From another point of view, though, the film seems to realize that a life exclusively defined through self-sacrifice for the family brings risks more serious than the thoughtless words of ingratitude to which she is humiliatingly subjected in these scenes. For Fifties' Mexican

---

[9] Deserving, in Fray Luis's terms, her family's gratitude, 'porque al oficio de la buena mujer pertenece, y esto nos enseña Salomón, aquí hacer buen marido y criar buenos hijos, y tales, que no sólo con debidas y agradecidas palabras le den loor, pero mucho más con sus obras buenas' (Luis de León 1963: 132) ('because it is woman's role, according to Solomon, to find a good husband and to raise good children, who will not only praise her through due and grateful words, but much more through good works').

audiences, the real prospect of poverty and homelessness for a career-less woman thrown out of her home by her husband would have seemed in times less responsive to the idea of women at work more than simply fanciful. While many advances in the emancipation of women had been made since the Revolution— the figure of Felipe Carrillo Puerto (1874–1924) is especially interesting in this respect—Mexican society's attitudes towards women, especially mothers, remained even by the 1940s and 1950s fairly conservative. Women had been holding public office since 1916, when Rosa Torres became the President of the Municipal Council of Mérida; feminist societies had been founded; areas like Yucatán had become centres for women's liberation; and divorce laws—even though regarded by some as double-edged, giving *carte blanche* for irresponsible behaviour by uncaring husbands—at least made it possible for women to be released from difficult marriages.[10] Nevertheless, the ideology of what Evelyn P. Stevens has called *marianismo*—a cult of 'feminine spiritual superiority, which teaches that women are semi-divine, morally superior to and spiritually stronger than men' (1979: 91)—ensured that whatever status mothers enjoyed remained to a large extent confined to domestic contexts, their power restricted to family affairs, although even here ultimately subject to the patriarchal law.

In *Susana*, Carmen represents all compromised and unappreciated mothers when in a third scene allowing her to express her anger, she vents her frustrations on Susana. Symbol of patience and endurance, the mother becomes for an instant a furious avenger, taking a whip to Susana, every lash delivered both a protest against the ungrateful behaviour of her son and husband caused by the presence of a woman unashamedly flaunting her sexuality, and a blow on behalf of all women against her submission to the social order's various repressions, especially of a sexual nature. Simone de Beauvoir's general discussion of a mother's resentments against the intrusions of a strange woman in the life of her son has a special relevance, especially in its diabolical references, to Carmen's attitudes towards Alberto in this film:

The hoax played on the devotee is exposed in the most merciless manner: his wife is going to deprive her of her functions. The hostility she feels towards this strange woman who 'takes away' her child has often been

---

[10] For details on the rise of feminism in Mexico, see Macías (1978).

described. The mother has elevated the brute, involuntary process of parturition to the height of a divine mystery, and she declines to admit that a human decision can have more weight. In her eyes the values are already established, they originate in nature, in the past: she misunderstands the worth of an obligation freely undertaken. Her son is indebted to her for his life; what does he owe this woman who was yesterday still unknown to him? It must be some kind of witchcraft that has enabled her to persuade him of the existence of a bond which up to now did not exist; she is scheming, not disinterested, dangerous. (1969: 319)

As Estela Welldon also puts it, 'motherhood provides an excellent vehicle for some women to exercise perverse and perverting attitudes towards their offspring, and to retaliate against their own mothers' (1992: 63). Even though here Susana is not Carmen's daughter, a drama of transferred hostilities is being played out, in which the various resentments of mother and offspring are being given expression. The abuse of the mother's power over the child—as also in *Ensayo de un crimen, Tristana, Los olvidados*, and elsewhere—leads to the child's desire to exact revenge in an ever-increasing spiral of perverse behaviour. As ever in Buñuel, the origins of perversity lie partly in culture and, as regards motherhood, its social constructions and expectations. When Carmen starts to lash out wildly at Susana, the film seems to be heading for a radical, disruptive closure, laying bare and fragmenting the injustices of a victimizing system. And even though outright subversion is avoided through the restoration of a fragile order, the scenes of her demented loss of control, as well as the chaos created earlier in the film, create an impact not totally smoothed over by facile resolution.

2.2. *Una mujer sin amor* and Romantic Love

'De manera que el hombre que acertare con una mujer de valor, se puede desde luego tener por rico y dichoso, entendiendo que ha hallado una perla oriental.'

Fray Luis de León, *La perfecta casada*

('So the man who finds a good woman can certainly consider himself rich and fortunate, having discovered an oriental pearl.')

PLOT SYNOPSIS: The narrative traces the emptiness of a marriage between an elderly, somewhat crudely materialistic, unromantic shop-owner, Carlos, and his young wife Rosario. A young, idealized engineer intrudes in their life and embarks on an affair that leads to the birth of Miguel, a brother for the legitimate son Carlitos. Years later, having rejected the opportunity of abandoning Carlos for Julio, Rosario receives word that Julio has died leaving his fortune to Miguel, whose paternity is known only to his mother. Becoming suspicious about his true relationship with his brother, Carlitos accuses his mother of adultery, and after a quarrel eventually becomes reconciled both with her and with Miguel, though with her husband's death, Miguel's impending marriage, and Carlitos's departure she prepares at the end of the film for a life of solitude.

Most critics join Buñuel in writing off *Una mujer sin amor.* 'Es la peor de las que he hecho' (Pérez Turrent and de la Colina 1993: 61) ('It's my worst film'). The critics, though, are too respectful of Buñuel's modesty here, and insufficiently mindful of his more general remarks elsewhere about the care and attention lavished on even his most commercial projects. This film was indeed another, like *Susana*, taken on for bread-and-butter reasons, a means of funding other projects closer to his interests. For some, its popular melodramatic form excludes it from serious analysis of the great Surrealist's work. But for all its various lapses, mainly the result of a ludicrous twenty-day working deadline, the film is another thoughtful mediation of attitudes towards the family and its various repressions of desire.

The credit sequence confirms the gloomy semantics of the film's title. While the names of the creative personnel roll on, at the right of the frame, a lonely woman stands by a window whose reflection on the floor, and just a little left of the window, provides the only source of light in the room. As a sort of prelude to the narrative, this image offers a compact expression of the film's attitude towards the confinements and obscurities of bourgeois marriage and the clear-sighted realities of life beyond. Within the constraints of the Mexican melodrama, the film reformulates the commonplaces of more respectable narratives of adultery (*Anna Karenina, Madame Bovary, David and Bathsheba*, and so on),[11] though here the popular cinema's greater edginess about

[11] The major Hollywood films based on these novels were *Anna Karenina* (1935), *Madame Bovary* (1949), and *David and Bathsheba* (1951).

transgressive desires ensures, as in *Susana*, that the ending, again ambiguously, is a happy one.

In its representation of Rosario's relations with husband and lover, the film covers the thematic ground of what, writing about romantic or ideal love, Jessica Benjamin has described as the belief that 'the man will provide access to a world that is otherwise closed to her' (1990: 116). Rosario's marriage to Carlos bears all the hallmarks, as he himself angrily points out, of a marriage of convenience. In this case convenience means exchange of poverty for the duties of sex and motherhood and access to the public world that her husband normally inhabits. Usually, though, in romantic narratives these advantages count for nothing without love. So it proves here, and the greater part of the film concentrates on the events leading up to and beyond a woman's quest for extra-marital romance.[12]

Ultimately, of course, the sanctioning of transgressive desires like adultery has only a temporary authority in popular films made largely in the shadow of an ideology prioritizing family over personal values. In keeping with such procedures, Rosario is forced to surrender the promise of romantic fulfilment to maternal duty, and is prevented from elopement with Julio. The sacrifice is made to seem all the more extreme through the husband's one-dimensional negative characterization in the film's routinely melodramatic reliance on excess. In order to highlight the sacrifices made for her child by his mother, Carlos is made to appear a violent, vulgar materialist, someone through whom the audience's seemingly conflicting desires for romantic fulfilment and family responsibility can be fully exploited. As a father, Carlos acts sadistically towards his son, Carlitos, refusing to hear his explanation of an offence at school, slapping him in the face, locking him up in his bedroom, less interested in the boy's welfare than in the slur that his behaviour will cast on his own standing and reputation. There is nothing here of Melanie Klein's 'Good Father', the man who not only fulfils his wife's wishes through having had the child in the first place, but who also derives 'an additional source of pleasure through the gratification of his feminine wishes by his sharing the maternal pleasure with his wife' (Klein and Riviere 1964: 81). What is most striking

---

[12] Agustín Sánchez Vidal (1984:146) sees this film as part of a family melodrama trilogy including *El gran calavera* and *Susana*.

in Carlos's treatment of Carlitos is, on the contrary, a displacement of 'sadistic wishes towards the mother' (ibid. 81), with no attempt at making any restoration to her. Eventually, when the child reaches adulthood, Carlos's attitude changes, his repressed hostilities towards his mother (neither seen nor referred to in the film) and displaced humiliations of his wife, Rosario, no longer as urgent now in old age as before. The individuality of the child, in any case now corresponding more to the father's sense of achievement and status (Carlitos becomes a doctor), means that the reflections on his own status are no longer identified with the failings of a naughty child.

Brutality is compounded with coarseness during his first meeting with Julio who, in this version of Maupassant's novel *Pierre et Jean* (also made into a film by André Cayatte in 1943), has rescued little Carlitos from the wilderness, his desired refuge from the home where he has been punished by his father. The novel has none of these preliminary explicatory scenes either setting up Carlos sen. as the brutish figure from whom his wife is desperate to escape or establishing Julio as the romantic alternative on which she pins her hopes. It introduces the reader to children already in their thirties and finds no room for lyricism and pathos, qualities so essential to film melodrama, especially the woman-centred narrative. Significantly, too, the film shifts the emphasis in its title away from the boys, stressing instead the woman's story, her subjectivity and heroic sacrifices, something that eventually exposes the contradictions of a Mexican ideology of womanhood restricting her, according to Octavio Paz, to being 'hech[a] a la imagen de los hombres . . . sólo un reflejo de la voluntad y querer masculinos' (1991: 41) ('made in man's image . . . only a reflection of masculine will and desire').

In the scene of Julio's invitation to the house, where Carlos expresses his gratitude for Carlitos's safe return, Rosario and Julio are often placed in shot together, varying a pattern in which either Rosario is isolated or Julio and Carlos, but never Rosario and Carlos together, appear in a two-shot. The divisions between the married couple, here expressed visually, are borne out by the dialogue, Carlos's uncouth and approving remarks about stereotyped male behaviour causing Rosario extreme embarrassment: 'Es Ud. joven. Apuesto que es Ud. mujeriego y jugador.' ('You're young. I bet you're a womanizer and a gambler.') Carlos's crass remarks and chauvinistic inferences about Julio, his assumptions about male patterns of behaviour in general, recall the ideologized males of many literary texts, such as Agata's husband, Nicanor Cruz, in *Todo verdor perecerá* (1941). No longer able to indulge in the conventional man's favourite sports, women and gambling, Carlos seeks vicarious pleasure through Julio's anticipated accounts of his exploits. The contrast between the intolerably gross husband and the dashing, sensitive young man—established through dialogue, visual composition, appearance, and behaviour—seems above all designed to make Rosario's eventual decision to remain with her husband all the more heroic, her sacrifice and the pathos demanded by the genre all the greater. The denial of an opportunity for surrender to romantic love draws on all the resources of the genre's enthralment to excess.

For all its melodramatic conventionality the pathos of Rosario's situation leads to all sorts of ambiguities about choices available to women. Whereas in a conventional melodrama romantic love is usually regarded by the text, whatever the actual qualities of the lovers, as a potential source of happiness, especially for the woman, in *Una mujer sin amor* romantic love is eventually seen as no less compromised by inhibitions and tyrannies of various kinds than marriage itself. *Amour fou*, given in Buñuel a Graciánmodified rather than a Bretonian force, may have its momentary and not-to-be-underestimated regenerative justification, but this is something often ultimately vitiated by other attitudes and preconceptions. Rosario's refusal to elope with Julio is the text's simultaneous deference to the ideology of motherhood and retreat from the illusions of romantic love.

On the surface, Julio represents an ideal alternative to Carlos. While Carlos is identified with the city and its corruptions—he is the owner, significantly, of an antiques shop—Julio is a civilized backwoodsman, a Rousseauesque man of nature, not just a city-dwelling engineer seemingly discontented with the frustrations of urban life and looking for the *barbarie* of nature and love. The film establishes a series of contrasts between (social) city settings identified with marriage, which is their symbol, and (antisocial) open-air ambiences associated with adultery. While Carlos is connected with interiors and the city, the limits of which define the meanings of socially accepted modes of behaviour, Julio is mainly associated with the transgressions symbolized by the wilderness.[13] But these are also sometimes confused, the illusions and frustrations of one crossing over with the consolations and stabilities of the other.

During the picnic in the country, a treat for Rosario and Carlitos while Carlos is away on business, Julio actually refers to the woods all around as his own, later slightly reformulating the remark, contenting himself with an expression of self-identification with the wilderness, on this occasion a piece of land he is working on in his capacity as an engineer. Later in the film Julio's association with the outdoors is restated during a conversation with Rosario by the river, a meeting during which she finally decides against abandoning her child and husband. These identifications of the lovers with the wilderness draw parallels between adultery and the imperatives of nature, but they also suggest, as Tony Tanner argues, that 'there is literally no enduring place in the world of social and natural cyclicity where the adulterous lovers can find a locale, a realm of their own' (1981: 34). Like outlaws on the run, Julio and Rosario find refuge only in each other's presence, and yet, as they strive to create a place of their own, their attempts to impose an order on the turbulence and frustration of their lives seem in danger of reproducing a similar set of disorders from which, above all, Rosario, like Emma Bovary and other famous literary and film heroines before her, seeks liberation.

The mother and wife, obedient to the demands of a brutish husband, is on the verge of compounding her subservience through a romance in which her identity and *raison d'être* will again be defined, in keeping with Paz's notion that the Mexican woman 'simplemente no tiene voluntad' (1991: 43) ('quite simply has no will of her own'), principally through subordination to the priorities of another man. Consequently, when Rosario finds herself in Julio's office—his official space, not the pastoral *mise-en-scène* of his private desires—she makes a remark that confirms her entrapment by attitudes that have destroyed whatever ambitions or initiatives towards autonomy she may once have harboured: 'Mi casa es ésta, mi marido eres tú.' ('This is my home, you are my husband.') These words invoke the familiar and

[13] In *Adultery in the Novel: Contract and Transgression* Tony Tanner refers to the idea of marriage's connection with 'the emergence of man's ability to establish boundaries' (1981: 60).

genuinely felt protestations of love, affirmations of a desire to be eternally in the company of the beloved, sentiments whose every syllable confirm unshakeable devotion. But, in the context of the various mechanisms of irony and excess in operation in this text, their resonances stretch beyond love's literal truths. Rosario's remarks also bear witness, in the light of her inner exile in adultery from her home, to the provisionality of the adulterer's place in the social world. Her place in the city and in the social fabric, symbolized by her status as wife and mother in the setting of her husband's home, is sacrificed for an unknown alternative. The fixity of marriage—its privileges as well as its disadvantages—is being put at risk in exchange for the instabilities of adulterous desire.

On the positive side, adultery implies not only transgression but also excitement, an act through which to feel truly alive, the gratification of an impulse acknowledging uncertainty and danger if not necessarily, as in de Rougemont's account (1956), death. But more negatively, of course, adulterous passion is often a desperate, ill-defined search for liberation from tyrannies in which the object of desire becomes the screen for fantasies of ideals hopelessly at odds with the reality of the individuals on whom they are projected. An illusion of this sort takes control of Rosario, who, like many fictional adulteresses before her, fails to come to terms with the reality of her unhappiness, to confront a need for assessment of her own value as an individual regardless of any considerations about her relations either with her children or with another man. So, her subjugation to Carlos almost succeeds in being reformulated in her relationship with Julio, to whom she seems ready to sacrifice her own individuality and her own space. Not only her home but also her very subjectivity will be surrendered for his. This is the negative side, taking to extremes romantic love's discovery of a self through the reality of the lover, an ideology bordering on self-effacement, so empty is the melodramatic woman's life without family or love, so paranoid her fear of solitude. Rosario is the film's equivalent of the Mexican women's magazine heroine, her attributes characterized by dependence, ineffectuality, humility, and passivity. As Cornelia Butler Flora points out : 'The heroine in Latin American woman's magazine fiction, regardless of class, tends to be either proud and arrogant—to be put in her place by the strong male—or to be gentle and self-sacrificing, passively awaiting the adored male' (Butler 1979: 69).

When Rosario and Julio touch on the theme of solitude, Rosario comments that there is no solitude when one has a child, the daily routines of childcare eliminating the possibility of intro-spection. The implications of the remark gesture not only to-wards the many fulfilments of motherhood but also towards the feeling that almost any time-consuming activity is tolerable as a way of avoiding confrontation with the realities of her situation. Yet, since the film cannot overtly approve of female introspec-tion (a process that may lead to meditation on her socially con-structed subjectivity), no mention is ever made of the more liberating potential of solitude. Until forced at the end by cir-cumstances to confront it, Rosario learns how to avoid solitude, how to occupy her time responding to her duties as wife and mother. Nevertheless, as in Sirk's *All that Heaven Allows* (1955), another woman-centred narrative tracing the sacrifices made by a mother for her children, *Una mujer sin amor* resists the regres-sive drives of the genre, finally confronting Rosario with the inconsistencies and confusions in which her life has been entan-gled. In *All that Heaven Allows* the mother stares at a blank TV screen, the children, for whom she unnecessarily sacrificed her lover, grown up and living elsewhere, their objections to his suitability as her husband no longer of any importance to them; in *Una mujer sin amor* Rosario is forced to confront her own soli-tude, refuses the company of her sons, at last recognizing the importance of introspection, reviewing her past and the direc-tion that her life has taken. As we see Rosario in melancholy, pensive mood, we are encouraged to feel that even if she had left Carlos for Julio she might not have freed herself, however ideal Julio might have turned out to be as a partner, from a spiral of self-defeating compromises.

The resistances to the ideological conformities of the genre are here not prompted by suspicions about the declared intentions or personality of the lover-hero Julio, whose air of sensitivity and attention clearly meet with the film's approval. Yet it is precisely because Julio is such an almost impossible paragon of sensitive masculinity that questions can be raised about the simplistic contrasts and exaggerations of melodrama and about the situa-tional ironies of the film, suggesting that, even though at first

Rosario would have enjoyed an ideal *Liebestraum,* the effect of
an attachment so engrossed in the virtues of her partner would
have again led to uncomprehending distraction from her own
place as a woman, and from questions about her own subjectivity, in the fabric of contemporary Mexican society. Julio's
extreme sensitivity is even reflected in his work as an engineer,
defined here as a calling identified not simply with practical but
also with aesthetic and creative sensibilities, in which designing
buildings becomes another clue of a sanctioned feminization.
Not content with this, though, the film develops further dimensions of situational irony in the idyllic pastoral scenes, at first
through the use of a close-harmony group, following patterns
already established in the Mexican melodrama (e.g. *Flor silvestre*)
and given a more mocking tone by Buñuel himself in *Gran
Casino,* heightening the ambience of passion through music:

¿De qué sirve querer | con todo el corazón? | ¿De qué sirve sufrir el
deber | respetando un amor? | Pa' mí sólo eras tú. | No por nadie jamás
| Eras sólo pa' mí | y besando la cruz | te lo puedo jurar.

(What's the point of loving with all one's heart? What's the point of
suffering in love? For me there was only you. Not for anyone else. Only
you for me and kissing the cross I swear it to you.)

As the trio sing, their lyrics prompt questions about duty and
fidelity. The song clearly refers to the wife's moment of truth,
hovering as she is between allegiances to her husband and to her
idealized lover. The music fills the night air, intoxicating the
couple as they put the child Carlitos to bed. The irony of the
lyrics, with its soft, lilting cadences and bitter-sweet tight harmonies, derives from the lovers' recognition that their mutual
feelings reach their climax as Carlitos goes to sleep. The clear
implications of this are that, in addition to seeking in each other
the fulfilment of romantic love, Julio searches for a mother in
Rosario while she pursues in him a Good Father. Julio initially
approaches Rosario through Carlitos, whom he rescues—in sharp
contrast to the little boy's father's act of rejection and its prelude
to his flight from home—and then befriends and takes on fishing
and boating expeditions. Both here and later on through his
legacy to his natural son Miguel, Julio is represented as the
Good Father, the symbol of equality and fairness, drawing sat-
isfaction and pleasure from the release of his own femininity
through the shared experiences of nurturing and caring for a

child. She has already heard him counter Carlos's uncouth re-marks about womanizing and gambling with a comment about welcoming the challenges of family life: 'Me apasionaría tener una familia.' ('I'd love to have a family.') Melanie Klein's de-scriptions of a more general process involving the complexities of sexual attraction highlight the particularities of the relations between Julio and Rosario: 'Her impressions of her father, her feelings towards him—admiration, trust and so on—may play a predominant part in her choosing of a love companion.' (Klein and Riviere 1964: 88). She goes on to remark that, if the rela-tionship between father and daughter is in some respects un-satisfactory, other male role-models from infancy (for example, a brother, cousin, or playmate) would modify or perhaps even supplant the original ideal. Her argument refrains from simplis-tically restricting role-model patterns of behaviour to childhood experiences, making the further point that 'Normal adult rela-tionships always contain fresh elements which are derived from the new situation—from circumstances and the personalities of the people we come in contact with, and from their response to our emotional needs and practical interests as grown-up people' (ibid. 89).

Whatever the case—whether as a result of childhood or of adult experience—Rosario's search for a Good Father figure fails to overcome her sense of marriage's sanctity, in this case as a site of heavily loaded social meanings from which liberation, as Tony Tanner argues, is always extremely difficult:

Marriage . . . is a means by which society attempts to bring into har-monious alignment patterns of passion and patterns of property; in bourgeois society it is not only a matter of putting your Gods where your treasure is. . . . but also of putting your libido, loyalty and all other possessions and products, including children, there as well. For bourgeois society marriage is the all-subsuming, all-organising, all-containing contract. . . . The central importance of marriage makes it clear why it was adultery rather than seduction . . . that became such a crucial subject. (1981: 15)

The narrative's refusal to contemplate an act of such extreme transgression against the social order allows the focus to switch to interrogation of the complexity of mother–son relationships. These become even more interesting as soon as Carlitos begins to suspect the truth about Miguel. Up to this point, and once he has become an adult, Carlitos is the narrative's method of questioning the basis on which men define and choose love-objects. An early scene involving Carlitos as an adult shows him pursuing a female colleague, making her a proposal of marriage. By now, like Miguel, he is a doctor, ready for settling down. Although he is himself pursued by a rather forward nurse, whom he repels partly because of her assertiveness, but also partly because of her social inferiority, his attention is focused on a colleague who tactfully rejects his courtship with the remark: '¿Por qué cambiar la amistad por el amor?' ('Why change friendship for love?') Directed at Carlitos, the remark seems equally aimed at the audience: are the vicissitudes and many failures of love really worth more than the reassurances of friendship? Only an equivocal answer is expected, of course, since family melodramas of this type, by Buñuel or anyone else, can only thrive on the audience's partial complicity in the celebration, whatever the costs, of romantic or ideal love. In this case Carlitos's love-object seems to follow Freud's description of the narcissistic, as distinct from the anaclitic, pattern, in which a man's choice of partner reflects not her resemblance to his mother, but to himself (1984*a*: 80–5). Both Carlitos and Miguel are attracted to a woman who seems in many ways different from their mother, something that ultimately suggests an unconscious rejection of her assimilation by an ideology of motherhood that has succeeded in denying her any other form of fulfilment, especially perhaps as regards career. Miguel's narcissism is ultimately redeemed by other gentler, more outward-going tendencies that make him far more approachable and desirable as a husband than Carlitos, whose resentments and inflexibility turn him into a more educated and potentially better-mannered version of his unreconstructed father.

Carlitos's unconscious repudiation of his mother in his (frustrated) choice of love-object, his quest for a narcissistic screen of desire (according to Freud not necessarily something incompatible with other more anaclictic tendencies), further projects his latent dread of women, making even more riven with pathos her eventual decision to burden her children with the full weight of her emotional attention. Carlitos's narcissism has originated, the text suggests, in the sacrifices made on his behalf by his mother. We are left to infer that, having decided against elopement with Julio, Rosario has over-valued her love for the children, especially at first Carlitos, but later Miguel, something that in the former has led to a view of women as the gratifiers of narcissistic desires, a process whose ultimate effects prevent the child and later the adult from responding to the reality of the female.

As soon as Carlitos suspects his mother of infidelity, these feelings of repressed hostility towards women—feelings born of claustrophobic maternal attention—take on a more unambiguous tone in his treatment both of Luisa, his brother's bride, and of his mother. Luisa becomes the target for sarcastic jibes about the irredeemable treachery and materialism of all women: '¡Qué seres sentimentales y desinteresados son las mujeres!' ('Women are such sentimental and unselfish creatures!') At his brother's wedding, he toasts, again sarcastically, 'la fidelidad de la mujer' ('women's fidelity'). His unresolved childhood fixations of mixed dread and desire towards his mother are given a visual formulation when, already beginning to be aware of his suspicions, Rosario tries to soothe him one night, a gesture merely serving to aggravate his hostility once he has seen her poring over one of Julio's old love-letters.

Carlitos's extreme reaction to his mother's past infidelity has a multitude of possible interrelated causes. These include the natural loyalty felt by a son towards his father, the sense of shame and rejection caused by a mother's deception, and a more general identification with the social order whose values have so shockingly been outraged. Carlitos's failure with women, symbolized by Luisa's rejection of him, his rather severe manner, his rough treatment of the nurse and, above all, his identification through a shared Christian name with his father, emphasize his failure truly to be reconciled with his mother's protectiveness, even over-protectiveness, behavioural patterns that confirm what Karen Horney, following Freud, has defined as the child's dread of women as a sex poised to reject and deride the male (1967: 133–46). Luisa's permanent and Rosario's temporary rejection of Carlitos the adult/child, the former preferring Miguel, the latter, for all her protectiveness and self-sacrifices, having contemplated abandoning him for Julio, bear out his worst fears. Luisa's preference for Miguel, Rosario's for Julio, even though finally refusing to abandon her child, inevitably match up to a fantasy of more virile, more phallically endowed rivals. Even the possibility of rejection by Rosario and Luisa leads to further anxieties caused by the frustration of a desire to prove his manhood. As Karen Horney puts it, the more he is rejected, the less able does the male become to satisfy that inner need: 'In sexual life itself we see how the simple craving of love that drives men to women is very often overshadowed by their overwhelming inner compulsion to prove their manhood again and again to themselves and others' (1967: 145). The pattern of repressed anger and anxiety cannot break free of its vicious cycle, the father Carlos becoming the son Carlitos, who becomes the father again, subjecting the reality of women to the tyrannies of childhood fixations.

None of these questions related to the neuroses suffered by men like Carlitos is resolved by the closure, which again, as in *El gran calavera*, *Susana*, and *La hija del engaño*, conforms to the pattern—as the brothers hug each other and cry out '¡Hermano!' ('Brother!')—of arbitrariness characteristic of melodrama. Most of Buñuel's happy endings, in auteurist as much as in commercial films like this, are complicated by irony. In the auteurist *Le Journal d'une femme de chambre*, ironic commentary on the prospect of marital bliss for the paired-off major characters—Celestine to the captain, Josef to a prostitute—is provided by thunder and lightning. In the commercial *Una mujer sin amor*, the memory-traces of the narrative and its exaggerations of character, *mise-en-scène*, and music (as the lush strains of Raúl Lavista's Brahmsian music flow over the enforced solitude of Rosario), like the arbitrariness of the sudden change of heart by a neurotic son who agrees to forgive and forget the past, undermine the closure. Rosario now has Julio's photograph on the mantelpiece of her lonely home. But in a film so committed to the definition of adult behaviour as something constructed out of the residues of infancy, a gesture of reconciliation so freely made has no more plausibility than the reality—as distinct from the romantic or idealized fantasy—of the man for whose heart a woman preferred in the end to remain at home.

2.3. *Los olvidados* and the 'Uncanny'

'¿Quíen es la Chingada? Ante todo es la madre.'

Octavio Paz, *El laberinto de la soledad*

('Who is La Chingada? First and foremost, she is the mother.')

PLOT SYNOPSIS: Pedro and Jaibo belong to a gang of delinquents in Mexico City. They steal from a blind man (Don Carmelo), who is eventually befriended by a young Indian boy abandoned by his father. They mug a helpless cripple and Jaibo murders another boy, whom he accuses of treachery. Pedro craves his mother's love. She refuses to show him any affection because he is the child of rape. She forces Pedro to surrender himself to the authorities, who send him to a reformatory. Jaibo, an orphan, seduces Pedro's mother. The two boys meet up again outside the reformatory. Jaibo steals money entrusted to Pedro by the reformatory governor and kills his friend. Jaibo is eventually shot dead by the police.

After the more muted impact of Buñuel's earliest Mexican melodramas, the appearance of *Los olvidados* in 1950 created the same sort of explosion as *L'Âge d'or* in Paris in 1930, and later *Viridiana* in Spain in 1961. Radical intellectuals on the Left attacked the film for its apparent endorsement of bourgeois values; leading Mexican politicians and public figures on the Right called for Buñuel's expulsion from the country (Buñuel was already by now a Mexican national). Jorge Negrete, the star of *Gran Casino* and president of the Actors Union, informed Buñuel that if he had been in Mexico at the time he would have prevented the film from being made. Eventually, though, following praise by Pudovkin in *Pravda* and the special Critics Award at Cannes, *Los olvidados* took its place as one of Buñuel's key auterist films.

Not obliged to work within the constraints of popular, commercial forms, Buñuel avoided a script based on a literary narrative, abandoned another project (*Mi hermanito, jefe*), and, on his producer Oscar Dancigers's advice, preferred instead to make a film inspired by newspaper accounts of urban squalor (including the detail, reproduced in the film's ending, of a boy's corpse found on a rubbish tip), descending into the underworld of the rougher parts of Mexico City, accompanied by Luis Alcoriza, the scriptwriter, and Edward Fitzgerald, the artistic director, spending around six months becoming familiarized with these areas, and even consulting psychiatrists on the problem of delinquency. In its portrayal of urban squalor through the lives of the delinquents Jaibo, Pedro, and their companions, and through its representation of the abandonment of the little boy later called Ojitos ('little big eyes') by his new friends, the film mirrors the realities of contemporary Mexican life in a way that highlights the betrayals of successive governments supposedly committed to social reform. At the time of the making of the film Miguel Alemán was president of Mexico. His presidency (1946–52) coincided, as Carl J. Mora remarks (1989: 75), with the Mexican film industry's Golden Age and a period of economic prosperity that, perhaps inevitably, failed to leave much impression on the lives of the very poor. Alemán's presidency is remembered, among other reasons, for the country's unprecedented progress in road-building programmes (Niedergang 1971: 265). It was also during his period of office that the University of Mexico was founded, but, to *los de abajo*, the illiterate and dispossessed of the time, advances in higher education and roadworks can hardly have been much consolation. For the lives of the most wretchedly poor, even the more socially orientated attempts at reform by an earlier president, Lázaro Cárdenas, failed to make much impression. By the time of the making of *Los olvidados*, Cárdenas's policy of distribution of land to the Indians—according to Niedergang, resulting in the transfer of 15 million hectares to over 80,000 farmers (1971: 272)—had been reversed, and Ojitos, the little Indian boy from the country (from Los Reyes) symbolizes the defeat of Socialism by the more Porfirian instincts of later governments.

The spirit of Porfirio Díaz lived on in Mexican society, epitomized in *Los olvidados* by the busker Don Carmelo, his squalid appearance and blindness expressions not only of economic and biological disadvantage, but of the survival in Mexican society of an impoverished, short-sighted, and ultimately destructive political ideal. Played by Miguel Inclán, a veteran of melodramatic villainy in Mexican films, Carmelo is Buñuel's indirect attack on 'strong' right-wing government, an uncompromising intertextual critique of pro-Porfirian films like Oro's *En tiempos de Don Porfirio*, the most successful film at the box office in 1939, starring Fernando Soler, stalwart patriarch of Buñuel's late Forties' and early Fifties' melodramas.

Cárdenas's departure from office, and with him the traces of *cardenismo*'s tentative Socialist orientations, led to a more bourgeois ethos politically, the restoration of respect for law, order, and religion, and a more neighbourly attitude towards the USA—tendencies very much reflected in the popularity of 1940s' family melodramas and comedies, with their representation of Mexican realities subservient to ideological processes of denial and

Utopianism. In this respect, as Mora has observed (1989), the effect of Eisenstein's presence and influence on the Mexican film industry following the abortive making of *¡Que viva México!* had been of ambivalent value. The lyrical style of Eisenstein, earning the approval of the great muralist Rivera and inspiring directors like Emilio 'El Indio' Fernández, led to the creation of images of extraordinary beauty, above all in the representation of the landscape and of indigenous life, while simultaneously encouraging distortions of contemporary realities through a tone of exaggerated celebration and Utopianism. This tendency is perhaps most forcefully epitomized by Fernández's *María Candelaria*, a film—along with *Nosotros los pobres* (1947)—with which *Los olvidados* seems at some levels to be in dialogue. If *Nosotros los pobres* provides Buñuel with his point of departure for an attack on the sentimental treatment of delinquency, *María Candelaria* perhaps provoked him not only into rethinking the treatment of the Indian—especially through its focus on the romantic couple played by Pedro Armendáriz and Dolores del Río—but also into idealizing the countryside through the Eisenstein-inspired photography of Gabriel Figueroa. *María Candelaria* sees Miguel Inclán in another of his villainous roles—this time as the *mestizo* shop-owner whose cruelty is directly responsible for the tragedy befalling the poor but noble Indian couple—one that overshadows his version of the unsentimentalized blind busker in *Los olvidados*.[14] Dolores del Río, who actually refused to be directed by Buñuel in *Doña Perfecta* (preferring Roberto Gavaldón), is as if also deconstructed in *Los olvidados* through Estela Inda, her high forehead, smooth, tightly-drawn facial skin over prominent cheekbones, and thick, curly, raven hair at once recalling and slightly redefining Dolores del Río's finer, slightly more ethereal indigenous features. Estela Inda's exhausted, urbanized look—perfectly suited to her one-parent family circumstances in the film—gives a rougher edge to her aura of full-figured, self-conscious sensuality, the aura of a woman whose sexual urges remain undimmed by violation, poverty, and death, and whose relations both with her own children and with others—especially the id-dominated Jaibo—are compromised by none of the more superficial elements surrounding the star meanings of Dolores del Río.

[14] While not appearing in *Los olvidados*, Pedro Armendáriz is used by Buñuel in *El bruto*, a film that deconstructs his stereotyped heroic roles in films like *María Candelaria*, *Distinto amanecer*, *Flor silvestre*, and so on.

In films like *María Candelaria* and *Flor silvestre* these qualities find their visual correlations in the photography of Gabriel Figueroa, whose lyrical Big-Sky Utopian New World landscapes are deliberately ignored in *Los olvidados* in favour of an image— still aestheticized—of urban deprivation. The nearest that the film allows him to get to capturing the shapes and patterns of nature comes in a scene where huge cactus plants force their way into the frame, stressing in the foreground the urgency and violence of sexual desire. Nothing here, then, of the reedy riversides and cloud-embroidered horizons of *María Candelaria*, most shots demanding lighting and composition that complement the wasteland ambience of Mexico's dispossessed.

These demystifying processes are inspired by a subversive, part-realist, part-stylized narrative rooted mainly in European but also, to a lesser extent, in Hollywood forms of Expressionism and, more generally, in the traditions of the Gothic (not just nineteenth- and twentieth-century English and American classics by Poe, Lewis, Maturin, the Brontës, and so on, but also their Hispanic variants in Quevedo, Goya, Rulfo, Cortázar, and others), all here given a sort of menacing quality inherited from one of Buñuel's favourite painters, Zurbarán (Buñuel 1982*a*: 51).

Reality is constantly under pressure here from unreality, as scenes demanding extremely stylized aesthetics reflect on and question the prevalence of others that seem, superficially, to bear out the film's prologue, where the incidents of the narrative about to unfold are said to be based on real people living in real cities. Many critics—e.g. Buache (1973) and Oms (1987)—have drawn attention to the parallels between *Los olvidados* and other delinquent-narrative films. *Los olvidados* could even be read as a critical commentary, above all, on the Hollywood films in this genre. It begins with a prologue reminiscent, in some ways, of the one in *Boys' Town* (1938)—'This is the story of Father Flanagan and the City for Boys that he built in Nebraska. There is such a place as "Boys' Town". There is such a man as Father Flanagan'—but even here the emphasis is different. While Hollywood prefers a dramatic, individualized tone, Buñuel opts for dispassionate, matter-of-fact documentary. As for narrative, whereas Hollywood mediates a romantic ideology in which, through the mechanisms of the patriarchal law (especially religion, in the form of Spencer Tracy's Father Flanagan, operating with the help of the other pillars of society: the press, social services, police, and capitalist enterprise), delinquents are cured of their deviant behaviour, *Los olvidados* offers no such optimism, affirming that even when individuals wish to reform, circumstances often conspire against them. So, Pedro seeks redemption, but Jaibo returns to destroy him.

The references to 'personajes auténticos' ('real characters') and the visual style of the documentary opening in *Los olvidados* (reflected in films like *L'Âge d'or*, *Las Hurdes*, and *La Fièvre monte à El Pao*) fulfil a desire not only to expose the horrors of contemporary living, but also to gesture playfully and ironically, even in this darkest of films, at realist or neo-realist forms of filmmaking (especially as characterized by Rossellini and De Sica in Italy) as well as to meditate self-consciously on the relations between film and viewer.

The tensions between realism and fantasy, involving playful narrative and structural subversion, can ultimately be related to Buñuel's fascination with the marvellous or fantastic elements of the ordinary, a tendency shared with some of his Latin American literary contemporaries, above all Cortázar (one of whose stories, *Las Ménadas*, he had planned to film). This is a tendency perhaps ultimately best understood through Freud's thoughts in 'The Uncanny' (1990), which also help clarify the film's preoccupations with the vicissitudes of family life.

Buñuel's constant remarks about a preference for a cinema of mystery and imagination undermine his own concessions to documentary and realism. Even at the end of his life, he was insisting that Surrealism was always something characterized not just by morality and revolution but also by poetry (Buñuel 1982*b*: 132). In his lecture 'El cine, instrumento de poesía' ('Cinema, Instrument of Poetry'), Buñuel remarks: 'El misterio, elemento esencial de toda obra de arte, falta, por lo general, en las películas' (ibid. 184) ('Mystery, the essential element of every work of art, is generally absent from films'), going on to refer, with less than total approval, to the influence of neorealism:

> El neorrealismo ha introducido en la expresión cinematográfica algunos elementos que enriquecen su lenguaje, pero nada más. La realidad neorrealista es incompleta, oficial; sobre todo razonable; pero la poesía, el misterio, lo que completa y amplía la realidad tangente, falta en absoluto en sus producciones. Confunde la fantasía irónica con lo fantástico y el humor negro. (ibid. 186)

(Neo-realism has introduced into cinematographic expression certain elements which enrich its language, but nothing more. The reality of neo-realism is incomplete, official; above all rational; but poetry, mystery, all that completes and enlarges tangible reality, is completely lacking in its products. It confuses ironic fantasy with the fantastic and black humour.)

The impact of neo-realism on *Los olvidados* cannot be dismissed as easily as Buñuel would like. Nevertheless, it is also undeniable that its contribution to the film is, to use Buñuel's word, 'completed' by the work of dream and fantasy. Neo-realism's origins lie in the ruins of German and Italian fascism following the end of World War II, meeting a need felt by Italian intellectuals on the Left to 'break with the cultural heritage of fascism and in particular with rhetorical artistic schemata which seemed to bear no relation to life as it was lived' (Cook (ed.) 1985: 36). It promoted an aesthetics, not by any means uniform, of visual authenticity, depending a great deal on location shooting, the use of non-professional actors, and thematics strongly informed by commitment to social reform, focusing on ordinary, everyday human experience. In this respect *Los olvidados* often parallels, say, *Ladri di biciclette* (1948) or *Roma, città aperta* (1945). Jaibo and Ojitos are played by non-actors, there is a great deal of location shooting, and the film carries a message—not perhaps at its deepest levels—about social injustice. But in its evocation of the realities of the *barrios bajos*, or poorer areas, of Mexico City, *Los olvidados* moves beyond the prose of documentary into the poetry of the Mexican Gothic, transforming dross into metaphor, the ordinary into the fantastic, the known into the unknown and disturbing. The process is already in evidence in one of Buñuel's youthful literary pieces, *Suburbios* (1923):

Suburbios, arrabales, casas últimas de la ciudad. A este conglomerado absurdo de tapias, montones, casitas, jirones mustios de campo, etc. se refieren estos motivos. . . . El bostezo inacabable del suburbio, sus ojos riveteados y marchitos, son siempre el maleficio tremendo de la ciudad. . . . Los habitantes han sido víctimas del mordisco rabioso que les produjo el alma del suburbio. (Buñuel 1982*b*: 91–2)

(Slums, outskirts, last houses of the city. This refers to that absurd conglomeration of walls, hillocks, little houses, dried up bits of field, etc. . . . The endless yawn of the slum, its eyes fringed and withered, are always the tremendous maleficence of the city. . . . The inhabitants have been victims of the rabid bite of the slum's soul).

Aranda claims (1975: 254) that this piece was written under the influence of nineteenth-century realist texts, but, even if he is right, its impact is made through metaphors (yawns, eyes, etc.) that provide a double focus on observed reality—seen through the perspectives of reason and the imagination—a process especially in evidence for the shooting of location and other scenes in *Los olvidados*. Buñuel himself draws on Breton to clarify the process: 'Lo más admirable de lo fantástico es que lo fantástico no existe, todo es real' (1982*b*: 186). ('The most extraordinary thing about the fantastic is that the fantastic does not exist, everything is real.')

Buñuel stresses that his commitment to fantasy and mystery does not imply repudiation of the preoccupations of ordinary daily life, affirming Breton's view that Surrealism is a *sous-* as well as a *sur*-realism, in which reality itself is the focus. One of the most striking ways in which *Los olvidados* reflects the ordinary realities of everyday life concerns its use of demotic language, above all in the discourse of the gang of delinquents, establishing an identity of rebelliousness, solidarity, or difference for the boys. Buñuel's films focus on the ordinary relations between men and women, but they do so through the complex processes of mystery and fantasy, metaphor and imagination. His films use the language of creative discourse, not of simple documentary.[15]

In *Los olvidados* the mysteries of human experience, the affront to the bourgeois order, and the explorations of family life are all expressed through melodramatic processes mediated through the Gothic mode. According to David Punter (1980), the Gothic is a complex term which, in its specific definition of novels written between the end of the eighteenth and beginning of the nineteenth centuries, calls to mind a poetics of terror, lugubrious settings, supernatural events, persecuted heroines, monsters, vampires, and werewolves. Yet the term has greatly broadened its horizons to cover twentieth-century writing both in English and in other languages, spreading into the cinema, above all into German Expressionism and Hollywood and British

---

[15] Monegal emphasizes this point: 'Buñuel es ante todo un poeta. No sólo antes de ser otra cosa, porque su vocación frustrada fuera la de escritor, sino por haber aplicado a su obra cinematográfica una concepción estética que desarrolló en el ejercicio de la literatura' (1993: 15). ('Buñuel is first and foremost a poet. Not only primarily because his frustrated vocation was that of a writer, but also because of having applied to his film work an aesthetics developed from the practice of writing.')

Hammer Horror. Partly taking their inspiration from the poetics of nineteenth-century novels, horror films sometimes retain the period settings, but they also sometimes resort to a contemporary environment for the representation of the monstrous. In both types, as in contemporary literary texts, there is a characteristic taste for saying and showing the unspeakable or the unwatchable, for transgression against taboo, for chaos over order, for challenges to the social order, and for confusions between natural and socialized forms of human behaviour, all expressed through a black humour and a form at odds with realism. Not in the strictest sense a horror film—because devoid of a sufficient number of necessary generic elements—*Los olvidados* nevertheless shares many of the drives and features of Gothic literature and horror films.

In dwelling on the monstrous and routine horrors of daily life, the film relies—sometimes indirectly (through its dehumanized setting, its interest in sexuality and violence, and through its concern with perception and audience response) but sometimes also directly (especially in the scene of Pedro's dream about his mother, Julián, and Jaibo)—on the orthodox elements of the mode.[16] *Los olvidados* demands consideration as part of Buñuel's wider, Sade-dominated attraction to the mode, an interest that led to a film script forged out of Mathew Lewis's *The Monk* (1796) (used as the basis for a film by Ado Kyrou, not by Buñuel himself, in 1972), and to others, like *Le Fantôme de la liberté*, where Buñuel includes a scene from a story by Bécquer, in which Gothic elements make their presence felt. *Abismos de pasión*, too, is not just a family-centred melodrama but also—its originally gloomy, chilly, northern setting transferred to the southern, desiccated, overheated world of Mexican society—perhaps Buñuel's most powerful engagement with Gothic. But while, with its unaltered nineteenth-century setting, its howling gales, passion-crazed characters, violence, and necrophilia, *Abismos de pasión* (Buñuel's version of *Wuthering Heights*) abides more strictly to the norms of the prototype, *Los olvidados*, with its contemporary settings, seems more interested in the exposure of what

---

[16] Agustín Sánchez Vidal describes Pedro's dream about his mother like this: 'Es una pesadilla que Buñuel maneja habilísimamente, jugando con todo el potencial irracional afectivo (y trágico) del Edipo' (1984: 130). ('It's a nightmare which Buñuel controls brilliantly, playing with all the irrational, emotional and tragic potential of the Oedipus complex.')

Freud described as the 'uncanny' elements of ordinary daily life.

Freud's essay on 'The Uncanny', like so much else of his work, lies at the heart of Buñuel films. The references to severed hands there must at least be partially responsible for the recurrence of the motif in *Un chien andalou* and *El ángel exterminador*. More specifically as regards this film's thematics, Freud's interest in eye symbolism—inspired by an analysis of Hoffmann's tale about the Sand-Man—is as crucially relevant as the essay's larger argument about contradictory feelings of security and insecurity arising from attitudes towards the known and the unknown.[17] Freud's definition of the uncanny as 'that class of the frightening which leads back to what is known of old and long familiar' (1990: 340) prompts a further thought that the uncanny also arises from the projection of unconscious fears and desires onto one's surroundings and the people with whom one comes into contact. As Rosemary Jackson puts it, 'Frightening scenes of uncanny literature are produced by hidden anxieties concealed within the subject, who then interprets the world in terms of his or her apprehensions' (1981: 64–5).

The film's interest in perception—reflecting the emphasis of both Gothic art in general and Freud's essay on the uncanny in particular—highlights the patterns of metamorphosis through which the ordinary, familiar settings, objects, or people encountered in normal daily life become transformed into sources of anxiety or dread. This is a pattern endlessly repeated elsewhere. *Nazarín*, for instance—a film stressing but also ironizing and questioning the benevolent impact of Christianity—shows Beatriz sometimes visualizing, through Nazarín's Christ-like example, a benign redeemer. Yet at one crucial point, in a dream, she sees a sinisterly contemptuous and laughing Baudelairean Christ, her repressed hostility and sexual obsessions transforming the familiar portrayal of the Good Shepherd into an unfamiliar—yet also familiar to her unconscious—figure of menace.

In *Los olvidados*, subjective shots and repeated dependence on eye and eye-related imagery force the viewer to see the familiar as strange or, more accurately, as projections of repressed strangeness and disturbance. This process of metamorphosis reaches its most complex formulation in the film's use of *mise-en-scène*,

---

[17] Eye imagery is also very much a feature of Surrealism. See e.g. Éluard (1939).

animals, and women characters. The cramped, over-populated shack dwellings of the local residents, wasteland open spaces, shadowy, narrow streets in nocturnal scenes, and the overhanging presence of the huge unfinished building—perhaps the most powerful image of the uncanny, in its skeletal framework exposing an inner structure of steely indifference and menace at the centre of a cruel and minatory social world—are all projections of disturbance and unease, a revelation of the darkness at the heart of modern urban living.

Like the physical structures, the film's various animals—dogs, donkeys, and birds (a dove, hens, a rooster)—belong to this pattern of Kafkaesque metamorphosis. For instance, dogs mysteriously appear in the night to follow Ojitos and Pedro after their encounter with Julián's father. But what seems ordinary and unexceptional here later becomes, through montage and dress, disturbing and eerie. Sometimes this has a darkly humorous quality, as when, while Pedro's mother and Jaibo make love indoors, the camera cuts to the two dancing dogs, their kitschy, human, clown-like costumes and posture providing wry commentary both on the animal desires of the unseen love-making couple indoors and on the irrationality and absurdity of instincts that gratify while making clownish fools of lovers.[18] On other occasions this process has a much more sinister dimension, as when, right at the end, a dog runs over Jaibo's dead body.

The donkey, too, becomes through context not just the harmless, friendly creature of Nativity Christmas cards or stories by Juan Ramón Jiménez or Robert Louis Stevenson, but also a figure of surrogate motherhood—her teats sucked dry by the famished Ojitos—for Peter-Pan-like boys looking for absent mothers and mother-substitutes. After Jaibo kills Pedro at night, it is the donkey that alerts Meche to what has happened. Aware that there has been some disturbance in the shack that has led to the animals' release, Meche urges her grandfather to take action. As the grandfather and Meche carry Pedro's corpse on the back of a donkey heading for the rubbish tip, the movement of the group in long-shot very much recalls—as Marcel Oms persuasively suggests (1987: 116)—the flight into Egypt of the Holy Family. In retrospect, therefore, Pedro becomes a darkly

---

[18] The dog as symbolic commentary on human love-making returns in *Tristana*, when, prior to the seduction of his ward, Don Lope ejects his dog from the bedroom.

ironic evocation of the sacrificial Holy Child and Meche the
normally recognizable and familiar, or *heimlich* ('canny'), Virgin-
surrogate, her complicity in an act not of maternal care, but
precisely its opposite, of cowardice and betrayal—taking Pedro
to the rubbish tip to avoid questioning by the police—revealing
the hidden menace of a child not exempted from the contagious
evils of material circumstances.

But perhaps the most complex use of animals involves the
appearances of various types of bird. If in his films insects are
Buñuel's most characteristic non-human actors, birds (appearing menacingly, for instance, in *Le Journal d'une femme de chambre*
and *Abismos de pasión*) are his most threatening ones. He himself,
off-screen, confesses his contradictory attitude to birds:

sentía rechazo. Un ave de cualquier clase, un águila, un gorrión, una
gallina, los sentía como elementos de amenaza. ¿Por qué? No sé. Es
algo irracional, relacionado quizá con mi infancia. Pero las aves
nocturnas, sobre todo un buho, o una lechuza, me resultaban simpáticas,
me atraían. (Pérez Turrent and de la Colina 1993: 51)

(I felt repulsion. A bird of any species, an eagle, a sparrow, a hen, I
felt them as threatening elements. Why? I don't know. It's something
irrational, connected to my childhood perhaps. But nocturnal birds,
above all owls, I liked, they attracted me).

In *El ángel exterminador*, a woman who emerges from a cup-
board which has been turned into a temporary lavatory by the
trapped guests exclaims that she has seen the countryside, an
abyss, and a hawk. Buñuel explains this remark autobiographi-
cally by saying that in the Aragonese village of Molinos where
he grew up there used to be a wooden lavatory on a precipice,
looking down over the abyss. One day, while relieving himself
there, he saw a black hawk fly past. The detail has its bizarre
Surrealistic place in the claustrophobic ambience of *El ángel exterminador*. But it is also another indication of a wariness of birds
finding its obsessive expression in a film. Surprisingly, perhaps,
in view of Goya's threatening owls and other owl-like monsters
(e.g. *Caprichos* nos. 36, 43, 61, and 72), nocturnal birds appealed
to him more. But daytime bird monsters are also as common in
Goya (e.g. *Capricho* no. 75, *Disparate* no. 13) as in Bosch's nightmare bestiaries. Paradoxically, day birds are for Buñuel the
nightmare creatures, but whatever ultimate explanations may
be appropriate for an understanding of the psychopathology of

their director, Buñuel's films use birds in varied patterns related to Freud-inspired but also socially determined notions of the uncanny. The association of birds with violence or death is a commonplace of Western art (e.g. Hitchcock in *Psycho* or *The Birds*), but for Buñuel the most immediate sources might well have been, beyond Goya and Bosch, mythological and classical traditions (e.g. Jupiter as swan, etc.) and Lorca's references to cocks in the *Romancero gitano* (1928), especially in the poem about the *piquetas del gallo*. The identification of birds and sexuality also occurs in Spanish slang, where 'pájaro' means 'penis', and women of no shame are said to be 'más puta que las gallinas' ('more whorish than a hen'). When one adds to these the memories of his upbringing in Aragón, among them those concerning boys' fears as they were relieving themselves about having their testicles pecked by birds, there is clearly enough of a potent mixture of visual and verbal sources here to make even the most hardened Surrealist squeamish about most species of bird. The association of birds with sexuality is reinforced by the further nuance that *huevos* ('eggs') is also Spanish slang for 'testicles'.

In *Los olvidados* these associations of birds with violence, death, or sexuality only become clear following recognition of their perfectly normal, logical presence in the shanty-town homes of the dispossessed in Mexico city. Animals often provide the inhabitants of the slums with their sources of livelihood. Chickens offering their eggs, or asses and goats their milk, ensure the survival of their destitute owners. Yet this cheek-by-jowl existence is spared even the slightest shred of sentimentality. The cohabitation of animals leads not to some pastoral idyll of creative or more natural human behaviour guided by instinct, but to an even more raging appetite for violence and destruction. Not even Pedro, described in the report by the warden of the reformatory as being fond of animals, flinches from bludgeoning two chickens to death in a displaced attack on all the figures of authority who have ever failed him. All the animals belong to a perfectly normal, familiar *mise-en-scène*, their qualities of unease only becoming apparent through projection onto them of repressed desires and anxieties. In every case Buñuel underlines their relevance to the dialectic of the uncanny through their identification with processes of perception reminding the audience of the transformation of places into settings made inhospitable not just through poverty and desolation—the result of

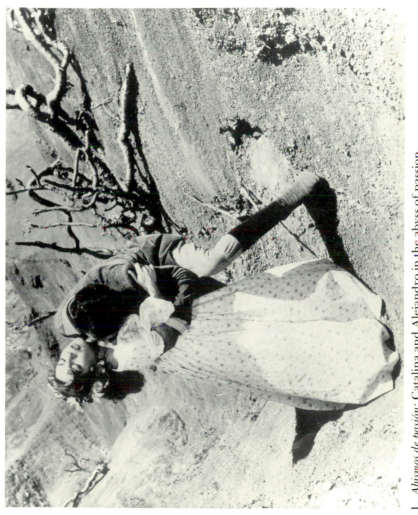

1. *Abismos de pasión*: Catalina and Alejandro in the abyss of passion.

2. *Le Charme discret de la bourgeoisie*: Life's a dream.

3. *Susana* and the 'daughter's seduction'.

4. *Una mujer sin amor* and melodramatic excess.

5. *Los olvidados* and Oedipal desire.

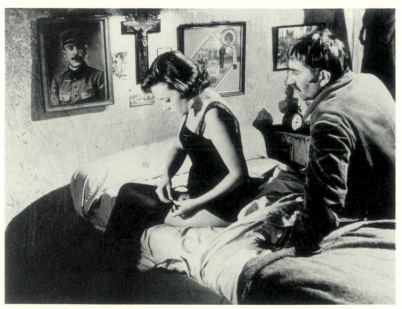

6. *Le Journal d'une femme de chambre*: In the lair of the Big Bad Wolf.

7. *Ensayo de un crimen*: Who is the dummy in the game of desire?

8. *El* and paranoid jealousy.

9. *Belle de jour* and the 'Sadean Woman'.

10. *Belle de jour* and the appropriated power of the look.

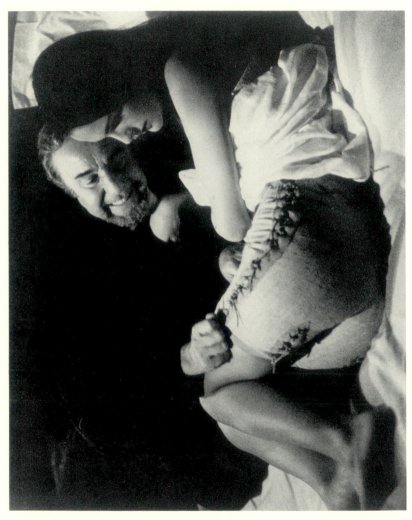

11. *Cet obscur objet du désir*: Sade crossed with Gracián.

political indifference on the part of successive Mexican governments in the Forties and Fifties—but also through psychological disturbance.

Developing Freud's comments on perception in the essay on the uncanny, Rosemary Jackson (1981: 45–6) refers to the regularity with which fantasy—another mode, related to the Gothic, with which *Los olvidados* has much in common—is often characterized by obsessions with perception or vision, associations which are frequently related to sexually defined traumas or desires. In *Los olvidados* the assault on the viewer's eye—a strategy traceable in Buñuel's work as far back as *Un chien andalou*, and continuing right up to the end with the attacks on Mathieu's field of vision by his *femme fatale* mistress Conchita in *Cet obscur objet du désir*—should therefore be read as a gesture of specifically sexual as well as of more generally social significance. This act of aggression is given its most dramatic form when, at the reformatory, caught sucking an egg by his fellow inmates, Pedro hurls its half-eaten remains at the camera lens through which the detached spectator has been observing the scene. The violence of the gesture recalls, as Marcel Oms notes (1987: 116), the offence, originating in *Un chien andalou*, against bourgeois perceptions of reality. Additionally, Pedro's furious delivery of the egg, which splatters all over the camera lens, attacks simultaneously the perspective of all who watch or judge him and his own eye, his own perception, which has blinded him—not, as in the story of Oedipus, for actually loving and being loved by his mother, but for trying vainly to love and be loved by her, an appeal for affection rewarded only with rejection and betrayals both by the police and his friend Jaibo. The behaviour of Pedro's mother accords with Estela Welldon's view that, whereas men's perversity is usually expressed through aggressive behaviour against others, women's perversity is normally manifested either through various forms of self-mutilation or through assault on their own children, who are regarded as extensions of their own bodies (1992: 8). The mother in *Los olvidados* also exercises power and acts perversely towards her own child. Her monstrous apparition in the dream seems to concur further with Kristeva-inspired theories of horror as abjection, especially as regards the representation of the monstrous-feminine (Creed 1993) in which the female monster appears as castrator and not, following classic Freudian theory, as castrated, as dreaded agent, not victim, of mutilation. As

Pedro's mother approaches him—seductively, menacingly—the raw meat she thrusts towards him is also readable at this level as her torn vagina, the object simultaneously of terror and desire. Yet since his mother's denials and rejections stem from her violation as a teenager by his anonymous father, the film gives a relatively sympathetic focus to this Mexican Medea, contextualizing in social and sexual terms the origins of her unbending hatred for her son. Like Oedipus he plucks out, albeit figuratively, his own eye, symbol of sexual as well as other types of knowledge, and hurls it at the viewer, a gesture of rage and defiance aimed equally at his mother—and, through her, all mothers—and at the social, moral, and metaphysical order of which he is the helpless and (invoking Freud's explanation of eye symbolism in the essay on the uncanny), in various senses, the castrated victim.

Yet as Jaibo and Pedro are friends—despite the violent end to their friendship that sees Jaibo kill Pedro—and could even be regarded as each other's *alter ego*, the eye is also Jaibo's, removed not by Jaibo's id-dominated but by Pedro's super-ego-led side of their double personality. While Jaibo never compromises his self-centred desires, Pedro constantly seeks accommodations with the world of what Lacan has termed the Symbolic (1970: 89–97). Like the significantly named Ojitos, who constantly seeks his absent father and submits himself to the law of the stern patriarch Don Carmelo, Pedro also looks for the approval of surrogate fathers, constantly gravitating towards figures of male authority, such as the owner of the forge or the warden at the reformatory. In contrast, Jaibo represents pure transgression, compromising others, indifferent to the suffering caused by his behaviour, remaining true only to his own self-centred desires, reaching back for a pre-Oedipal, Imaginary self, contemptuous of the Symbolic order from which he seems convinced that it is virtually impossible to be released.

When the blind man mutters the first two words of the proverb 'Cría cuervos . . .' ('Raise ravens . . .')—the rest, '. . . y te sacarán los ojos' ('. . . and they will peck out your eyes'), left unspoken—we become more than ever convinced that his blindness represents, beyond a physical defect, not just a refusal to see the world as it really is, instead of through the banalities of Porfirian prejudice, but also the revenge of the forces of the Imaginary returning, in yet another addition (spoken, not seen) to the film's aviary of doves, hens, roosters, and now ravens, to pluck out the eyes of a social reactionary. The bird imagery in his song—'Mas si el dolor hacia tus puertas llega | Y si anida en tu pecho un cruel sufrir . . .' ('But if sadness calls at your door | And if a cruel suffering nests in your breast . . .')—stresses this further significance, even though he himself remains unaware of it.

Buñuel's own dismissive remarks about Don Carmelo's representation of pet phobias about blind people[19] fail to undermine the force of the character as a target for the film's assault on the politics of authoritarianism and prejudice.[20] But, as Carlos Saura's *Cría cuervos* (1975) points out in its intertextual commentary on *Los olvidados*, the brood of ravens who return to cause such damage to their masters are not content with settling political scores. They also seek revenge for the havoc caused by sexual disturbance and repression. This is, of course, the sense in which references to eyes in Hoffmann's 'The Sand-Man' are mentioned in Freud's 'The Uncanny': 'he puts the eyes in a sack and carries them off to the half-moon to feed his children. They sit up there in their nest, and their beaks are hooked like owls' beaks, and they use them to peck up naughty boys' and girls' eyes' (quoted in Freud 1990: 349).

The twinning of Jaibo and Pedro, as two sides of the conflict between the forces of the Symbolic and the Imaginary, leads to the exposure of the female as another of the film's sites of the uncanny. In some ways *Los olvidados* reproduces, once more in a film by Buñuel, the ambience of Sade's *The 120 Days of Sodom* (1785), a place committed to transgression of taboos of all types: on this occasion it is not just, for instance, attitudes towards physically handicapped individuals like the blind man or the cripple that are subverted, but also in particular the incest taboo. Even the cripple is related to the thematics of perception, since the wooden box he uses as transport has 'me mirabas' ('you were looking at me') written on one of its sides.

As many have remarked, the attitude of both Pedro and Jaibo —two more sons of La Chingada, film equivalents of Octavio Paz's orphan-myth explanation of Mexican history (1991)— towards Pedro's mother is one largely motivated by the repulsion/

---

[19] For his unsympathetic attitude towards the blind, see Buñuel (1982a: 272).
[20] For Víctor Fuentes the attack on Carmelo is an attack against the Father (1993: 107).

attraction felt towards the 'other'. When Jaibo looks at her wash-
ing her legs and feet, he is drawn to her erotically, an attraction
that eventually leads to their sexual union, but in a way that
summons up images of his own mother, a 'family romance' fantasy through which the mother, dead or perhaps only absent,
has become in his imagination an altar Virgin Mother. This
transgresssion of a most sacred taboo leads not only—after the
gratification of sexual desire—to rejection by the mother of her
lover/son, but also ultimately to death. As an id-driven character, Jaibo can say and do things denied to Pedro. On the other
hand, Pedro's dreams release desires repressed in his unconscious. From this point of view, what is particularly striking in
the famous dream sequence that has so engrossed its many
commentators is that the dream narrative in which Pedro is
approached by his mother, at first without and then with that
piece of glistening raw meat, is prefaced by the descent of a
chicken from the top to the bottom of the frame, chicken feathers
also a little later on in the sequence floating in slow motion
across the camera's field of vision to obscure the view. The dream
is the film's most unmistakable moment of Gothic—a corpse
flowing with blood, chiaroscuro lighting, whistling winds, thunder, a diabolical, sexually self-conscious Madonna, provocatively
lifting her skirts and approaching, in slow motion, her vulnerable boy-child—calling up what Karen Horney in a discussion
of wider issues calls via Freud 'men's dread of women' (1967:
133–46). The chicken and chicken feathers emphasize the atmosphere of dread, especially of sexual dread. Pedro's attack on
the chicken at the farm and his mother's vicious assault on a
rooster that constantly harasses the hens (the latter incident also
rightly seen by Gwynne Edwards (1982: 99) as a reconstruction
of Jaibo's murder of Julián) are clearly charged with sexual
meaning. Whenever roosters or hens appear elsewhere in the
conscious lives of the characters, they become projections of
repressed unconscious desires and anxieties, especially those
associated with the breaking of the incest taboo, thus contributing to the film's creation of an ambience of the uncanny.[21] The

---

[21] For all his devotion to the authoritarian politics of Porfirianism, the blind Don
Carmelo may be another symbol of all who break this taboo. His blindness may be
not just a comment on his failure to see through the tyrannies of authoritarian
politics. Have his eyes been pecked out by the avenging forces of patriarchy for
transgressions against a sexual law?

ghostly appearance of the mother in the dream and her forbidding presence in the rest of the narrative as a figure of dread and
cruelty suggest, furthermore, a projection of what Sara Kofman
has called a feeling of uncanniness in the face of the 'abrupt
reappearance of what one thought had been overcome or lost
forever' (1985: 56). What men reject in themselves they project
onto women. The feminine, the maternal in the male, is displaced onto the female who, through no fault of her own (the incident of Pedro's mother's violation stressing the point), is turned
into an image of dread, of familiarity made unfamiliar, kept at
a distance in a context of socially constructed, unapproachable,
uncanny entrapment. For Karen Horney, the pubertal boy already 'fears in women . . . something uncanny, unfamiliar and
mysterious' (1967: 141). For Buñuel, as well as for Jaibo, Pedro,
Ojitos, and Don Carmelo, women, failing to reach the standards
set by the demands of a family romance, become instead the
uncanny monsters of frustrated desire.[22]

[22] In her excellent book on Hitchcock, Tania Modleski (1988) considers the 'uncanniness' of the female body in *Vertigo*.

3
Male Desire

'Todo cuanto obró el Supremo Artífice está tan acabado que no se puede mejorar, mas todo cuanto han añadido los hombres es imperfecto: crió lo Dios muy concertado y el hombre lo ha confundido.'

Gracián, *El Criticón*

('Everything created by the Great Architect is so perfect it cannot be improved, but everything added by humans is imperfect: God created it all harmoniously and man has disturbed it.')

EVEN though women provide the main narrative focus in various films (e.g. *Tristana, Viridiana, Susana, Una mujer sin amor*), Buñuel more regularly prioritizes masculinity and the orientations of male desire. From the earliest ones to the very last, the films dramatize the highs and lows of male subjection to the vicissitudes of desire. Less lyrical than some of the other celebrants of *amour fou*—because more familiar with the traditions of *desengaño* associated with the work of the great Spanish writers, especially his fellow-Aragonese mentor Gracián—Buñuel leans towards narratives exposing the dangers as well as the rewards of sexuality. His males usually suffer from a common affliction, defined by Peter Middleton in a general discussion of masculinity (1992) as a failure to direct their gaze inwardly, towards a healthy introspection of their motivating forces. Suffering for love and seduction by the temptations of 'obscure' (partly because uninvestigated) desires are not in these films patterns of behaviour restricted to the young. Middle-aged and even elderly, as well as youthful, lovers are condemned to endure the torments of raging passions.

From the adolescent social pariah Jaibo to the child-like nephew in *Le Fantôme de la liberté*, the pubertal, metallic-toothed gangster in *Belle de jour*, or the elderly necrophiliac Don Jaime in *Viridiana*, Buñuel's films explore the urgent drives of men seeking

through the transformations and regenerative power of love release from habit, outmoded traditions, dreary routines, or even
the self. In most cases desire has a heterosexual orientation,
though occasionally—especially in *Un chien andalou* and its coded
reference to Lorca through the figure of the disorientated andro-
gyne poking with a phallic cane at the severed hand in the
middle of a busy street—male homosexual desire earns acknowledgement if not necessarily either serious interest or approval.
Buñuel is clearly edgy about the subject, expressing doubts, for
instance, in *Mon dernier soupir* about Lorca's homosexuality (1982*a*:
75). Of all the other films, *El* comes closest if not to actually
recognizing homosexuality, at least to creating an ambience in
which the neurotic behaviour of its main character can be most
clearly understood through reference to Freud's writing on paranoia (1979), regarded in some instances as having its roots in
repressed homosexuality. Although such a reading is dismissed
by Buñuel himself (Pérez Turrent and de la Colina 1993: 81),
this in itself, like his disavowals of Lorca's homosexuality, is a
form of repression, part of a characteristic pattern of dismissiveness about his work, motivated to a certain extent by modesty
or weariness of deep critical readings, but also by a strategy of
camouflage and evasion.

Buñuel's denials, of course, additionally confirm the limitations of authorial control over the material and operations of the
text and its reception. Although on the basis of moments like
these the films can be accused of failing consciously to address
questions of homosexuality, some of the outrage that initially
greeted the scene where a middle-aged bourgeois attempts to
pick up the juvenile delinquent Pedro in *Los olvidados* seems over-
sensitive, since Buñuel's target there was pederasty not homosexuality. Even so, characterized neither by homophobia nor by
a conscious desire to represent the realities of homosexual experience, Buñuel preferred to devote himself to the project of
representing and interrogating male heterosexual desire.

Sometimes, through inner strength or through an aleatory law,
men experience no difficulty in enjoying good relationships with
women. Valerio (Georges Marchal) in *Cela s'appelle l'aurore*—
perhaps too virile for his cosseted wife, yet enormously attractive
to his more sensual colleague (Lucía Bosé)—is an obvious example. But more usually love makes fools of men, not only because they repeatedly fall for unsuitable women, but often also

because circumstances—usually associated with childhood experience—have made them unfit for the women they desire. The first category—men in some way or other deceived or exploited by designing women—includes among the more interesting examples Vázquez in *La Fièvre monte à El Pao*, Pedro in *El bruto*, or Mathieu in *Cet obscur objet du désir*; the second, Archibaldo in *Ensayo de un crimen*, or Francisco in *El*. Among the many minor characters who fall into this second category none is more fascinating than Martin, the manservant in *Cet obscur objet*, who, we suspect, speaks both for himself and for Buñuel's darker self when he remarks that a friend of his considers women to be 'sacs d'excrément' ('sacks of excrement').

The stars playing the major roles in these films, whether by choice or necessity, reflect the focus of Buñuel's interest in different aspects of male subjectivity. Even though less tightly organized around a structure as elaborate and powerful as the Hollywood star system, the European or Mexican films made by Buñuel, whatever hesitations he may himself have had about the use of well-known actors and actresses, rely to a certain extent on the audience's knowledge and perceptions of major stars in these roles. The Mexican films exploit for box-office purposes the popularity of, say, Pedro Armendáriz, Fernando Soler, Jorge Negrete, or Arturo de Córdova; the international films, that of, for example, Fernando Rey, Gérard Philippe, or Francisco Rabal. Although David Bordwell (1979) is probably right in suggesting that the art film is orientated towards a process of textual unification through authorship rather than through genre or stars, the importance of stars even in art films, including Buñuel's, cannot be underestimated.

As an example of Buñuel's use of a star in the role of a male largely untroubled by the more negative complications of sexuality, Francisco Rabal—as Jorge in *Viridiana,* as Hippolyte in *Belle de jour*, or as Nazarín—shows how the interactions of role and star persona inform the meanings of the text with the mediated significance of ideals of masculinity in circulation in Spain or Mexico in the Fifties and Sixties. In Hispanic film, serious analysis of stars is virtually non-existent. And although it is instructive to compare studies of stars in the Hollywood cinema, discussion of male stars in Hollywood has too often focused on the male pin-up either as equivocal icon of beauty at once affirming and disavowing homosexual desire or else as screen emblem of patriarchal power and prejudice.[1] Examples of the former include feminized, aestheticized men like Montgomery Clift, James Dean, or Tyrone Power; of the latter, the 'Big Bad Wolves', Gable, Tracy, Wayne, or Flynn.[2] Theorizing the male in the art cinema is still in its infancy, but Edgar Morin's highly influential, insufficiently acknowledged, and ground-breaking work on stars (1960)—stressing the complexities of audience identification with objects of desire or ego-ideals—is a useful beginning for consideration of Buñuel's use of stars.

As both object of desire and ego-ideal, appealing as much to men as to women and to all sexual orientations, Francisco Rabal emerges from the Spanish film industry and its rudimentary star system bringing with him for Buñuel's Hispanic audiences a range of meanings identified with a whole series of films which, if not restricting him to a narrow range of roles, nevertheless played on specific qualities. The most interesting of his films from this point of view is *Nazarín*. Quite apart from the raw material of looks, voice, gesture, and so on, Rabal's off-screen presence, primarily identified with proletarian origins and public defences of Marxism, inevitably helped colour audience reception of his film roles.[3] These, and a tough but also sensitive and confident masculinity—characterized by rough features, a deep growl, and a face lined with experience—combine with the intellectual and social identifications with Marxism to establish the outlines of the persona. Rabal is a darker, Spanish Richard Burton: powerful, sensitive, thoughtful, proletarian, hard-living and hard-drinking, and eroticized. All of these qualities are in evidence in his three Buñuel roles. In *Viridiana* and *Belle de jour* the impact of these attributes cuts through the opportunism of Jorge in the former and the kitschy parody of the Bogart-raincoated gangster Hippolyte in the latter. In neither film do either Rabal or masculinity come under any threat. In *Belle*, as Hippolyte, he is so self-assured about his virility that he even agrees to let his young companion first sample the new arrival *chez* Mme Anaïs. In *Viridiana* both the dark, sexually self-conscious maid and the fair, frigid novice of desire ultimately capitulate to

---

[1] For trends in discussions of male stars, see Neale (1983), Dyer (1982), and Babington and Evans (1993: 227–37).
[2] See Joan Mellen's treatment of the 'Big Bad Wolves' of the Hollywood Cinema (1977).
[3] For a full survey of Rabal's career, see Canovas (ed.) (1992).

him. Rabal is perhaps Buñuel's dream of masculinity, a wish-fulfilment of self-confident maleness of the sort to which he him-self, *tío* ('uncle') to his *sobrino* ('nephew')—playful terms that hint at a dream autobiography—seems drawn as ego-ideal.[4] All these qualities are, however, placed under threat in *Nazarín*, a film not only—for Hispanic audiences—ironizing roles in Spanish films made by Rafael Gil on religious subjects, e.g. *Sor Intrépida* (1952), but also restating the theme running right through Spanish lit-erature of the higher man's triumph over sexuality and domes-ticity. By the end of the film Nazarín may have become aware of the futility of Christianity as a force for good, but he remains a citadel of purity, having successfully withstood the assaults on his manhood by Beatriz and Andara, his independence, at least from women, allowing him to continue his life's journey unin-hibited by the laws of desire.

The majority of Buñuel males find difficulty in resisting the lure of unsuitable women, their sincerity and masculine self-assurance no match for the *mujer devoradora* of films like *El bruto*, *La Fièvre monte à El Pao*, or *Susana*. Pedro Armendáriz shares with Rabal qualities of strength and nobility but, whereas Rabal, though capable of gentleness, is also always clear-thinking and experienced, Armendáriz is more innocent, an overgrown child, the power of his manly frame undermined by a baby-face too vulnerable to the snares and allures of *El bruto*'s tenement *femme fatale*, Katy Jurado, here embodying none of those qualities of loyalty and endurance characteristic of her role in *High Noon* (1952), instead releasing the turbulent drives of a fatal passion that no child-brute could resist. Another child of desire, Gérard Philippe, somewhat unconvincingly makes a late retreat from the enslavements of perhaps the most famous of all *mujeres devoradoras* of the Mexican cinema, María Félix, here again, though a little less venomously than in *Doña Bárbara* (1943), a woman taken in adultery, a scheming Bathsheba deceiving an elderly husband with various of his colleagues, including even-tually the virginal Gérard Philippe as Vázquez.

While Rabal is a wish-fulfilment dream, Philippe and Armendáriz are nightmare figures of innocent masculinity placed under constant threat of castration by phallic, predatory,

---

[4] Buñuel and Rabal were clearly very close, as Buñuel himself remarks in his autobiography, where he points out that, while he referred to Rabal as his nephew, Rabal referred to him as his uncle (1982a: 299).

pre-Oedipal vamps, although even here Buñuel hints at the experiences or disturbances of childhood that make men regress towards the choice of domineering, potentially castrating women who lead or threaten to lead them to destruction. In the second category of Buñuel males, the focus is on the neuroses, traumas, and desires of the men themselves, all of whom are in various unambiguous ways portrayed as individuals adversely affected by childhood experience. Men like Francisco in *El* or Archibaldo in *Ensayo de un crimen*, though outwardly conventional, are inwardly the dark introjections of a collective male psychopathology of self-doubt and destruction. The autobiographical resonances of Fernando Rey's playing of his Buñuel roles has already been discussed. But, as both Buñuel himself and his widow Jeanne admit, autobiographical traces are also in evidence in *El*, its star, Arturo de Córdova, embodying—in Morin's terms (1960)—not so much an object of desire as a sort of egoideal underside, a nightmare self of male anxiety (Rucar de Buñuel 1991: 108). In their explorations of male subjectivity these films uncover a palimpsest of contradictory motivations and desires. Often drawn to women as potentially civilizing influences, Buñuel's males are also invariably repelled by the sexual power of the female. Recent writing on masculinity that has highlighted the 'difficulties of difference' illuminates some of the greatest complexities of Buñuel's treatment of male subjectivity and desire (Rodowick 1991). On the one hand, anticipating these defences of masculinity, the films avoid a naïve position in which 'men can only be acceptable if they forsake their masculinity' (Seidler 1994: 114) as they explore the aspirations and frustrations of the male. On the other, there is a clear sense—conscious or unconscious—that 'what goads the male subject forward on his Oedipal quest is the dread of the abject mother' (Rutherford 1992: 180). Fearing feminization and humiliation through contact with women, many of Buñuel's males, like those referred to by Rutherford, often resort to violence, fighting over the body of the mother, a figure both loathed and idealized, displaced onto the obscure female objects of desire from whom they seek retribution as well as gratification.[5]

[5] Jonathan Rutherford (1992), Victor Seidler (1992), and Peter Middleton (1992) are among many who have recently been directing attention towards masculinity, above all heterosexual masculinity and its own legitimate fields of enquiry.

Francisco in *El* is Buñuel's clearest dramatization of this tension, given its most perfect formulation in Arturo de Córdova's
playing of the role. In a film made in Mexico some years before
El, Julio Bracho had already explored through *Crepúsculo* (1944)
the more neurotic side of Arturo de Córdova's persona. As a
kind of prelude to *El*, *Crepúsculo* stresses the more intense—
perhaps slightly more unbalanced—nature of a man obsessed
with a beautiful woman in a narrative eager to make an early reference to Oedipus' self-mutilation. Again the narrative hinges
on a triangular relationship between two male friends and the
woman they both desire. Whereas, in *El*, Francisco successfully
woos Gloria away from her fiancé (discovering that his self-
destructive *amour fou* respects no bonds of friendship), in *Crepúsculo*
the Arturo de Córdova figure, Alejandro, takes no such action,
preferring instead the crepuscular world of adultery and frustrated desire, seeming to approve of his self-definition as 'el más
incurable de los enfermos' ('the most incurable of sick persons'),
a condition finally leading to suicide. He is still the picture of
agitation and intensity as Agustín, ready to kill for honour in *For
Whom the Bell Tolls* (1943), one of several films he made in Hollywood. Visually, Arturo de Córdova belongs in the same class as
those paragons of Hollywood middle-class patriarchy, groomed
to perfection, not a bristle of their crisply trimmed moustaches
out of place on razor sharp profiles. Neither rugged nor manfully
indifferent to the finer nuances of personal appearance—as, say,
were Spencer Tracy or John Wayne—Arturo de Córdova has
more in common with stars like Zachary Scott (playing against
type in *The Young One*), Ronald Colman, or even, more sinisterly,
Basil Rathbone, their dark pencil-thin moustaches and mono-
chrome hair and eyes not so much signs of narcissism as of
conservatism, in their eager adherence to classical styles of dress
and grooming perfect icons of bourgeois standards.

So, in *El* Arturo de Córdova's outward conformism makes all
the more powerful and disturbing the inner turbulence and chaos
of a mind on the verge of nervous breakdown. The superficial
visual endorsement of the Oedipal order is here no guarantee
against unconscious wishes to break its various taboos. Like the
Fernando Rey characters, like the various other men caught in
the crossfire between desires to conform or to rebel against patriarchal laws, Arturo de Córdova as Francisco in *El* represents
Buñuel's male in crisis, his subjectivity threatened by powerful

Oedipal traumas, his desires largely spared the necessary liberating processes of introspection. Simultaneously the victims and
aggressors of desire, Buñuel's Oedipal males are blinded not
only by their own gestures of self-mortification, but also by a
failure to interrogate the causes and motivations of their repetitive and ultimately self-destructive passions. Struggling to assert
themselves, to break free of laws of surplus repression, they find
themselves—like Don Lope in *Tristana*, first a rebel and then a
conformist—compromised and trapped by their various predicaments, hopelessly failing to see the construction of their own
masculinity in discourse and representation, ignoring the consequences of a process making of even the unconscious—that place
of supposedly liberated desires—the game reserve of the various
strategies of a predatory ideology.

3.1. *Ensayo de un crimen* and Oedipality

'It is not good that man should be alone.'

Genesis, 2

PLOT SYNOPSIS: In a flashback narrative, Archibaldo confesses to
crimes of intention, if not of actual deed, against women. His taste
for murdering women has originated with the gift from his mother
of a musical box which he imagined had magical properties. Ever
since thinking the box, and not a stray bullet from a revolutionary's rifle, had been responsible for the death of a disciplinarian
governess, Archibaldo has been obsessed with a desire to murder
attractive women. In adult life he tries to murder four women:
a nun, Carlota, Patricia, and Lavinia. Three die (none killed by
him), but Lavinia is paired up with him at the film's conclusion.

Of all Buñuel's films *Ensayo* seems most conspicuously to bear
out Barthes's view that all narratives are structured around the
mechanisms of the Oedipal myth:

Plaisir Oedipéen (dénuder, savoir, connaître l'origine et la fin), s'il est
vrai que tout récit (tout dévoilement de la vérité) est une mise-en-
scène du Père (absent, caché ou hypostasié) ... (1973: 20)

(An Oedipal pleasure (strip, know the origins and the end), if it is true
that every narrative (every disclosure of truth) is a *mise-en-scène* of the
Father (absent, hidden or hypostasised).)

The repression of the female that this process seems to imply is denied total efficiency in Buñuel's films since, as everywhere, resistances to patriarchy recur constantly, sometimes unexpectedly. In this film, for instance, the narrative's drives are aimed at an exposure of Oedipal disturbances defined as ultimately responsible for the leading character's neuroses. These are revealed through displaced frustrations and hostility towards Archibaldo's mother, feelings expressed as a desire to murder the 'Bad Object' women he pursues, but also through a critique of the social order of which he is the neurotic, terrorizing agent and victim. Through its interest in key questions of psychological and ideological disruption, and the darker motivations of desire—Archibaldo (Ernesto Alonso) has tried, even though unsuccessfully, to murder five women—the film maintains its characteristically Buñuelian tone of comedy.

Most obviously, the closure conforms to the practice of comedy's preference for happy endings. Here, as if adhering to some Surrealistic form of *deus ex machina*, the most suitable of the women Archibaldo has failed to murder appears magically to accompany him out of the frame to a joint future of relative, even if necessarily ambiguous, happiness. While this upbeat scene is layered with multiple ironies, the film avoids the ruptures and despair of the restricted number of films made by Buñuel in overwhelmingly tragic mode. Here, whatever final destiny awaits the odd couple, setting off for a life perhaps of endless—and perhaps eventually tiresome—mutual practical jokes, the emphasis lies on recovery and reaffirmation. The desire for social reintegration, exemplified by the union of Archibaldo and Lavinia (Miroslava Stern), also very much belongs to the domain of comedy—as does the film's commitment to a belief in the possibility of love and the need, above all, to risk failure in the pursuit of fulfilment. In Buñuel's post-lapsarian garden of death as well as of delights, a kind of mortal redemption is sometimes made possible through tolerance and recognition of common frailties. It is perfectly true, as Raymond Durgnat points out (1968: 96), that, in granting other characters the pleasure of committing Archibaldo's crimes for him, the film offers a jaundiced view of a world in which destruction is an all too common, even banal, feature of ordinary human behaviour. But in denying Archibaldo this pleasure the film seems also eager to show that his complicity does not preclude the possibility of grace.

At this level, the film's comedy derives partly from frustration and also from the salvation of the comic hero from his own darkest instincts. The grace favoured upon him in this way, frustrating but also miraculously delivering him from evil, is prompted by the film's recognition of the frequent origins of criminality (not just Archibaldo's) in Oedipal confusions. So, as he himself explains to Carlota, the comic anti-hero here is both sinner and saint, ideologized into aberrant behaviour but also in revolt against ideology, a rebel at once trapped by socialised, mechanical forms of behaviour and also free to be their scourge. Like Bergson's mechanical man, Archibaldo is an automaton programmed by Oedipal decree into routine behavioural patterns. On the other hand, like the Bakhtinian comic hero, he is also as if seized by a carnivalesque, festive madness that surfaces in ludic forms of activity with which he has been identified since early childhood.

Following on from a discussion of Derrida's linking of awareness and playfulness, Andrew Horton in a recent analysis of film comedy defines the comic as a form of play, thriving on self-consciousness, producing a text that is 'plural, unfinalised, disseminative, dependent on *context* and the intertextuality of creator, text and contemplator. It is not, in other words, just the *content* of comedy that is significant but also its 'conspiratorial' relationship with the viewer' (1991: 9). Horton then distinguishes between Oedipal and pre-Oedipal comedy, and specifically refers to Buñucl's comedy—with its emphasis on wish-fulfilment and dreams—as a variant of the latter. According to Horton, Buñuel's comedy is not Oedipal because it avoids accommodation, compromise, social integration. Attractive in general terms, the division seems too schematic, especially as regards *Ensayo de un crimen*. Accepting the Oedipal and pre-Oedipal categories, it would seem more useful to regard Buñuel's films as being driven by the simultaneous operation of both tendencies, sometimes in harmony and sometimes in conflict. In *Ensayo* the comic hero's murderous designs on women refer back to Oedipal disturbance, seeking their elucidation through accommodations with the social order, while glancing even further back to unsocialized, wilder forms of transgression. What is certainly true of *Ensayo*, as of many other films (e.g. *Cet obscur objet*), is its exemplification of the 'conspiratorial' relationship with the viewer.

But this process, and the stress on Archibaldo's ludic, transgressive patterns of behaviour, ultimately requires consideration from the perspectives of Oedipal desire. According to Freud, the boy-child's identification with his father, his ego-ideal, coincides with an 'object-cathexis' with his mother (1985: 134). Eventually these conflicting drives are resolved through the child's recognition of his father's symbolically-sanctioned power to castrate, an awareness that either leads to continued identification with the mother (seen as castrated), or with the father, the latter course clearing the way for a normal male identity. This measure is a necessary prelude to socialized masculine subjectivity and the boy's awareness of his own legacy of power and authority which in due course he will exercise himself. Freud recognized that this rite of passage is rarely free of complicating factors making simple, hermetically sealed definitions of masculinity and femininity virtually impossible. The boy's rejection of the mother in favour of the father leads to a devaluation of the mother's femininity. But pre-Oedipal memories and desires, free of post-Oedipal impairment, are not redirected with comprehensive success along socially approved routes, since as Freud argues, pre-Oedipal desire never totally vanishes (1985: 134). Reworking Freud's theories, Lacan defines the pre-Oedipal as the world of the Imaginary, the post-Oedipal as the Symbolic, the former conceived as a clear danger to what Frank Krutnik refers to as the 'phallic economy of identity and desire' (1991: 83), the latter as the sphere of patriarchal law. Krutnik goes on to define—in a passage of primary relevance to the world of Surrealistic *amour fou* and Buñuel's neurotic lovers—the implications of the boy's choices between the Symbolic and the Imaginary:

the woman is constituted as a source of 'imaginary plenitude', and she becomes invested with an authority that can be validated as superior to the divisions of the phallic regime. This tendency is at its most extreme in fantasies of *amour fou* where the desire to 'fuse' with the woman achieves its ultimate realisation in death. . . . In the *amour fou* fantasy, the male 'contracts' himself to the woman as a means of directly opposing his post-Oedipal pacting with the Law of the Father. (1991: 83)

In *Ensayo* the narrative follows the traumas of the boy-child who has failed to negotiate Oedipality *en route* to his acquisition of conventional, socialized masculinity. Veering between what many theorists—e.g. Gilbert and Gubar (1979)—have defined as the polar opposite stereotypes of women as virgins or whores, saints or witches, Archibaldo displaces onto the women he desires (and desires to kill) the repressed love/hatred of his own mother. The film is another of Buñuel's narratives in which motherhood is seen to be a cause of difficulty. Three of the women he wishes to murder are whore/witches, the other two virgin/saints, though each group also has the potential to develop the attributes of the other. Once Archibaldo's flashback begins, his narrative opens with reference to a virgin/saint, his mother, and concludes with the only woman successfully to avoid death either directly or indirectly through Archibaldo's involvement, the whore/witch Lavinia, whose dummy other self, however, is satisfactorily consigned to the flames of his kiln.

Archibaldo is Buñuel's case history of a boy's failure to move beyond attachment to identification with his father. As a result of this process of submission to pre-Oedipal regression, he becomes not only disqualified from the rights and privileges of phallic power, but also condemned to find only unhappiness and disruption in his pursuits of love, leaving him fixated on his mother in endless affairs in which he becomes both the rejected and rejecting subject/object of desire.

The first scene of Archibaldo's childhood parades a phantasmagoria of Freudian symbols stressing the child's fixation: a toy train runs around in circles on its miniature track, and Archibaldo is found hiding in his mother's wardrobe, wearing her high heels and corset. In exploring through flashback memories of childhood the roots of criminal instinct in the adult, the film also hints, in view of Buñuel's equivocal attitudes to the matter, at the possibility of a latent homosexuality frustrating the likelihood of normal relations with women. The boy's exaggerated attention to grooming, establishing cliché links between prissy, narcissistic drives and unarticulated suggestions of homosexuality, is a further sign of excessive interference by a mother whose appearance confirms another stereotype of crude discussions on the origins of homosexuality. Glamorous and over-indulgent towards her son, she is also a betrayer, abandoning the child for an evening out with the father, who remains an extremely shadowy figure, absent to the point of virtual invisibility in relations with his son. The mother's bribe to appease her son's jealousy and anger at her absence is the gift of a music box, a Pandora's box of libidinal pleasures that until the very last moments of the film will continually attract and repel the boy throughout his adult life. The box plays a sprightly tune accompaniment to the dance of a female figurine whose circular movements—arms aloft, skirt raised to reveal spindly legs—repeat the restricted itinerary of the train, both affirming and disavowing the pleasures of sexual desire.

The gift is also a mark of female collusion, stressing not only power over the male, since both mother and governess are identified with discipline, but also the association of women with falsehood. On his mother's instructions, the governess attempts to divert his attention with an involved fairy-story account of the music box's origins. The story she invents is also significant for its thematics of suspected female treachery: the music box, once the property of a genie, has the magical power, as soon as its music begins to play its sickly tune, to kill the object of its owner's hostility. When the king is deceived by his prime minister into believing his wife has betrayed him, the music box's magic effects are released against her and she is killed. Here, in miniature, the history of male scapegoating of women is summarized in a narrative told by a colluding woman who has introjected a mythology of female treachery, further fuelling the twisted desires of her mother-fixated charge.

The boy's response leads to displacement of his anger towards his mother onto his governess, who in some senses, above all as a disciplinarian, represents the mother: he aims his music box at her, hoping its magical properties will despatch her into oblivion. A stray bullet from a revolutionary's rifle flying in through the window puts an end to the unfortunate governess's life, and from that point on Archibaldo is obsessed with a displaced desire to kill his mother through attempts to murder a series of variously desirable and repellent women with whom he comes into contact. As he surveys her corpse, concentrating on the trickle of blood running down her stockinged leg, the perspective through which he will establish his adult sexual relations becomes clear, bearing out Foucault's view about subjectivity's constitution in relations of power (1984). Archibaldo's dependence on force, his desire henceforward to impose his authority over women, stems directly from a feeling of powerlessness.

The emotional blackmail previously guaranteed in infancy to ensure his mother's gratification of his desires begins to lose its effect as he grows older. Lacking power over his mother, the boy resorts to violence against her, but through the punishment of

other women, the triadic relationship between mother, governess, and boy providing the model for the future. The process of
splitting women into saints/virgins or whores/witches corresponds to the patterns of displacement discussed in Bruno
Bettelheim's analysis of the Hansel and Gretel fairy-tale (1988:
159–65). Archibaldo's fixation with his mother, his refusal or
inability to submit himself to the due processes of Oedipal development, highlight attempts to deal with reality through regression and denial. At this level, the mother (previously regarded
as saint/virgin, the gratifier of desire) becomes the witch/whore,
through whom desire is frustrated:

Severely upset that Mother no longer serves him unquestioningly but
makes demands on him and devotes herself even more to her own
interests—something which the child had not permitted to come to his
awareness before—he imagines that Mother, as she nursed him and
created a world of oral bliss, did so only to fool him—like the witch in
the story. (Bettelheim 1988: 163)

Realizing that the mother, source of such overwhelming pleasures and control over him, is capable of what he regards as
betrayal, the boy determines never to allow a woman to exercise
such power over him again. In most cases, of course, the conflicts raging within the child between the rival claims of the
Good and Bad Mother are, if not wholly, at least largely resolved. But where resolution is impossible, this process, with
serious consequences for women trapped in the power structures
of relations with men, is of further interest in highlighting patterns of male violence against women as being to a large extent
prompted by the fear and hatred of the male's displaced recognition of his own inner femininity. Characteristically 'feminine'
qualities of softness, tenderness, and intimacy, developed through
the bonding of mother and child, become a source of aversion
and contempt as a result of this act of maternal betrayal, destined for assault on the mother-surrogate screens of his own
projected phobia and dread.

In Lacan's reformulation of Freud, though, desire is caused
above all by a lack, an absence of the object of desire: the mother
from whom the boy has been separated and whom he constantly
seeks and punishes in the women he meets in adult life. In the
case of *Ensayo*, the price for Archibaldo's entry into the world of
the Symbolic is extremely high, including above all the loss of

his obscure object of desire, his mother. The boy realizes not only that he is denied access to his mother, but also that she desires and is desired by the father. Of all the women Archibaldo pursues only the governess seems to be unattached to a male, but her identification with the father, through the mother and through service in his household, is indisputable. Significantly, all the other women are involved not just with men but with patriarchal figures: the nun with a heavenly father, Carlota with the architect (often a symbol of order in Buñuel's films, e.g. *El*), Patricia and Lavinia with elderly sugar-daddies, Lavinia often referring to her lover publicly not as her lover but as her father.

The attempts at murdering all these women therefore include the further Oedipal nuance in Archibaldo's as yet unresolved inner conflicts and desires of an assault through the mother on the phallic power of the father.[6] Even though the male partners of these women seem to have a largely undifferentiated symbolic force as embodiments or agents of a patriarchal law, the women are grouped into the saint or witch categories—the saint represented by the nun and Carlota (Ariadne Welter), the witch by the governess, Patricia (Rita Macedo), and Lavinia (Miroslava Stern). The nun's saintliness is carried by the significance of her vocation, though even here there are embryonic signs of wickedness emphasized through the pretty cosmeticized features of the minor actress playing her (Chabela Durán) and the way her presence triggers off Archibaldo's memories of the dead governess's bloodstained legs. More elaborately developed is Carlota, whose saintliness is expressed not only through demure gestures and genteel etiquette, but also through overt identifications with the Virgin Mary. She first appears in the film praying in her own apartment chapel. When Archibaldo arrives with a bunch of flowers, she offers these with his approval to the Virgin. Even when in his imagination Archibaldo acts out her murder, suspecting her of infidelity, he forces her first to kneel down and to recite the 'Dios te salve' ('God Save You'), a slightly more sombre prayer anyway than the 'Ave María' ('Hail Mary'), picking it up at the crucial moment when the text refers to exile and associations with the original image of female corruption, Eve: 'A ti clamamos, los desterrados hijos de Eva. A ti suspiramos

---

[6] On Sade's notion of murder as the climax of erotic excitement, see Víctor Fuentes (1993: 71).

gimiendo y llorando en este valle de lágrimas . . .' ('We appeal to you, we the exiled children of Eve. To you we plead, wailing and weeping in this vale of tears . . .').

Carlota's submission to Archibaldo's demands represents her forced awareness of her identification with Eve and with all sinners, especially females. She is shot dead while lying on the nuptial bed, in Archibaldo's eyes the symbolic site of all women's (especially all mothers') betrayals, even those conforming on the surface to the saint/madonna stereotype. Even Carlota, ultimately perhaps only a callow madonna, identifies herself with transgression, pursuing an affair with a married man, the flawed architect-patriarch (and not Archibaldo) turning out eventually to be the man who actually succeeds in killing her.

The whore/witches, set up as the major targets of Archibaldo's displaced aggression, also reveal in all their wickedness positive transgressive qualities of which the text clearly also approves. At first sight, Patricia seems to reflect Archibaldo's mother's glamour and taste for excitement and for going out, although her aura is rather more raucously vulgar. Patricia is a spectacle of the powerful woman, giving orders to her more feeble, wasted-looking lover 'Willy' (in view of the film's later parodic reference to American tourism through a group of English-speaking characters, a seemingly intended pun on male potency under siege by assertive femininity). Willy's enslavement through desire to a woman who takes the wheel of their car, who asserts and flaunts her sexuality to the point not only of collusion in but also of exploitation of her own fetishization by the system, risking her relationship with her lover by stretching his jealousy to the limits of endurance, sets up the perfect target for Archibaldo's repressed Oedipal hostility towards the threatening, powerful woman. At the roulette wheel, spending Willy's money freely, she suddenly removes a high stiletto-heeled shoe, thrusts it under the chin of the man sitting beside her and comments on its expensive Parisian quality, remarking significantly that the fit is not perfect. This characteristically Buñuelian little cameo of foot fetishism, to which the woman herself draws attention, pointing out its difficult accommodation to the reality—as distinct from the male fantasy—of women's lives, represents the text's awareness of the objectification and the 'conspicuous consumption' of women, highlighting women as either willing or forced items of exchange value in the social order.

The witch/whore is both trapped in modes of self-destructive behaviour and also enabled through her self-conscious sexuality to acknowledge more openly the drives of the libido. Her relentless, fast, and high-pitched patter, her crude innuendo and vulgar laughter, and her expensive jewellery and cheap behaviour mark her out—in a dreary, conformist world—as a positively transgressive character, alive at least for all her crudity, however positioned by her ageing lover and would-be assassin. Her apartment *mise-en-scène* emphasizes her ambivalent status in the bourgeois order. Among other significant items projecting a varied image of contradictory desires, the photographs of musclemen, *toreros*, and rugged film stars—including one of the arch-patriarch himself, John Wayne—not only confirm her enthralment to patriarchal norms of masculinity (something caught by her framing with Willy in the casino mirror), but also represent her willing surrender to the libido. The film gives her a final stamp of approval through Willy's remark about her irrationality: 'Es la mujer menos razonable del mundo' ('she is the least reasonable woman in the world'). Willy means that she lacks common sense, but the text, in view of its Surrealistic master's enduring celebration of the irrational, asks the viewer to regard this defect —exemplified by Patricia's loud, colourful vulgarianism—as life-affirming, evidence of a character ruled less than the majority by the austerities of the super-ego, in her excess motivated by what Freud called the primary process and the liberated codes of the pleasure principle. This is the woman of whom a friend at the casino remarks: '¡Qué mujer tan interesante! ¿Verdad Archibaldo?' ('What an interesting woman! Don't you agree Archibaldo?'), and about whom Archibaldo replies: 'La asesinaría con mucho gusto' ('I would kill her with pleasure').

No conformist male can tolerate the threats to order and inner control of a pleasure-ruled woman. As a dull, frail-looking father figure, Willy has every reason to fear rival courtship; as a mother-fixated regressive, Archibaldo is at once attracted and repelled by the memory of his mother's distant betrayals. Patricia's suicide note neatly summarizes the impossibility of the whore/witch's situation: 'Me es imposible seguir soportando la vida que llevamos. No quiero que me veas bonita cuando esté muerta. Por eso me mato en esta forma. Ojalá mi sangre pese sobre ti mientras vivas.' ('I cannot go on living as we do. I don't want you to see me pretty when I'm dead. That's the reason I'm killing myself this way. I hope my blood weighs heavily on you while you live.')

We might feel this is another Gilda-text forcing Patricia/Mame to take the blame and punishment for sexual disturbance and unhappiness. Perhaps so, but at least Buñuel makes sure the lover is spared none of the responsibility for his share in the confusions and sadness leading to an act of such desperation. It is a further instance of the film's *huis clos* relationships, hellish encounters between lovers locked in increasingly intolerable forms of intimate confinement: 'Ya estamos acostumbrados al infierno.' ('We're used to the hellishness.') The infernal imagery arises naturally out of the film's patterns of witch/whore references. But among Archibaldo's potential victims none is more diabolical than Lavinia, the woman in whom he finally meets his match.

Significantly, he comes across her in a jeweller's shop, where they both vie for the music box that Archibaldo has lost since childhood. Archibaldo is never conscious of the fact that, in desiring the music box, Lavinia emphasizes her unwitting identification with its original owner, his mother. The second time Archibaldo and Lavinia meet she is sitting in a bar with a group of American tourists, lecturing them on Mexican history. Lavinia's function as tourist-guide indirectly recalls Diego Rivera's mural 'Touristic and Folkloric Mexico' (1936), where a haughty American symbolically rides an ass through a crowd of exotic, tourist-welcoming Mexicans wearing various types of mask and colourful, buffoonish costumes. Self-trivialization through tourism is given a slightly different perspective in Buñuel's more playful, less nationalistically touchy images, where, anyway, Lavinia is always in control, often treating her eager flock contemptuously. Her embodiment of transgression is established as soon as Archibaldo catches sight of her at the opposite end of the bar, seeing her through the flame of a candle on his table. The memory of this second encounter, as he later informs her, remains strongly etched in his mind: 'Me atrajo desde que la vi rodeada de llamas como una pequeña bruja condenada a la hoguera, mi pequeña Juana de Arco.' ('I was attracted to you seeing you surrounded by flames like a little witch condemned to the stake, my little Joan of Arc.') The religious aura excites him, confirming Buñuel's abiding interest as a Surrealist in the heightening of erotic experience through religious transgression, seeking the marvellous through the transcendental. But the reference to Joan of Arc also further emphasizes Archibaldo's recognition in Lavinia of the active, assertive woman prototype. When, in Marina Warner's account, the historical Joan was brought to trial, she was accused of three crimes: 'the unwomanliness and immodesty of her costume; the luxury of her state; the carrying of arms. Her transvestism offended; it was a potent strategy for change' (1983: 150). Neither Lavinia nor Archibaldo's mother is a transvestite, but their expropriation of male power corresponds to the crime of which Joan was accused, and of which her transvestism was denounced as being the visual symbol and proof. Capable of arousing, as Marina Warner argues (1983: 209), both respect and horror in the male, the Amazon woman or the Ayesha standing resplendent in the flame affronts the social order, earning in this text (for Buñuel as much as for Archibaldo) an equivocal force of fascination and revulsion. Lavinia recalls the witch-characters of Carlos Fuentes in texts like *Aura* (1962), *La muerte de Artemio Cruz* (1962), *Zona sagrada* (1967), Ciro Alegría's *El mundo es ancho y ajeno* (1941), Cortázar's La Maga in *Rayuela* (1963), and García Márquez's *Cien años de soledad* (1967), while also referring back to practices in colonialist Latin America that Ruth Behar has defined as the 'Castilian tradition of sexual magic and witchcraft' (1984: 183–5). Denied power in the public domain, women, even respectable ones, often resorted to the secret world of witchcraft in search of remedies for reducing tyrannical husbands to impotence.

At first arousing Archibaldo's horror, Lavinia eventually earns his respect because, in addition to projecting what—in a discussion about witches—Jung (1959) refers to as the male unconscious's dreams and psychotic fantasies, she is also the only woman who, through the equally strong addiction to irreverence and sense of playfulness, appeals to his own instinct for creativity. Lavinia's attraction to Archibaldo endorses Buñuel's celebration of ludically irrational and transgressive behaviour. When she brings her troupe of eager but wearisome tourists to visit his workshop, she significantly describes him as 'un artista original que no sigue reglas' ('an original artist who doesn't follow rules'), recognizing in him a fellow transgressor against the social order. But shared happiness, here as almost anywhere else in comic narratives, triumphs over adversity only after the successful negotiation of various ordeals.

Before the film closure's ironic celebration of their union, various demons require exorcism. Lavinia must first come to realize that gold-digging from an elderly protector who not only suffers from an excess of jealousy but is also a police informer is an unreasonable price to pay for material security. For his part, Archibaldo must also recognize that his monstrous aversion to women, the psychological block preventing him from developing a normal relationship, originates in his regressive desires and pent-up hostility towards his mother. Once they are locked in mutual fascination, these perverse lovers, with their complex traces of autobiographical Buñuelian obsessions, play out a battle of wits leaving each other intrigued and absorbed by shared drives and fantasies. Lavinia plays a trick on Archibaldo—who later takes his witty revenge—informing him that if he wishes to see her again she can be found working in a downtown shop in Mexico city, failing to warn him that the woman employed there is a dummy made in her image, one of several for which she poses in her career as a model.

Archibaldo's playful deceptions simultaneously project his own fantasies and attract Lavinia in their ludic inventiveness. He brings home one of the Lavinia dummies, dresses her up, and seats her in his living-room, ready for her to be introduced, as his cousin, to the real thing. Once Lavinia sees her double, a teasing, extremely playful game begins in which both male and female alternately respond to and identify themselves with the dummy, her other self. Kinship with Archibaldo has already been established through the pretence that they are cousins. At one point—transgressing the taboo on first-cousin sexual relationships—Archibaldo kisses and fondles the dummy, and is disciplined by the real Lavinia as he threatens to extend his sexual advances beyond propriety. Later, while Archibaldo is absent from the room, she herself exchanges her clothes for the dummy's so that, as it were, she takes her place, now accepting, now rejecting socialized constructions of femininity.

These comic strategies of masquerade and identity, of fantasy and taboo-transgressions, stress the empathy between rebel heroes, both respectful as well as irreverent towards the prohibitions of the social order. Constrained by the compromises of ideology (which for a woman include her victim status, and for a man embrace hostilities towards both the witch/mother and disavowed feminine tendencies), these characters are also part of Buñuel's comic dramatization of the wilder forms of desire. The games both characters play include a fondness for masquerade, Archibaldo impersonating his mother, Lavinia—in a hyperbolized version of a socialized identity—her own dummy. Buñuel intends this most characteristic of comedy's stock devices to be part of his complex thematics, not merely suggesting a simplistic contrast between appearance and reality but, far more interestingly, serving as an essential component of the text's celebration of release and disorder. Masquerade, transvestism, reversals, all blend in with the overall comic tone of the film, even if more violent human instincts are never far removed from the surface. Frustrated, through her unexpected departure, by his failure to murder Lavinia, Archibaldo satisfies his Oedipally twisted desires by burning to death her other, the dummy. The dummy, of course, both is and is not Lavinia. In real life Lavinia represents female assertiveness and autonomy. In the shop window, mute, lifeless, specularized, deprived of autonomous subjectivity, she represents the ideologization and commodification of women, the expression of female 'otherness', silenced, immobilized, and eternally subservient to the demands of male fantasy.

The more monstrous version of this process is mediated through Archibaldo's attack. Left alone, once the real Lavinia has disappeared with her gaggle of 'gringuitos', he reverts to regressive—even primitive—behaviour more worthy of Neanderthal modes of courtship, clasping the dummy by the hair, knocking her onto the floor, dragging her towards the kiln. *En route* her limbs begin to sever themselves from the torso, her dismemberment further proof of her fetishization. Eventually she is hurled into the kiln, her demonic master looking on with demented relish at the witch's burning, but, as the camera cuts from the decomposing wax on her face to the frenzied stare of her executioner, the film establishes another link between victim and judge, saint and sinner, guilty and innocent. If the dummy is the visual image of women's objectification by the worst excesses of the social order, Lavinia herself, alive, witty, inventive, and irreverent, is also proof of energetic resistance, the representation of the film's belief in the possibility of a woman more than capable of holding her own, combating the forces intent on her victimization.

These identifications between protagonist, victim, and audience once again highlight the text's patterns of self-consciousness. Furthermore, the confessional structure—Archibaldo's narration of his foiled desire to murder various women—is, as in other films, not only motivated by a desire to focus on a character driven by guilt to be shriven by a figure of authority—on this occasion a judge—but also to expose, in this precursor of postmodernist aesthetics, the text's artificiality. The artist figure here, Archibaldo the potter, represents Buñuel the auteur, establishing, as Andrew Horton (1991) defines it, that conspiratorial relationship with the spectator, here mischievously identified by Buñuel with the listening judge as a figure of authority. We too become judges and confessors, not innocent bystanders, our laughter at the absurd antics of Oedipally traumatized men and ideologized witch-like *femmes fatales* a response once again not of the Hobbesian but of the empathetic Freudian type, forcing upon us the recognition of a shared fate in the construction of fantasies and phobias by which all are compromised.

In recognition of that common fate and collective responsibility, Buñuel frees Archibaldo—even if only temporarily—from the curse of the music box and its Oedipal spell, arranges for Lavinia's magical appearance beside him at the end, and sets them both off together on a journey of provisional fulfilment. At the end Archibaldo discards not only the music box but also a cane. As he does so, we wonder whether in throwing this unmistakably phallic possession away there is the suggestion of a desire to be free both of Oedipal inhibitions and of sexuality itself. Abstinence, the film seems to be saying, is the only guarantor of genuine peace of mind. And yet, the ending is left open. We remember that the box, fought over with Lavinia at the jeweller's, was lost once before, only to turn up again to haunt Archibaldo. In all probability the vaginal or womb-like box and the phallic cane will reappear to plunge their owner into yet more sexual chaos and confusion.

3.2. *El*: Fetishism and Paranoia

'O, say; as summer flies are in the shambles
That quicken even with blowing. O thou weed
Who art so lovely fair and smell'st so sweet
That the sense aches at thee!
Would thou had'st never been born.'

Othello, IV. i

PLOT SYNOPSIS: Francisco, a paranoiacally jealous man, falls in love with his friend Raúl's fiancée Gloria, whom he first sees in church. He marries her but becomes increasingly tormented by the thought of her attractiveness to other men. At one point he breaks down and seeks the comfort of his manservant. Eventually, his derangement leads to failed attempts on her life. Gloria informs her ex-fiancé of the sufferings she endures in her marriage and, after Francisco decides to retreat to a monastery, she finally marries Raúl. The film ends as they both visit him there.

Buñuel's exploration of male fetishism reaches its most elaborate form in *El*. Here, in a way rivalled only perhaps by *Le Journal d'une femme de chambre*, fetishism opens up a realm of perverse desire including confusions caused by forms of paranoia. In their hyperbolized formulation fetishism and paranoia lead to a deeper awareness of the socialized constructions of masculinity. Based on an autobiographical novel by Mercedes Pinto, *El* reviews a topic much discussed in Hispanic art, especially the honour plays of the Golden Age. As many social anthropologists have argued *vis-à-vis* Hispanic culture as a whole (e.g. Peristiany (ed.) 1965), jealousy acquires more poignancy in societies, especially Mediterranean ones, where women have traditionally been the standard-bearers of male honour. The film offers through horror and comedy *grand guignol* spectacles of paranoid jealousy, its focus consistently remaining on exposure of social pressures and determinants.

Fetishism here highlights the film's interest in male power; paranoia, its threatened erosion. Freud's discussion of fetishism has at least three levels of primary interest for a discussion of *El*. First, its concentration on the idea that the fetish is a substitute for 'the woman's (mother's) penis that the little boy once believed in and . . . does not want to give up'; second, its configuration as a 'token of triumph over the threat of castration and a protection against it'; third, its impact in preventing the fetishist from becoming a homosexual, 'by endowing woman with the characteristic which makes them tolerable as sexual objects' (1981c: 352–4). Since Francisco, the fetishist in question, is excited by feet and shoes, it is of further interest that 'the foot or shoe owes its preference as a fetish—or part of it—to the circumstance that the boy peered at the woman's genitals from below, from her legs up' (ibid. 354).

The references to repressed homosexuality and its possible

relevance to Francisco's state of mind demand consideration through questions relating to paranoia. For the moment, what needs stressing is Francisco's fetishism as affirmation of the desire for power over women, a process avoiding engagement with the realities of the woman to whom he professes devotion. Foot fetishism also succeeds here at the very least in distancing the male from the female, converting her into a screen for projection of disturbed fantasies and desires. Troubled by the prospect of loss of control over her, the jealous male fetishizes the woman he desires.

The film also traces the gradual loss of control over his own actions by a man, who in some senses resembles Calderón's reputation-obsessed husbands, someone further described by Carlos Fuentes as a 'middle-class Othello' (1978: 57), whose preliminary appearances convey seemingly unassailable authority and power, attributes validated by his close involvements with the Church. Early moments in the film identify Francisco with religious imagery in a way that reinforces notions of power, though by the end religion has been steadily equated with gradual disintegration and madness. Francisco's language often relies on sacred or pious references, as when urging his wife Gloria to treat him as her confessor or when, in an early aside, he chides her mother with the suggestion that, although not a bad woman, Gloria is in need of discipline: 'No es mala pero necesita que se le sermonee bien.' ('She's not a bad woman, but she needs to be given a good sermon.') More significant identifications with religion include Francisco's close friendship with a priest, performing the duties of acolyte in church services—especially the Maundy Thursday feet-washing ritual—and, most disturbing of all, something stressed by the film's title and its indirect allusion to the Old Testament Jealous Deity, his quasi-blasphemous identification with God himself. In this respect, it seems natural that his favourite place for an evening or afternoon out with his wife is not the cinema or the races or some other place of less demanding concentration, but up a church bell tower, a height from which to survey, as a contemptuously detached Olympian, what he regards as a wretched humanity toiling and rushing around like futile insects worthy only of extermination. His actual words are: 'El egoismo es la esencia de un alma noble. Yo desprecio a los hombres, ¿entiendes? Si fuera Dios no les perdonaría nunca.' ('Egotism is the essence of a noble soul. I despise men, do you see? If I were God I would never forgive them.')

The remark gestures awkwardly to notions of self-love, traditionally regarded—implicitly, for example, in Fromm's discussion on Meister Eckhart (1968: 49)—as the highest love of all,
the love of God for himself. But Francisco's egocentricity (unlike, for instance, St Teresa's, whose introspection prepared her
for worthiness of God's favour) is a perversion, self-love here
defined by cruelty and scorn, not harmony and love. In a frenzy
of egocentric perversity, revealed in the film as being in large
measure determined by the demands of culture, Francisco even
turns his venom on Gloria, attempting—in a scene anticipating
not only others by Buñuel, but also Hitchcock's *Vertigo* (1958)—
to hurl her into the abyss, his wife, like everyone else with whom
he comes into contact, bearing the brunt of his fury and despair.
Self-love of this kind links up with Buñuel's interest in the
provisionality of power. However, the focus here falls not on the
timeless thematics of earthly vanities. Rather, it seems to be
specifically related to historically contextualized meditations on
the clash between modernity and tradition, above all in the realm
of the senses.

Francisco is tradition's martyr. His treatment of Gloria, wavering between reverence and sadism, now eulogizing her beauty or
spirituality, now attempting to sew up her vagina, reveals the
heavy price exacted by tradition. No longer in *El* content to
expose some of the more harmlessly ludicrous forms of bourgeois
tyrannies—as when in *Un chien andalou* the dead hand of culture
is portrayed through the image of priests and dead donkeys
pulling against the urges of the imagination—Buñuel seems here
in bleaker, crueller mood, more governed by the aesthetics of an
Artaud than by the drives that led, for instance, to the making
of a film like *Ensayo de un crimen*. Yet, the text seems to be saying,
if even Gloria, Francisco's primary victim, can be relied on to
feel compassion for, as well as fear of, Francisco, the viewer
should be capable of nothing less, treating him as both victim
and agent of the perversions and cruelties of the bourgeois order.
If Jeanne Rucar's remarks about the film's autobiographical
traces are accurate, Buñuel had no other option than to dramatize his own displaced paranoia through a balance of sympathetic as well as critical rhetoric. The anecdote about his influence
in securing her a job, which, unknown to her, he himself paid for
to keep his young fiancée out of mischief in a Spanish friend's

shop in Paris, is the most extended of many references in her autobiography seeming to validate the impression of a complex relationship between Francisco and Buñuel (Rucar de Buñuel 1991: 41).

The emotionally crippling influences of culture, something of which Buñuel seems to be proclaiming himself a victim, are given visual expression in the film's elaborately constructed *mise-en-scène*. Throughout the film, Francisco is engaged in a long and futile battle with unseen, unnamed opponents over lands claimed historically as his family's, property now appropriated by rival claimants. Once more, a battle is fought out here between tradition and modernity. Significantly, too, the land in question is in Guanajuato, one of Mexico's prettiest, but also eeriest, colonial cities. During the scenes of the couple's honeymoon visit, the architectural sublimity of the city is caught in various shots of a picture-postcard or tourist-documentary kind. But even here, the city's identification with the darker side of culture—especially perhaps as regards implicit evocations of colonialist tyrannies—is wittily suggested when Gloria takes Francisco's photograph as he stands behind a heavy, wrought-iron grilled gate, a shot crudely but effectively stressing entrapments behind façades of order and tradition.

The moment recalls a similarly ironic use of *mise-en-scène* during the dinner party to which Francisco has invited Raúl and Gloria, along with other guests, as part of a strategy to lure his future wife away from her current fiancé, his boyhood friend. As the guests retire to the drawing-room after the meal, a woman guest plays Chopin at the piano while dust begins slowly but copiously to blow into the room. A sign of inner turbulence caused by sexual agitation, the dust emerges from a room in which pure chaos reigns, where, among the piles of jumble, Pablo the valet is searching for another chair. Like Guanajuato and its cemetery of publicly displayed mummies, juxtaposing tourist attractions with macabre relics, and like Francisco himelf, whose veneer of composure, fastidiousness of appearance, and sartorial elegance mask the inner derangement of a man driven to the verge of dementia, the house is another of the film's symbols of order under threat from various forms of confusion. Just as he has been dispossessed of hereditary domains in Guanajuato, so too the house in Mexico City is gradually invaded by alien elements, its presence suddenly jeopardized by otherness and difference, in the shape of a wife threatening to desecrate the premarital inviolability of its owner's hermetic egocentricity.

Among other things, Francisco's egocentricity is a study of solitude failing to recover any sense of unity with the natural order. Francisco's residence includes acres of garden where, rather than represent liberating instinctual drives or primordial union with nature, ancient trees symbolize the weight of outmoded tradition. The trees and the house are linked with Francisco's father and grandfather, their presence providing yet more evidence of failure to break free of the past and its various determinants. Nature, imprisoned in the hot-house climate of repressive ideology, is beginning to take its own revenge, returning, as in some of the more gruesome stories by Quiroga, in monstrous form, breaking out grotesquely all over Francisco's house, supreme symbol of the twisted social order. The encroaching menace of nature heralds the eventual disintegration of that order, as the interior of Francisco's house, like the inner recesses of his degenerating mind, seem to reproduce in their Gaudiesque art-deco patterns the monstrous return of the repressed. In many indoor scenes at the house Francisco is framed against a background of shrubbery and plants seen through windows. The rooms are themselves congested with flowers, especially phallic lilies in vases; chandeliers with elaborate structures resembling miniature trees hang from the ceilings; painted leaves on door panels and squiggly lines on walls suggest the onslaught of irrational, natural forces, returning monstrously to challenge the inflexibilities and claustrophobic social structures of a decaying inherited order.

At one point at the dinner party, guests comment on the interior décor of Francisco's house. The camera then accompanies Raúl's references to Francisco's father's inspiration for its design in the 1900 Paris exhibition with shots of the balcony and ceiling, showing the clash between Gothic lines of columns and pillars as straight as the index finger of St John (as another order-obsessed character remarks in *Cet obscur objet du désir*) and the fussy art-deco arabesques of resurfacing desire.[7]

Even in the most trivial ways, Francisco's idiosyncrasies of gesture and manner defer to an inevitable process of colonization by the returning repressed. The detail of his zig-zagging

---

[7] The remark is taken directly from *La Femme et le pantin* (1981: 77).

walk, replacing the straight, direct approach with meandering incertitude when he reaches a point of no return in his descent into madness, confirms the disintegration of a man whose obsession with order once impeded even a moment's rest on a bed over which hung a slightly crookedly placed picture of the Virgin. By the end, the *mise-en-scène* of eccentricity and egocentricity, of a space affirming not only the triumph of civilization over nature, but also the isolation of the hyperbolized spokesman and victim of that triumph, becomes the setting simultaneously of horror and comedy.

Expressionistic shadows—inherited from the Twenties' German films that Buñuel so admired and wrote about (Buñuel 1982*b*)—begin to colonize Francisco's space, his place of definition. In this redesigned setting the monster is imaged not only as the perpetrator of cruel or sadistic acts against defenceless victims—like the Caligaris and Fredersons of German Expressionism—but also as someone experiencing loss of control and power and, since on this occasion the monster is male, mutating into femininity. It is significant in this context that prior to his final brutal assault on Gloria, an act stressing his definition as a monster of desire, Francisco enters his valet's bedroom, bursting into unmanly tears as he begins to explain the causes of his unhappiness.

The identification of male monsters or their victims with loss of authority and a certain tendency towards feminization, has lately become a subject of much debate in film (Hutchings 1993), but the difference between recent Hollywood films and Buñuel's treatment of the monstrous male is that, whereas in the former this may often reflect an unconscious process, motivated partly by a backlash against gay- and feminist-inspired alternative forms of masculinity, in *El* the comic treatment of the monster suggests not only sympathy for Francisco but also awareness of the rigidities of introjected traditional forms of masculinity that have helped lead to his condition. As the viewer's responses and identifications shift between victim and victimizer, between sadistic and masochistic pleasures, the erosion of the male's legacy of a traditional masculinity highlights not only the pathos of its disintegration, but the tyrannies of which it is often capable.

The masochistic pleasure aroused by the spectacle of characters victimized by others, or by the confusions of an introjected order, is discussed in a Deleuze-inspired feminist study of the films of Marlene Dietrich by Gaylyn Studlar (1988). For Deleuze (1971), as for Studlar and Hutchings, sado-masochistic desires are not, contrary to Freudian theory, complementary but opposed. Whereas control is the hallmark of sadism, an affirmation of post-Oedipal identifications with the Symbolic order, masochism reactivates the urges and instincts of pre-Oedipality (Studlar 1988: 38), in which the male masochist takes up the position of child, the female becoming the agent of his fantasy, a disciplinarian object of obscure maternal desire. Whether one accepts the Freudian view of the interrelationships of sado-masochism or the Deleuzian revisions (1971), where the two become split, it seems clear that audience identification with the masochistic monster of *El,* Francisco, opens up questions about the structures of patriarchal forms of subjectivity in which the conventional male's relationship to the Symbolic order is placed under unbearable strain. In the particular case of Francisco, moreover, his masochistic desires for Gloria are further complicated by paranoid jealousy, a condition which in its most extreme form, as here, is sustained, according to Freud, by neuroses born of repressed homosexual desire.

In 'Some Neurotic Mechanisms in Jealousy, Paranoia and Homosexuality', Freud distinguishes between three kinds of jealousy: competitive, or normal; projected; and delusional. For Freud, normal jealousy lacks more than rudimentary analytical interest, though even here it is something not completely rational, with deep roots in the unconscious. Projected jealousy refers either to actual infidelities or repressed impulses towards infidelity in men or women. In the case of repressed impulses, these can often become so strong as to need release through projection onto one's partner. Delusional jealousy also has its roots in repressed desires for infidelity but, crucially, 'the object in these cases is of the same sex as the subject. Delusional jealousy is what is left of a homosexuality that has run its course, and it rightly has its position among the classical forms of paranoia' (Freud 1979: 199).

Looking at paranoia in *El* from these perspectives helps clarify not only some of Francisco's idiosyncratic forms of behaviour but also Buñuel's wary attitude to the subject. There are no random homophobic remarks in *El* like Don Andrés's in *El bruto*: 'En mis tiempos los hombres no eran tan mariquitas como ahora' ('In my day men weren't the queers they are today').[8] And even if no direct allusions are ever made to homo-sexual desire, the various indirect references arising out of the film's obvious awareness of Freud's essay on jealousy and homo-sexuality make it a site, neither progressive nor regressive, for opening up questions about these related matters. For all his transgressions against various forms of established order, Buñuel is not, after all, outside culture, his films sometimes colluding with—as well as, more usually, challenging—the Symbolic law, their resistances to bourgeois norms at once conscious and un-conscious, compromised as well as uncompromising.

Francisco is clearly suffering from paranoid jealousy, not of the projected sort: first, never having had intimate relations with a woman he can harbour no feelings of jealousy of a partner's relations with another man before marriage to Gloria; secondly, his desire for her is prompted by the sight not at first of female but of male naked flesh. Once the credit title sequence ends, the camera takes up its position inside a church where the ritual cleansing by the priest of the altar boys' feet on *Jueves Santo* is watched with some intensity by Francisco. The camera zooms in on the priest's face as he kneels down to take into his hands a boy's bare foot. The camera cuts to a close-shot of the boy looking down at the priest. Later in the sequence there is a shot of a whole row of altar boys' feet. Eventually, this is followed by a close-shot of Francisco; cut to a closer shot of the priest this time kissing the boy's foot; cut back to Francisco looking at this incident; he begins to turn his face slowly towards the right-hand side of the frame; cut to a close-shot of a woman's feet in smart leather shoes (men's shoes are at left and right of the frame), as the camera now begins to move, giving us a subjec-tive shot (that is, taking up Francisco's point of view), gliding along a row of shod feet belonging to worshippers at the service, eventually stopping at Gloria's (though at this point neither Francisco nor the viewer knows that these are her feet and shoes), before moving up her legs, from her feet to her face, which is quite still; cut to a close-shot of Francisco looking now at her face; cut to Gloria, who remains still, then lowers her eyes, paralleling the gesture of the boy whose feet were washed and kissed by the priest; cut to Francisco looking; cut to Gloria, who

---

[8] See Buñuel (1982a: 263) for the anecdote about Pedro Armendáriz's refusal to wear a short-sleeved shirt for fear of being thought a homosexual.

again lowers her eyelids; cut to Francisco, looking towards the left of the frame; cut to Francisco moving away from the group involved in the ceremony. From one point of view, Francisco's scanning of the rows of feet, moving from boys to woman, arguably represents the quest of a predatory heterosexual male, skipping past the serried ranks of, to him, uninteresting boys' feet, looking for and then finding the only object of his sexual desires, a woman. But from another point of view, Francisco's own *via crucis* towards his obscure object of desire suggests that his route towards the female is only accessible through the male. The homo-erotic meaning is further reinforced by the parallel shots of the young boy and Gloria, both characters becoming the objects of the male gaze, both characters—through the demure gestures of closing eyelids and slight inclination of the head—unified in their appeal to Francisco, who unconsciously displaces his homo-erotic sexual desires onto the paranoid dream screen of his hapless eventual wife.

The homo-erotic subtext—disavowed but sometimes liberating itself from its multiple constraints—resurfaces even more clearly with Francisco's realization of his marriage's final collapse. In another of Buñuel's scenes of male bonding between master and valet, Francisco enters Pablo's room at night, surprisingly in some respects for a man so in thrall to order, to unburden himself of his desolation and failure. In contrast to his master's Mexico City apartment *mise-en-scène* of warring reason and instinct, the room inhabited by Pablo exteriorizes the banality but also the confident masculinity and inner freeedom of a man spared the torments of his paranoid master. On the walls of Pablo's room are pinned up the posters and related paraphernalia of an enthusiasm for cycling. There is even a bicycle parked on one of the tables. The room has none of the fussy feminine décor sometimes associated with the rest of the house. Cycling here, another of Buñuel's many images of movement, suggests freedom, providing a contrast with the symbols of confinement with which Francisco is so often identified. In this context, though, sport also connotes manliness, a reading confirming the viewer's earlier suspicions of Pablo as a man of heterosexual desires in the scene of his pursuit of a household maid. Thus, whereas Francisco is a man of inner schisms, of disavowed or unacknowledged sexual ambivalence and confusion, Pablo epitomizes untroubled heterosexual masculinity. Where Francisco is unable through paranoid jealousy to relate normally to Gloria, Pablo has no difficulty in expressing and pursuing his interest in the harassed maid, even though she seems more horrified than thrilled by the overture.

It is in this ambience of confident heterosexual masculinity that the paranoiacally jealous man seeks comfort. The measure of Francisco's loss of power and growing alienation from the patriarchal order is his willingness to appear dishevelled, weeping, distraught—all conventional markers of femininity—before a man who is both his social inferior and emblem of the socialized concept of masculinity which, at one level, he strives to epitomize. Whatever intentions Buñuel may have had about this scene, its effect is to stress the more than fraternal nature of the bonding between the two men. The feminization and submissiveness of Francisco becomes intensified through his lack of embarrassment over sitting on the edge of Pablo's bed—while, in pyjamas, Pablo still lies in it—and through his explanation of his troubles in language that could easily be transferred to a scene involving his mother or another woman: 'Necesito a alguien que me quiera, que me comprenda.' ('I need someone to love me, to understand me.') At the very least, this remark to a valet is incompatible with Francisco's status, a gesture of verbal intimacy paralleled by Pablo's gentle touch of Francisco's arm. These moments exposing the complex motivations of acknowledged and repressed desires towards Gloria and Pablo, whatever the effect of censoring mechanisms imposed on them either consciously or unconsciously by Buñuel, do at least seem to encourage a pursuit of their origins in the traumas of childhood experience. On the one hand, Francisco's conscious rationalization of his attraction to Gloria—'dulzura, esa especie de aura de bondad, la resignación' ('sweetness, that type of aura of goodness and resignation')—may not be consistent with his traditionalist sympathies. On the other hand, although he may often be too reductive and too simplistic in his own analysis of what is clearly represented as an obsession of great complexity, he does acknowledge, elsewhere, that desire is ultimately rooted in the experiences and remorse of the past:

El rayo no nace de la nada, sino de nubes que tardan mucho tiempo en acumularse. Este tipo de amor se está formando desde la infancia. Un hombre pasa al lado de mil mujeres y de pronto encuentra a una

que su instinto le dice que es la única. En esta mujer cristalizan sus
sueños y sus ilusiones, los deseos de la vida anterior de ese hombre.

(Lightning is not created from nothing, but from clouds which take a
long time in forming. This type of love begins to grow in childhood. A
man passes by a thousand women and suddenly he finds one who, his
instinct tells him, is the only one. In this woman are crystallized his
dreams and expectations, the desires of his earlier life.)

The Olympian imagery of a self defined through the determinants of religion persists here, but the more interesting part
of this speech delivered by Francisco at the dinner party, encouraging once more an appeal to psychoanalysis, refers to childhood influence. The *flechazo*, or spark of affinity, of an *amour fou*
releases feelings nurtured and stored up in the earlier life of the
male, all of them ready to be released and projected onto that
one-in-a-thousand women whose own individuality is both ignored and overwhelmed in the process. If the male lover's desire
is the product of childhood experience, it is significant that in
this film we are given the following information about Francisco:
1) his childhood friend was Raúl, who is now his rival in love
and from whom he eventually steals Gloria;[9] 2) mention is made
of his father and grandfather, but not of his mother.

The discovery that Gloria is his childhood friend's *novia* may
be read as further grounds for the diagnosis of Francisco's condition as paranoid, homosexually repressed jealousy. The references to his father and grandfather, the architects not only of the
house and its grounds but also of the ambience, or ideology,
in which Francisco grew up, confirm his life in the shadow of
patriarchy. The absence of any reference to the mother at once
disavows maternal/feminine influence and suggests an obscure
displacement of a desire for her.

The search by Francisco for a mother—real or imagined—in
adult life leads to infatuation, or *amour fou*, with Gloria, the sweet,
good, resigned, and submissive mother figure, the 'Gloria in
excelsis Deo', the 'Gloria' whose definition lies not in her own
individuality, but in her capacity for exultation of the divine-
like, jealous 'El', the mother prouder of her son's achievements
than of her own, something stressed in poses suggesting a mother–
child relationship. The man to whose 'aire de dominio, de

---

[9] On the idea that men often secretly desire the men in the lives of the women
they pursue, see Girard (1969) and Sedgwick (1985).

seguridad' ('air of authority, of security') she was initially attracted has all but vanished by the end of the film, his quasi-divine self-possession and authority reduced to a shadow. At this level, the film's title *El* seems no longer simply to refer to Francisco or to the emblematic authority of an internalized patriarchal culture, but to an ill-defined, disavowed search by Francisco for a repressed 'El', an ideal perhaps not of difference but of sameness, given a complex, unconscious expression in the confused definitions and actions in scenes involving, especially, Pablo and Raúl.

The point is, finally, given a humorous reformulation in the detail of the moustaches worn at different stages in the film by Francisco and Raúl. This doubling (stressed through references to childhood friendship, to their shared desire for Gloria, to their comparable social status in the community) is given a further witty emphasis through the sporting or not of a moustache. During his marriage to Gloria, outwardly appearing to be the confident icon of patriarchy, Francisco has a moustache, while Raúl, denied access to Gloria at first, does not. When Raúl is married to Gloria at the end he wears a moustache, while Francisco, by now a monk, does not. Clearly the moustache here is a sign of psychological and social significance, reinforcing Buñuel's view, expressed in his essay on Adolphe Menjou's moustache, that moustaches rival eyes as one of the audience's best routes to the depths of a personality (1982b: 168). In the monastery social laws of the kind in operation in the outside world do not apply, so symbols are mere vanities and forbidden. More than that, though, as well as being, consciously, the symbol of phallic power and conquest, of which only the genuinely virile man is worthy, the moustache is also, perhaps unconsciously, a mark of sameness, at once acknowledged and disavowed by the film. The paranoid Francisco has become a social outcast, tormented by contradictory desires. But in his final defeat the film parallels the expository, illuminating force of what *vis-à-vis* his own work Dalí called 'paranoiac-criticism'. As Wallace Fowlie puts it: 'The paranoiac is the man who appears to have a normal kind of health and attitude, but who privately is fashioning the world in accordance with his own desire and the imperviousness of his desire' (1963: 113). Francisco's desires, like Séverine's, become incompatible with the values of the world he wishes to inhabit. While Séverine succeeds in making the necessary adjustments and compromises, Francisco finds his place in it intolerable.

3.3. *Cet obscur objet du désir* and Sado-masochism

'If God afflicts your enemies, surely that ought to suffice you. It is both mean and presumptuous to add your torture to his!'

Emily Bronte, *Wuthering Heights*

PLOT SYNOPSIS: On a train journey from Seville to Paris, a middle-aged man, Mathieu, recounts to fellow passengers in his compartment the story of his infatuation and cruel treatment by Conchita, whom he had first met as a servant at his brother's house. Conchita blows hot and cold, alternately humiliating and tempting Mathieu, always refusing, however, to surrender what she claims is her still-intact virginity. Eventually, after buying her a house in Seville, Mathieu is locked out and has to watch Conchita making love to her young lover El Morenito. At the end of the train journey, Mathieu and Conchita are reunited. The torments of desire have not yet run their full course.

Whereas in other films he limits himself to individual moments of confessional flashback narrative—e.g. in *El*, where Gloria confides in Raúl, or in *Le Charme discret*, where various characters describe their dreams—in *Cet obscur objet*, as in *Ensayo de un crimen*, Buñuel relies almost entirely on this mechanism. Flashbacks may sometimes occur in a narrative unprovoked by a character —in *Un chien andalou*, for instance, the time settings of the film keep changing without any manipulation by any of the characters —but the confessional flashback is triggered off by a character narrating some event from the past either to another character or, more directly, to the viewer. In general, flashbacks, confessional or otherwise, provide variation in narrative mechanisms, undermine the artificial order of chronology and linearity, encourage detachment and conceptualization, and place in question the premisses and events of the frame-text to which they belong. These are effects much in evidence in *Cet obscur objet*. Additionally, flashbacks provide interiority for the leading characters of the narrative. Writing in a passage of some relevance to *Cet obscur objet*, M. Turim remarks that 'flashbacks in film . . . often present a past like a dream, waiting to be interpreted' (1989: 18). He goes on to say that the spectator 'hears' the flashback from the position of the analyst, thus becoming identified not simply with the narrator but with the analyst as well (ibid.). The psychoanalytical, and also religious, features of confessional flashback structures clearly appealed to Buñuel—the lapsed but still traumatized Catholic Surrealist—and *La Femme et le pantin*, the original novel by Pierre Louÿs on which *Cet obscur objet* is based, clearly fuelled such interests: 'je n'observe jamais sans pitié le besoin qu'ont les âmes simples de crier leur peines dans le désert' (1981: 51). ('I never observe without pity the need of simple souls to cry out their sorrows in the wilderness.')

Confession—its importance to sexual narratives recognized by Foucault in *The History of Sexuality*—here leads to knowledge not only of male subjectivity, but of the power relations within which it operates. *Cet obscur objet* bears out Foucault's claims that we have become a confessing society (1984: 59).[10] As Mathieu's confession attempts to order, to confirm, or even to imprison reality, to view it from his own perspectives, the film introduces a series of images associated with confinement—the train compartment, the mousetrap, the Paris bedroom, the house in Seville from which Mathieu is debarred—all of which to some extent provide reminders of the entrapments of language and ideology. But a narrative starting out as a project of male self-justification eventually becomes the medium of the return of the female repressed, a text freed from the constraints of the Symbolic law.

Through its confessional structure the film belongs to a dominant mode of twentieth-century art, something reflected by the cinema in both its art-film and popular traditions. As an example of the latter, arguably the entire work of Woody Allen, and of the former, many of the films of Fassbinder, can be read as autobiographical psychopathologies.[11] Without recruiting members of his own family or entourage (as in Fassbinder's case), or acting in his own films (as in Allen's) to work through his private neuroses and obsessions, Buñuel nevertheless manages to surround *Cet obscur objet*, as almost all his other films, with an autobiographical aura even more emphatic than usual.[12]

[10] For a full treatment of the trend towards confessional narratives, see Tambling (1990).
[11] For a discussion of Woody Allen and confessional narrative, see Babington and Evans (1989), and, for Fassbinder, see Hayman (1984).
[12] Though Buñuel does appear himself in *Un chien andalou*, *Belle de jour*, and *Le Fantôme de la liberté*.

The reappearance for a fourth time of Fernando Rey in a key part reprises consistent processes of introspection. In so far as these are directed inwardly towards questions of male subjectivity and desire, they are developed nowhere more vigorously than through associations with this most conspicuous of *alter egos*. In *Cet obscur objet* the Rey persona provides through the role of Mathieu a final opportunity for analysis of the fiendish pleasures of *amour fou*, a sweet but destructive confusion respectful neither of status nor of age. Like the Gene Hackman character in *Night Moves* (1975), Mathieu is Buñuel's testament to the scars inflicted on the hearts of even aged lovers. As the Hackman character ruefully observes, age offers no remedies for the pain of love, and Buñuel provides further painful evidence through Mathieu.

As he begins his confession, like the picaresque anti-heroes of Spanish literature Buñuel claimed to like, Mathieu seems motivated both by a need for self-justification and for expiation. Having only Mathieu's account of his troubled affair with Conchita, absolution can only be provisional, especially since the narrative he carefully constructs fails to prevent subversive resistance to the truth of his version of events. True to form, Buñuel is in ambivalent mood, seeking the sympathy of the viewer for common human failings, acknowledging the guilt and accepting the penance for emotional crimes and misdemeanours. Partly drawing closer to Mathieu through his self-protective rhetoric about the perfidies of his irresistible *belle dame sans merci*, we become simultaneously distanced through awareness of his complicit or implicit involvements in outmoded victimizing strategies towards women.

For all Mathieu's care and attention in creating an impression of injured innocence, he ultimately fails to resist the pressures of the text's parallel commitment, mainly through comedy, to the exposure of unreconstructed forms of masculinity. Like the heroes of Screwball comedy, he is a figure—here more hyperbolized than his Hollywood predecessors—of conformist masculinity, subjected to endless comic humiliations by a Katharine Hepburn equivalent (the hybrid Angela Molina/Carole Bouquet) exacting female revenge, as Michael Wood argues (1981), for male failures to notice and to react to the reality of women, a defect of perception emphasized through Mathieu's treatment of the two women (radically different in most respects) who play the

part of Conchita as if they really were the same.[13] Mathieu's
traditionalist masculinity comes under fire as, all around, terrorist bombs explode, sights and sounds not just of a politically
agitated decade, but also of an all-out attack on personal and
social realities, while nearer to him a New Woman has been
firing at the conventional prejudice of which he remains in some
respects unfashionably guilty. In the unreconstructed fantasy of
the traditionalist male, women exemplify the various stereotypes
to which feminist writing has drawn attention. Here Conchita is
not only, as Linda Williams rightly argues (1992), specularized,
trapped in various postures of display for the gratification of the
male gaze, but also identified as a figure of sexual cruelty releasing masochistic desires. Like other Buñuel males in middle or
old age, Mathieu is to a certain extent drawn to a woman's
powerlessness, here associated both with her servant-class status
and with her youthful innocence.

On this occasion, though, as distinct from the blonde-fixated
Buñuel lover (e.g. Jaime in *Viridiana* or Husson in *Belle de jour*),
Mathieu is attracted to darkness of appearance as well as to ill-
defined, opaque motivations of desire, a seduction inspired by
the novel's revelation of Mathieu's lack of experience of blonde
mistresses: 'Je n'avais jamais eu de maîtresse blonde. J'ai toujours
ignoré ces pâles objets de désir' (Louÿs 1981: 49). ('I'd never
had a blonde mistress. I have never had knowledge of these pale
objects of desire.') Failing to be stirred by the challenge of outwardly frigid blondes, Mathieu expresses through attraction to
darkness his pursuit of sexually uninhibited and self-conscious
women. Conchita's youth and apparent inexperience help further the cause of his singular designs. Relations with a more
mature woman, someone more his age, might have brought the
versatility of sexual experience but, in addition to the obvious
delectations of her fresh beauty, a young woman is both free
from the memory traces of previous sexual liaisons and as yet
unmarked by the possible disillusionments, demands, and anger
of middle age.

These reflections recall similar behavioural patterns in the
portrayal of other characters, especially *Tristana*'s Don Lope.
Enjoying a reputation as a roué, a Don Juan with many trophies

---

[13] Paul Sandro interestingly notes the reverse process, in which 'Mathieu has one
body but two names, since only one of the Conchitas calls him Mathieu; the other
calls him Mateo' (1987: 142).

taken from the field of sexual conquest, Don Lope attempts to
settle finally for the companionship of a young girl, an apparently defenceless ward through whom to stave off the loneliness
of advancing old age. His pursuit of Tristana, the child who will
become the monster of desire, seems as much motivated by frustrations with older, worldly-wise women as by lust for the virginal waif in his custody, the *tabula rasa* of unpoliticized manners
and perceptions.

Linda Williams argues that male power is exercised in *Cet obscur
objet* through Mathieu's controlling gaze (1992: 185–209), a
strategy, however, given its most ambiguous exposure in the
scene where Mathieu climbs onto a chair to spy on Conchita
and her young lover Morenito. As elsewhere, though, the gaze
is returned by Conchita, deflecting Mathieu's outrage at the
challenge to his libidinal and proprietorial rights over her through
her own look of contempt and ridicule. While the camera frames
Mathieu against the window panes above the bedroom door (as
it will also later hold him against the grilled patio gate from which
he views the love-making—fake or real?—between the youthful
couple) any idea that the gaze is always inevitably male in Western
art, a view seemingly endemic to much writing on spectatorship
in the Hollywood cinema, loses much of its credibility.

Buñuel may well be a director compromised by all sorts of
prejudices against women, but he is also someone clearly aware
of prejudice, recognizing the various tyrannies to which they
have often been subjected—by men as well as by colluding
women—and as eager to interrogate these as the drives which
often lead women to make men the fools of desire. Mathieu's
look belongs to the past, in some ways understood, perhaps even
to a certain extent respected, but now defined as outmoded,
regarded as a hindrance to the needs and interests of the modern
woman. On the one hand, the woman seen by Mathieu is neither Angela Molina nor Carole Bouquet but an exchangeable
sexual property: 'Conchita', or, to use the slang Latin American
meaning of the word, the 'cunt', or obscure object, of his unsat-
isfied desires. On the other hand, the woman seen by the viewer
is more than sexually defined, refusing all decision-making on
her behalf by others—including her mother, who has sold her
into marriage with Mathieu—and insisting on taking responsibility for her own life.

The redirection of the gaze towards Mathieu succeeds in

transforming the conventional male into an object of ridicule. Through the treatment he receives from the modern woman his posture recalls the buffoonish characters of farce, like, say, the Cervantes or Lorca stage *celoso*, the *senex* who must give way to the young Turks in the brave new world of sexual equality. Caught in the frame of his own bedroom window, Mathieu plays out Buñuel's comedy of male desire, trapped by his own masculinity, incapable of liberation from attitudes and habits of mind eternally driving him into spirals of ever-increasing unhappiness, incapable of seeing women beyond the limits of his own or other men's desires. He is Buñuel's representation of a pathetic masculinity from which the modern woman is in flight. Mathieu's absurdity is finally exposed by Conchita in another of the tragicomic scenes of male humiliation, where she dances flamenco naked in front of Japanese tourists: 'Je ne suis à personne. Je suis à moi. . . . Je n'ai rien de plus précieux que moi.' ('I don't belong to anyone. I belong to myself. . . . I have nothing more precious than myself.') This is extremely close to the novel's wording, although missing in the film is a final reference about her refusal to be bought by anyone: 'Personne n'est assez riche pour m'acheter a moi-même' (Louÿs 1981: 141). ('No one is rich enough to buy me.') The remark is an unnecesary addition to a clear enough expression of a woman's right to self-determination and fulfilment.

In this scene Conchita is played not by Carole Bouquet but by Angela Molina, the warmer, more sensuous, and more approachable of the two actresses, her more playful self giving way here to a desire to explain to the disorientated, time-warped male the true object of female desire. Freedom, even if it cannot ultimately be achieved, since most people are programmed for conjugal living, is what Conchita seeks but may never find. The difference between Mathieu and Conchita lies clearly in their relative ability or failure to recognize the traps in which each is caught, rather than in the degree of freedom each has managed to earn. Failing to acknowledge his own entrapment, the essentialist male can only react to Conchita's transgression against the order he defends by relying on familiar methods of protest. Bewildered by her unconventional behaviour, he resorts to traditional threats and sanctions: 'Si tu restes un jour de plus dans cet endroit c'est fini entre nous.' ('If you stay in this place one more day it's all over between us.') Mathieu seems incapable of shaking off a belief in the male's natural authority over women, a failure that provokes a significant reaction from Conchita: 'Tu ne m'as jamais compris.' ('You've never understood me.')

The solution to the great enigma of Freudian psychoanalysis here resists the comprehension of the supremacist male, his defaults of perception largely the result of sexual fantasies projected onto the unrecognized, unfocused reality of women. Mathieu is a secular variant of the man who has seen but not understood. As if to stress the point, Conchita continually refers to his eyes—in bed, for instance, or in the flamenco for Japanese tourists scene, where she remarks: 'Si tu savais combien de nuits j'ai pensé à tes yeux!' ('If you only knew how many nights I have thought of your eyes!') The remark is ambivalent, simultaneously drawing attention to the scopophilic, sexually defined desire of the male to see as well as to understand the female, while also highlighting the mesmeric power of the look from which the female sometimes seeks release; for, if the film is concerned to explore the male's desire for the female, it also describes how and why, even under the most seemingly unfavourable circumstances, the female is also drawn to the male.

Freud's discussion of sado-masochism helps clarify important issues raised by a film not averse to dramatization of some of the more controversial elements of the novel's original treatment of the relations between the sexes. The novel includes many scenes where Mathieu not only describes but also takes pleasure in his violent treatment of Conchita:

Que voulez-vous? Je la frappai encore. Et brutalement, d'une main dure, de façon à me révolter. Elle cria, elle sanglota, elle se prosterna dans un coin, la tête sur les genoux, les mains tordues. (1981: 168)

(Well, so what? I hit her again. Brutally, with a hard hand, in a way that revolted me. She cried, she bled, she crouched in a corner, her head on her knees, her hands contorted.)

When Mathieu questions her behaviour, Conchita replies:

Pourquoi tu me battes, Mateo? Quand je sens ta force, je t'aime; tu ne peux pas savoir comme je suis heureuse de pleurer à cause de toi. Viens maintenant. Guéris-moi bien, vite! (1981: 169)

(Why do you hit me Mateo? When I feel your strength, I love you; you cannot know how happy I am to cry because of you. Come now. Cure me well, quickly!)

In what Michael Wood has rightly referred to as a 'particularly murky subject' (1981: 330) the film shows Mathieu striking Conchita, but it is left to the misogynist Martin, his valet (a character invented for the film, in keeping with Buñuel's fondness for the type),[14] to revel in the spectacle of Conchita's pain. So, Martin—the initials of both men's Christian names reinforcing their identity—projects the 'murkier' elements of Mathieu's obscurer desires, though even here Buñuel's wit, perhaps covering up the traces of his own darker thoughts, creates further patterns of displacement in having Martin also distance himself from the cruder forms of sadism by inventing a misogynistic friend, thus absolving himself—like Buñuel—though perhaps not wholly convincingly, from more explicit forms of resentment against women. If Martin's sadism represents Mathieu's displaced desire to punish women from a distance, Mathieu himself, unable to resist the sexual allure of women, plays out at one level the cruder instincts of authoritarian masculinity.

In 'The Economic Problem of Masochism' Freud describes three forms of masochism: erotogenic, feminine, and moral (1984*b*: 415).[15] The first refers to the physical pleasures of pain, the second to the feminine position adopted by the individual, regardless of gender, and the third to the need for punishment felt by the ego. In all three forms, Freud is as usual primarily concerned with perversion. While many aspects of Mathieu's attraction to Conchita can be explained in all sorts of ways that cannot really be described as perverse (her youthfulness, beauty, *otherness*, the grounds for attraction between any pair of lovers), there remains one element of his continuing involvement with a woman who repeatedly causes him pain, but to whom he consistently turns, that can be partially explained through perspectives adopted by Freud.

At one level, though Mathieu's pursuit of Conchita is fuelled by the pleasures of deferral, her refusals of sexual favours (which at one point include the wearing of a formidable chastity belt)

[14] Also appearing, for instance, in *El*, *Le Charme discret*, *Robinson Crusoe*, *El ángel exterminador*, the valet reproduces the *gracioso/galán* relationship of Golden Age Spanish drama, in which, as well as providing the more vulgar foil to the hero's overblown ideals of love, the servant figure also acts as a kind of shadow, or *other*, to the *galán*. Buñuel has also confessed to fantasizing that he would have enjoyed being a *mayordomo* himself (Pérez Turrent and de la Colina 1993: 164).

[15] In defining masochism as something ultimately inseparable from sadism, as sadism turned in on itself, Freud's theory is at odds with Deleuze (1971).

keep ablaze desires that with fulfilment risk extinction.[16] At another level, though, Mathieu's persistence, very much paralleling Freud's notion of 'feminine' forms of masochism, suggests a desire to place himself in the position of the feminine, a position primarily defined by passivity and, consequently, motivated by a return of his own repressed:

The obvious interpretation, and one easily arrived at, is that the masochist wants to be treated like a small and helpless child, but, particularly, like a naughty child. It is unnecessary to quote cases to illustrate this; for the material is very uniform and is accessible to any observer, even to non-analysts. But if one has an opportunity of studying cases in which the masochistic phantasies have been especially richly elaborated, one quickly discovers that they place the subject in a characteristically female situation; they signify, that is, being castrated or copulated with, or giving birth to a baby. For this reason I have called this form of masochism, *a potiori* as it were ..., the feminine form, although so many of its features point to infantile life. (Freud 1984*b*: 416–17)

Application of these notions to Mathieu's involvement with Conchita leads to an awareness of the extent to which at unconscious levels their parent–child relationship (he is in his fifties; she is described as only 18 in the novel) is inverted. In a visually less colourful equivalent of the relationship in *Le Fantôme* between the bare-buttocked M. Bermans and his obliging, leather-clad, and whip-administering *dominatrice*, Mathieu here becomes the child, Conchita the parent or instrument of authoritarian discipline. Her moments of clear-sighted self-assertiveness, lucidly articulating desires for independence from authoritarian constructions of female subjectivity, succeed in drawing attention to pleasures of spectatorship often rooted in reductive forms of representation. Mathieu's punishment by Conchita is therefore partly motivated by an attack on dominant forms of masculinity often leading to such reductive constructions. In so far as his masochism is further defined as feminine, it may be regarded as another process through which the text both acknowledges and places in question the male's encounter with the feminine. Mathieu's irresistible pull towards Conchita is in part a representation of male desire no longer simply disavowing difference. It is the dramatization of a masochistic fantasy forcing men to

---

[16] In her autobiography, Jeanne claims that if he had lived in the Middle Ages Buñuel would certainly have used a chastity belt on her (Rucar de Buñuel 1991: 41).

address questions of femininity, to submit to certain processes of feminization.

For her part, Conchita's persistent involvement with Mathieu betrays, in its less progressive drives, a desire for self-annihilation, for submission to the Law of the Father. The choice offered to Conchita is between Morenito (slim, athletic, young, good-looking, her contemporary in dress, manner, and behaviour) and Mathieu, a father figure twice her age. From one point of view, attraction to Mathieu represents a desire for order and stability, qualities more identified with maturity than with youth. Morenito may offer her adventure and vigour, but the modern man will treat the modern woman without the respect associated with old-world courtesies. From another, Conchita's pursuit of Mathieu suggests a desire simultaneously for acquisition of patriarchal authority and assertion of her own masculinity. Significantly, Conchita has no father, only a mother, their combined efforts in exploiting Mathieu underlining a pattern of female recuperation or assertion of pre-Oedipal masculinity partially externalized and displaced onto Mathieu. In this respect, therefore, it seems highly reasonable that Conchita should seek endless deferrals of sexual fulfilment with Mathieu. The image of Mathieu as paternalistic bogyman, as source of parental discipline, is further stressed through the Surrealistic spectacle of the grubby sack full of unseen, probably unmentionable objects (excrement? blood-stained lingerie? sado-masochistic paraphernalia? or just the crosses of neuroses, obsessions, or phobias borne by common humanity?) carried around by Mathieu, or by an unidentified character at the beginning, or placed in a shop window or lying in piles at the railway station. Is the sack, as Michael Wood interestingly wonders, 'an *objet trouvé et retrouvé*' whose interpretation would 'spoil its gratuitous presence' in a film 'amused by the inevitable victory of interpretation over life' (1981: 338)? Or is it a visual representation of the proverbial warning to naughty Spanish children that, unless they behave, 'vendrá el hombre del saco y te llevará' ('the man with the sack will come and take you away')? For, like the children in the train compartment listening to Mathieu's admonitory narrative, Conchita is herself a child, listening to the truths of the social order embodied in Mathieu, unwilling and unable to treat their mediator as a lover in the truest sense, keeping him at a distance as a distrusted and envied figure of awe, dread, and power, an icon of privilege, the supreme bearer of the phallus, both ridiculed and desired.

4
Female Desire

'Estas machorras son así: cuando podían estar haciendo
encajes o confituras de manzanas, les gusta subirse al tejado
y andar descalzas por esos ríos.'

Lorca, Yerma

('These Amazons are like that: when they could be making
lace or apple jam, they prefer to climb up onto the roof and
go wading barefoot through rivers.')

VICTOR J. SEIDLER's reminder (1991) that ever since the Enlightenment masculinity has been associated with rationality,
femininity with irrationality, seems especially appropriate for the
framework of a discussion on Buñuel's representation of women.
For the international Surrealist struggling to free himself from
the primacy of reason, submission through *amour fou* to a female
order of unreason seems only natural. But for the Aragonese
provincial, partly moulded by a predominantly Catholic culture,
an embrace of the feminine risked opening up a Pandora's box
of dreaded, ultimately equivocal pleasures. This inner conflict
reflects itself in a duality of approach noticeable throughout the
films. Characters like Lope, Pierre, Mateo, and Alejandro, among
others, hurl themselves at women, sacrifice their independence,
lavish care, attention, and material rewards on the Tristanas,
Séverines, Conchitas, or Catalinas in their lives, only to be
spurned, humiliated, or even destroyed by these irresistible sirens.
Nevertheless, despite the more dominant male perspective,
Buñuel's films set out occasionally to adopt, as far as possible,
the woman's view, seemingly aware of what Foucault (1984) has
defined as the sexualization of the individual through various
forms of discourse including, of course, psychoanalysis, a discipline with its own special history of strategies for imposing processes of control and normalization over the female subject.

As a result, in Buñuel's films women are sometimes not simply
the fantasies of male dread or desire, but characters existing in

their own right whose realities and experiences the films strive to reflect. Even so, career women are conspicuously absent, and if female characters do have jobs they are usually the stereotypes of nursing (*Le Fantôme de la liberté*) or domestic service (*Le Journal d'une femme de chambre*). Women's issues in Buñuel's films are related to the pressures and constraints of relations between the sexes or within the family. This is so for minor as well as for major roles. As an example of the former, the cameo appearance by Muni, one of Buñuel's regulars, the maid *chez* Mme Anaïs in *Belle de jour*, is especially interesting. Absent in the Kessel novel (1980) on which the film is based, her invention for the film seems designed partly to add homeliness and realism to the more exotic ambience at the chic Parisian house of shame, and partly to draw attention through her relationship with her blonde teenage daughter—perhaps a budding Séverine—to the hazards of raising a child in an urban environment.

The proletarian mother's struggle to protect the interests of her child is a motif repeated in *Tristana*. There, Lola Gaos—wizened, weasel-faced, husky-voiced—lends to the part of Saturna an aura of proletarian disadvantage mixed with menace, an almost ascetic form of self-sacrifice and subservience to a colonizing ideology. Saturna, symbolically, is the devouring, castrating mother who has introjected feelings designed more to uphold the structures of a conservative social order than to nurture either her own assertiveness or the urgent needs of a disabled (figuratively as well as literally), disorientated, and idle adolescent son. Although there is very little here of the maternal self-sacrifice, displacement of desires, and ambitions of some of the Mexican melodramas (especially *Una mujer sin amor* and *Susana*), Saturna is one of many women in Buñuel's films seemingly too ideologized for truly independent action.

These failures of independence are often given a fatally destructive form, as in Tristana's capitulation to a system of which she eventually becomes both the agent and the victim. Other films, perhaps especially *Susana*, seem to bear out Foucault's notion of the 'hysterization' of the female body (1984: 104). Here Susana's body, to borrow Pat Caplan's Foucault-inspired phrase *vis-à-vis* a general discussion of female sexuality, is 'thoroughly saturated with sex' (1991: 7), a caricature form of sexual self-consciousness. But on other occasions submission to the dominant order takes a more muted, less exemplary form, as when, for instance, Viridiana surrenders to the inevitability of material demands, failing in her mission to become some modern St Teresa equivalent, or a more ascetically inclined Dorothea Brooke, carving out for herself a mission and purpose beyond the confines of domesticity. As well as perhaps being in some ways pre-Oedipal nightmare figures of Buñuel's dread as well as desire, Viridiana, Tristana, and Susana are all women clearly ill at ease in roles assigned to them by circumstance: Susana and Tristana turning into socially bred monsters of desire, Viridiana giving up the struggle for independence much less dramatically, accepting her fate with resignation and disillusionment rather than through hysteria.[1] In some cases, as in *El gran calavera*, a woman seems content to avoid any struggle, remaining comfortably and happily within the limits of an identity defined for her by a benevolent, charismatic patriarch.

Among all the various forms through which women's subjectivity is constructed, the most problematic relates to sexual desire. Buñuel's films rely on some of the most glamorous, sexually self-conscious female stars of the commercial Mexican and international art-film cinemas: e.g. Catherine Deneuve, Jeanne Moreau, Simone Signoret, Stéphane Audran, María Félix, Silvia Pinal.[2] These actresses contribute, at least in part, to the projection of an eroticized aesthetics. Buñuel and his producers may have had a primarily, though not exclusively, male spectator in mind when these actresses were contracted, but in the light of recent theorizing about spectatorship it has become clear that either as ego-ideals or as objects of desire these stars are equally interesting—for consumption as well as for deconstruction—to audiences of all sexualities, whose responses will usually be 'bisexual' rather than limited to individual orientations.

The analysis of female stars in mainstream cinema has moved beyond simplistic 'images of women' approaches to the point where, even though radical feminism continues to condemn all such representations as hopelessly compromised by patriarchy, a libertarian tendency (exemplified perhaps most provocatively

---

[1] For a fuller discussion of these matters in *Viridiana*, see Fiddian and Evans (1988: 61–70).
[2] On stars in general, see Richard Dyer (1979), the chapter in Pam Cook (ed.) (1985), and Christine Gledhill (ed.) (1991). On European women stars, see Molly Haskell (1987: 277–322). On Catherine Deneuve, see Ginette Vincendeau (1993).

by Linda Williams) adopts a more complex attitude to female erotica. To some extent this is a view inspired by Foucault's concentration on 'the desire not only for pleasure but also for "knowledge of pleasure", the pleasure of knowing pleasure' (Williams 1989: 3) and the exposure of the failure of the history of sexuality to 'imagine their pleasures outside a dominant male economy' (ibid. 4)

So, although Jeanne Moreau in *Le Journal d'une femme de chambre*, Silvia Pinal in *Simón del desierto*, María Félix in *La Fièvre monte à El Pao*, or Simone Signoret in *La Mort en ce jardin*, all to some extent succumb to fetishized or male-constructed images of femininity, it is frequently the case that in their disruptive presence in the narrative (working both consciously and unconsciously through both diegetic and non-diegetic mechanisms) these stars represent female impulses reaching out for self-definition beyond the limits of conventional male prejudice. In *Le Journal*, Jeanne Moreau's self-conscious sexuality is placed in the service of a mission—admittedly, ultimately compromised—to reclaim space for the feminine and to avenge a brutal attack on a young female through strategies that call up all sorts of maternal feelings lying outside the order of 'dominant male economy', prefiguring some of the attitudes theorized by feminists like Nancy Chodorow (1984), Luce Irigaray (1974), Adrienne Rich (1981), and others. In *Belle de jour* the thematics of sexuality itself offers Buñuel an opportunity for exploration of the 'Sadean woman's' multiple desires, given measured formulation through twinning with questions about the representation of sexuality, a process exploring the relations between erotica and pornography. The buxom presence of Simone Signoret in *La Mort en ce jardin* or Catherine Deneuve's exposure in various states of undress—including the *de rigueur* costume of bra, panties, stockings, and suspenders that Buñuel, no scourge of conformity here, claims most excited him (Pérez Turrent and de la Colina 1993: 60)—pander to the male while also dramatizing the whole complex issue of the representation of the body and its contribution to an aesthetics of exploitation which remains candid enough to acknowledge rather than to repress its pleasures, for women as well as for men, for repressed ideologues as well as for liberated Sadeans.[3]

---

[3] For Víctor Fuentes, women in Buñuel are able to take the initiative because they are not so burdened with repression as men (1993: 60).

4.1. *Le Journal d'une femme de chambre*: Mothers and Daughters

'I could never see a man I really cared for being hurt.'

Kitty, in *The Killers* (1946)

PLOT SYNOPSIS: Célestine arrives from Paris to take up her post as a chambermaid in a bourgeois country house. There she arouses the sexual desires of the servant (Joseph), the master of the house (Rabour), his son-in-law (Monteil), and the next-door neighbour (Captain Mauzer). Rabour, a shoe fetishist, dies half-way through the narrative. Monteil's suit is rejected. Célestine is attracted to Joseph but, when she suspects him of being the rapist and murderer of her protégée, the child Claire, she determines to help the police trap him. Joseph is sent to jail and Célestine settles for respectability by marrying the Captain.

Perhaps more than usually so in a film by Buñuel, the relations between men and women in *Le Journal d'une femme de chambre* belong to a structure of dichotomies including contrasts established most obviously between children and adults, black and white, country and city, bourgeois and proletarian, upstairs and downstairs. While the film's narrative is inspired by Mirbeau's novel (1968) and shares some features with Renoir's earlier film (1946), its pattern of binary opposites perhaps takes its most significant thematic lead from indirect references to the fairy-tale about Little Red Riding Hood. In this film—in contrast to Renoir's, where Joseph's victim is not a little girl but Rabour's neighbour, the Captain—an adult woman's identification with a little girl provides one of the main keys for unlocking various issues involving female desire.

The film has a dual structure. The first part concentrates on the arrival of Célestine at the Monteil household. Her intrusion in this closed, fairly eccentric and repressed world acts as a disturbance, a questioning of the bourgeois order. In the second part, though apparently weary of the eccentricities of this world, Célestine changes her mind about leaving the house and, on the point of boarding a train bound for Paris, decides instead to return and help discover the identity of the man who has raped and killed the little girl, Claire, with whom she had developed a loving relationship. This dual structure at all times prioritizes the role of the female as active participant in the narrative. Although the character of Célestine is still compromised both consciously and unconsciously in certain ways—her role as a chambermaid in itself identifying her with a classic male sexual fantasy—she is nevertheless one of several Buñuel heroines (others include Séverine, Conchita, Susana) who take the initiative, striving to shake off attempted impositions of identity inseparable from male approval. In Buñuel's films this is something never wholly achieved, but the determination to be self-motivated is often vividly dramatized.

In conforming to the standards of the wilful Buñuel heroine, Célestine is also the inquisitive stranger who becomes for a little while the scourge of the bourgeois order by which she is eventually (though not unexpectedly) seduced. Like other Buñuel outsiders —Alejandro, for example, in *Abismos de pasión*—she holds up a mirror to prejudice and horror, becoming a figure through whom taboos are broken and a whole society shaken out of its emotional and moral torpor. Her arrival from another world (the city), her different ways, her outspokenness, and even her sex are all represented as a trouble, a provocation to her employers and, through them, the audience. Appearing as an investigative figure in the second part of the narrative, she appropriates the role and narrative function of the male detective figures of French (e.g. Melville) as well as Hollywood *film noir* (e.g. Hawks, Wilder, Powell), in the process discovering that her mission to find the little girl's killer is inseparable from her quest for her own sexual and personal identity.[4]

These questions are given formal emphasis through the use of the wide-screen (Franscope) format and a searching, restless camera. Charles Barr's (1974) references to Cinemascope's potential for creating meaning through horizontal structures and depth should be kept in mind in *Le Journal*, where horizontality is immediately established in the opening shot of the countryside taken from a fast-moving train, a shot that emphasizes the panoramic survey of a bourgeois world on the point of being invaded by Célestine, whose investigative role is further stressed by the roving camera. There is a certain irony in the film's use of the wide screen: released from the stuffiness of urban living, Célestine will find in the open vistas of the countryside and its middle-class inhabitants a world no less socially or morally stifling. On

---

[4] Virginia Higginbotham rightly argues that the diary format allows Buñuel to focus 'upon intimate details of the process by which a shrewd, compassionate outsider capitulates to a system she deplores' (1979: 118).

the other hand, the restlessness of the camera is highly suited to the film's dynamics. Jean-Claude Carrière describes Buñuel's increasing taste for a moving camera as 'hypnotic' (1978: 93), and, although the remark is primarily designed to describe the effect of this constant movement on the audience, there is also a sense in which the camera reflects the hypnotic effect on the Monteil household—both upstairs and downstairs—of Célestine's ubiquitous presence. As regards the relations of depth created by wide-screen photography, Célestine's investigative role is given even further emphasis through the regular close-ups of the clutter of interior *mise-en-scènes*, animals, insects or parts of the human body, the symbolic focus of interior as well as exterior realities.

The main reversal of the detective/*film noir* pattern is in the film's replacement of a man by a woman as investigator, a process that results in setting up the male as well as the female as enigma. Although the film dispenses with the diary (voice-over equivalent) format of the Renoir version, enough care is taken elsewhere through other devices to underline the processes of self-assertion and introspection identified with the heroine. The most obvious strategy for this arises from the impact of the part of Célestine, played by Jeanne Moreau, a star whose meaning was already associated with transgression, self-conscious sexuality, and independence. Her appearances in films like *Les Amants* (1959), *Jules et Jim* (1961), and *La notte* (1961) express a sensuality whose force emerges as much from cerebral allure as from blatant carnality. Though identified with love—another woman tells the Moreau character in *Les Amants*, 'l'amour te réussit' ('love suits you')—she is also an independent woman, explaining her addiction for buying clothes as a form of self-indulgence or self-assertion: 'Pour moi. . . . Pour être à la mode. . . . C'est mon droit.' ('For me. . . . To be in fashion. . . . It's my right.') The stress is on self-fulfilment, her remarks here not simplistically prolonging a stereotyped identification of women with a trivial passion—in this case, clothes—but stressing through the language of fashion a desire to define her own space and identity. Her lover's remark 'je t'aime parce que tu es différente' ('I love you because you're different'), equivocally referring to social as well as to psychological *otherness*, has an application beyond the narrative constraints of this film.

Eroticized, like many other European female stars of the period, including Brigitte Bardot, Claudia Cardinale, or Gina

Lollobrigida, Jeanne Moreau has an added dimension of intellectuality or introspection, expressed in a variety of ways, partly
the result of appearances in work by art-film directors like Malle,
Truffaut, and Antonioni, but also partly because her looks have
that mixture of sensuality and power, flaw and perfection, that
deservedly earns comparisons in the Hollywood cinema with
Bette Davis. In *Jules et Jim* her intellectuality is stressed through
the endless analysis and theorizing of her appeal by rival lovers.
Her identification there with Greek ideals seems designed as
much to launch quasi-Socratic arguments about the meaning of
beauty as to flatter the attractiveness of a striking woman. The
intellectual, blemished qualities of the Moreau look are transmitted through her high-domed forehead and hollow cheeks.
The slightly tired, saucer-shaped eyes convey sensuousness
modulated by intensity and melancholy. The lips, more than
usually swollen, have their Bardot-like pouty sensuality offset by
a droopy expression born perhaps of experience and disenchant-
ment, or even, as the voice-over defines it in *Jules et Jim*, of
disdain. All of these qualities, as well as a relaxed, mature approach to sexuality, exemplified by her nakedness at one point
in *Les Amants*, play into the character of Célestine in *Le Journal*.

   Jeanne Moreau's self-control and assertiveness find their thematic and visual equivalents in the film's use of space; for,
whereas Célestine's main narrative function seems related to her
intrusions in the various spaces of characters in and around the
Monteil household, trespassing on their privacy, interrupting
activities like Mme Monteil's ablutions in the bathroom, or
Joseph's polishing or cleaning, no one other than the maid
Marianne (Muni) ever intrudes on hers. In a room of her own—
Virginia Woolf's prerequisite for a woman's sanity—Célestine
retains, as far as possible, momentary self-control. Whereas
she disrupts the order of social and psychological structures—
refusing ultimately to accept the hierarchical laws governing the
lives of most of the other characters—she remains at many levels
and for long periods free of such disturbance herself. Her friendship with Marianne confirms her solidarity with the menial and
marginalized, though this is an issue more elaborately developed
in her relationship with Claire. Nevertheless, Célestine's relations with Marianne revealingly highlight differences of emphasis between the two film versions.

   In the Renoir, Célestine attains self-awareness when she sees her own behaviour reflected in the deferential attitudes of the scullery maid Louise, whom she meets for the first time at the station: 'When I saw how you acted at the station, I saw what was wrong with me.' There, an attractive, smartly dressed, confident, and beautiful woman played by a major romantic star of the Forties, Paulette Godard, looks at a dowdy, subservient, extremely plain young woman, and surprisingly discovers in the scullery maid's willing deference to authority (especially male authority) and in her resigned acceptance of ill-treatment as the price of ugliness, a reflection of her own introjected attitudes and conditioning. In some ways, this is the female equivalent of *The Picture of Dorian Grey* (1944),[5] the character's inner self here reflected not onto a portrait but onto a live mirror of socially constructed subjectivity. Célestine catches herself in the equivalent of the Lacanian mirror stage (1970), both recognizing and mis-recognizing her place in the Symbolic order, seeing for once not the outwardly beautiful woman on display for society, but its inwardly ugly and disempowered victim. This is the point at which she determines to assert herself through resistance to the social order and identification with the plight of all victimized women, among whom she has now finally begun to number herself, refusing to take the post as chambermaid unless her appointment also means reinstatement of the wretched Louise.

The maid is differently focused in Buñuel, who has no place for this early scene involving the two newly appointed domestics. Here Célestine arrives at the station, is met by Joseph, and is then taken to the Monteils', where Marianne (Louise's equivalent) has already been working as a maid. But even without the railway scene Marianne's relationship with Célestine also serves to highlight social, especially female, forms of victimization. Marianne is played by Muni, a Buñuel regular sometimes identified (as here) with abject subservience, at other times with limited forms of daring transgression, including blasphemy—as when she confesses her dislike of Jesus Christ in *Le Charme discret*—and prostitution, in her role as maid *chez* Mme Anaïs. Muni's docile look of a friendly, somewhat timid labrador, her eager-to-please eyes, soft, unaggressive contours, and hushed voice—signs of deference to dominant males—become a focus here for related

---

[5] Interestingly, also starring Hurd Hatfield, the lead in Renoir's *Diary of a Chambermaid*.

questions of social and sexual exploitation but, whereas above all through the railway mirror-scene Renoir stresses the primarily social implications of female victimization, Buñuel's focus here is mainly sexual. Fixated on her master (Michel Piccoli's M. Monteil, a nervous chain-smoking model of bourgeois futility, sex-starved and dominated by a frigid, personal-hygiene obsessive), she welcomes the scraps of attention eventually cast at her once her idol realizes that pursuit of Célestine has foundered on his preposterous declaration of a specious *amour fou*. While Renoir's multi-focused film stresses social questions among its many issues, Buñuel's heavily emphasizes sexuality, exploring wild and domesticated desires, taking the audience to the limits of sexual experience, revealing the uncontrollable power and irresistibility of sex drives, forcing a realization of the extent to which desire simultaneously ennobles and demonizes, exalts and trivializes, men and women.[6] Muni as Marianne is the underside of Célestine: not just a portrayal of pathetic surrender to the social order, but the representation of commodified sexuality, denied status and dignity, prepared to be used and discarded for a moment's intimacy. What to Monteil is no more than the gratification of a fleeting urge is to her a desperate measure for recognition and love. Both women are united through Monteil's designs on them; but, while Célestine refuses his distorted sexualized projection of female identity, retaining her dignity, defining her subjectivity in ways that do not exclude—but are not totally dominated by—sexuality, Marianne has no option from her position of powerlessness and inner desiccation other than to accept it. A single shot catches the poignancy of powerlessness and solitude. Looking forward to her moment of intimacy in Monteil's company, Marianne begins to weep. Are these the tears of anticipated pleasure, of gratification that someone as lowly as a scullery maid has attracted, even if only in primitive ways, the interest of a man, or are they the tears of a brutally clear awareness of her plight, perhaps even of the film's deeper thoughts about the inescapable solitude of the human condition and of the provisionality and futility of all human quests for happiness? In its pathos, the moment embraces all such possibilities.

   The more sombre implications of such questions are further

[6] Agustín Sánchez Vidal considers Buñuel's film more corrosive than Renoir's (Sánchez Vidal 1984: 280).

explored through the victimization of the little girl Claire, another casualty of brutal male desires, another female with whom Célestine finds common cause. Both Muni and Claire provide Célestine—and, through her, the audience—with the clues to the darker areas of male desire, as reflected in their treatment by Monteil and Joseph. The pairing of Célestine and Claire formulates questions given a more analytical frame of reference in recent feminist studies of female subjectivity and desire, above all those elaborated by Nancy Chodorow concentrating on questions about the 'reproduction of mothering'.

Reacting against Freudian and Lacanian claims for the masculine as normative and the feminine as deviant, feminists like Chodorow have theorized male and female subjectivity through reformulations of the Oedipal process, especially in its relations to female subjectivity. An object-relations theorist, Chodorow is interested both in exploring the asymmetrical organization of gender—something conditioned by and underscoring the association of women with mothering—and, in the light of this emphasis on the mother–child relationship, in considering the social bases for the child's complex subjectivity. An important stage of the argument relates to a redefinition of the pre-Oedipal phase, in which it is claimed that the male's development, involving a denial of the primary identity—its initial object relations with its mother—is not paralleled by the female. Moreover, the boy's repression of his identification with his mother leads to feelings of separation, detachment, and difference, while the female, mothered by another female, experiences no such loss, and develops a greater feeling of oneness with an external reality. Although it fails to 'account for differences between men and the effects of class and race' on the formulation of masculinity (Rutherford 1992: 37), there are important sociological implications in Chodorow's work, especially as regards moves towards redefinitions of role and gender absorbing revisions of the nature and function of mothering (1984). Her argument proposes that there are no grounds for tying women to parenting on the basis of 'instinctual nurturance' (Chodorow 1984: 28). Various theories from anthropology, psychology, and psychoanalysis are all ultimately discounted, leading to the conclusion that women are tied to parenting because of lactating and pregnancy functions, not because of instinctual drives for nurturance beyond these functions. More radical feminists like Adrienne Rich (1981) have criticized Chodorow's failure to develop the implications of the symbiotic relationship between mother and female child to a point of fuller recognition and exploration of female relationships and lesbian friendships.[7]

Whatever their limitations, Chodorow's theories of mothering seem relevant to the question in *Le Journal* of Célestine's identification with the cause of women generally and with Claire's plight in particular. Célestine's involvement with Claire highlights the inner structure of her own socialized subjectivity, her figuration as subject and object of sexual desire, and her role as displaced or surrogate mother. The pairing with Claire occurs almost immediately. The little girl wanders into the downstairs world of the Monteil household and seems to be admitted quite naturally to their company by all the domestics, although nothing is disclosed about her family circumstances. Her admission to this world offers no reassuring contrast between the ease and informality of one social class (rural, proletarian) and the malaise and informality of another (the upstairs world of their masters), since form and protocol are equally powerful arbiters of behaviour here, especially when Célestine is forced to vacate Joseph's chair at the dining table. As Buñuel refuses to make sentimental class distinctions, this is not a more relaxed Utopian world, of the kind described by Renoir, where M. Monteil is often seen being pampered by domestics, seeking refuge from the severities of his disciplinarian, forbidding Mrs Danvers of a wife (played by the same actress, Judith Anderson). Nevertheless, Claire's welcome in *Le Journal* into a private world testifies to the greater flexibilities of rural society. Yet it is left to Célestine to provide the child with the sort of intimate attention she clearly seeks.

---

[7] Writing by Chodorow and Rich belongs to trends in feminism seeking to overturn Freud's male-centred theories of sexuality, preferring to highlight female genitalia not as an absence but as a presence in its own right, discussing notions of female pleasure outside phallic terms of reference. This has led to writers like Cixous and Irigaray developing 'utopian' solutions involving celebration of the female body and its pleasures through an *écriture feminine*, or to Derrida-related notions of feminine writing as *différance*. These issues are succinctly expressed, and the various contradictions of Cixous's anti-essentialist, 'bisexual', text-based articulations of sexuality and desire clearly exposed, in Moi (1985). For arguments related to the various dangers as well as the many insights of such theories, see the excellent review of these trends by Jackie Byars (1991). For an equally stimulating analysis of Hollywood melodramas with mother-related questions, see Linda Williams (1987). Other books on the topic include those by Mary Ann Doane (1988), Lucy Fischer (1989), and E. Ann Kaplan (1992).

Early examples of the growing identification between the child and the recently arrived outsider are Célestine's offer of an apple —something she denies Joseph—and of a bed when it becomes too late for the child to return home on her own. The offer of an apple has been read as one of several moments in Buñuel's films—the most obvious other example is the gift of a pineapple to Nazarín—when human beings are shown to be capable of acts of generosity and kindness. As Gwynne Edwards argues (1983: 48), this gesture clearly has biblical connotations, but, although on each occasion the character receiving the gift is in some way associated with innocence, Célestine's kindness goes beyond the representation of innocence, and beyond expressions of humanity and protectiveness, to suggest precisely the opposite, the triumph of experience. In *Tristana* the heroine recalls through her offer of an apple to the boy Saturno Adam's temptation by Eve, arousing the boy's sexuality *vis-à-vis* an object of desire—Tristana herself—towards whom he will feel a mixture of awe and dread. Saturno's wish to see Tristana's breasts is eventually granted. But, when he does catch sight of them, his face is gripped by an expression of horror rather than of pleasure. In *Nazarín* the offer of a pineapple has significance beyond pathos or empathy, drawing attention as well to the hero's foolish embrace of abstract, sexless forms of Christian charity. So, in *Le Journal* there is indeed, as Gwynne Edwards observes, an affinity between the two females, indicated by the offer of the apple, but this is a gesture that, beyond its assertion of innocence, signifies female rather than more general forms of solidarity, an action that looks ahead to Célestine's determination to expose the cruel motivations of perverted male sexuality. Célestine's decision to reverse her plans for returning to Paris are prompted by a desire not only to find Claire's killer, but also to explore her own sexual urges and to identify herself with Claire's victimization. Additionally, though, gestures like the offer of an apple or the use of her bedroom, or tucking the girl up in bed, suggest the expression of a mothering instinct, behaviour that seems to bear out some of Nancy Chodorow's theories about its socially constructed reproduction.

Célestine's actions do not simply mark her out as a character with normal philanthropic instincts. They also establish her as someone whose maternal, nurturing qualities demand consideration within the framework of debates—perhaps only faintly highlighted by the conscious drives of the text—about the various biological or social determinants of mothering. Claire is simultaneously the child through whom Célestine's mothering instincts—both biological and social—are strongly aroused, and a mirror of her own subjectivity. The focus on children, at once mythologized and abused even in Sixties society, remains throughout the film. Adults are often linked with children, their behaviour frequently defined in terms of regression, play, or innocence. The most glaring example of this identification is the Captain, reverting to childhood forms of behaviour especially in his long-standing feud with Monteil, tipping rubbish and throwing stones over the hedge that divides their properties. His petulant behaviour towards his neighbour is defined as childish, and he is also fondly described by his motherly bed companion, the servant Rose, as an infant: 'Il est drôle; un enfant; comme il est jeune pour son âge!' ('He's amusing, a child; how young he is for his age!') On another occasion she remarks: 'Mon Dieu quel enfant' ('Good Lord, what a child!'), after his confrontation in court with Monteil. Less direct but more complex forms of regression include, above all, the fetishistic behaviour of Monteil's father-in-law Babour. Fixated on shoes, Babour is another of Buñuel's retarded males, the peculiar form of his fatal obsession—leading him eventually to suicide—ultimately understandable perhaps through reference to Freud's remarks about castration fears (1981c: 351–7). Joseph, perhaps the least obviously infantile of the characters, is also described as a child, significantly by Célestine herself: 'Et maintenant, mon petit Joseph, dis-moi que c'est toi qui l'as tuée, la petite Claire' ('And now, my little Joseph, tell me it was you who killed little Claire').

The mothering instinct, something from which in other films some of Buñuel's males are often in flight (e.g. *Los olvidados*, *Susana*, *Tristana*), surfaces here in Célestine's complex attraction/ aversion to Joseph. Her description of Joseph as a child suggests that, even under the unlikeliest circumstances, cultural as well as biological maternal feelings pull the female towards the male. But, through association with Claire, Célestine is also herself a little girl, the little girl who has introjected the ideology of mothering while remaining simultaneously the submissive daughter in search of the dominant father-figure male.

At one level, the relationship between Claire and Joseph recalls the fairy-tale about Little Red Riding Hood. There is even a direct reference to the story when, before he marries Claire in the woods, Joseph cries out: 'Fais attention au loup!' ('Look out for the wolf!') As Bruno Bettelheim observes (1988: 166–83), this fairy-tale describes the female child's drive towards sexual independence and maturity. Red Riding Hood has discovered the beauty and allure of an attractive but also highly dangerous outside world of sexual desire. On her journey to her grandmother's she must choose between the reality and pleasure principles, between the perilous wood and the safer routes towards the comforts of home. Along the way she confronts in the wolf not just a representation of male sexual predatoriness, but also the mirror image of her own asocial, animalistic urges, something also related, according to Bettelheim, to the 'Daughter's unconscious wish to be seduced by her father (the wolf)' (ibid. 175). The final meaning of the story is summarized like this:

Deviating from the straight path in defiance of mother and superego was temporarily necessary for the young girl, to gain a higher state of personality organisation. Her experience convinced her of the dangers of giving in to her oedipal desires. It is much better, she learns, not to rebel against the mother, nor try to seduce or permit herself to be seduced by the as yet dangerous aspects of the male. Much better, despite one's ambivalent desires, to settle for a while longer for the protection the father provides when he is not seen in his seductive aspects. She has learned that it is better to build father and mother, and their values, deeper and in more adult ways into one's superego, to become able to deal with life's dangers. (ibid. 181)

As Tom Milne (1978), Gwynne Edwards (1983), and Agustín Sánchez Vidal (1984) have already noted, Célestine's determination to discover the identity of Claire's murderer includes, as Buñuel's own screenplay notes testify, strange, confused forms of attraction as well.[8] The importance, though, of Célestine's fascination should not be read simply in terms of a desire for rough, crude, animalistic forms of sexual fulfilment, exemplified in the portrayal of rampant, unreconstructed masculinity through Joseph the terrorizing Bad Father figure (as distinct from the

---

[8] In the original script, Buñuel's direction reads: 'Joseph pose une main sur l'épaule de Célestine [this does not actually happen in the film], qui le regarde comme si elle était étrangement fascinée par cet homme qu'elle soupçonne d'un crime, attirée par lui' (Buñuel 1971 b: 86). ('Joseph places his hand on Célestine's shoulder and she looks at him as if she were strangely fascinated by this man whom she suspects of a crime, attracted by him.')

Good Father, the Captain whom Célestine eventually marries). Equally important is Célestine's internalization of an ideology which defines the fulfilment of female desire through the quest for subservient forms of object relations.

Though clearly separate, these different impulses of desire— a simultaneous embrace of wild, rough, perverse pleasures and an assimilation of the victimizing norms of the social order— belong to a pattern of creative textual contradictions of a kind often found in Buñuel. Human personality cannot be understood, as Bettelheim implies, without acknowledgement of contradictory impulses operating at its centre: 'Fairy stories speak to our conscious and our unconscious and therefore do not need to avoid contradictions, since these easily co-exist in our unconscious' (1988: 174). So, simultaneously mother and little girl, Parisian adventuress and rural Red Riding Hood, in search of a Big Bad Wolf Father (Joseph) and Good Patriarch (the Captain), Célestine is the text's inscription of the female in the Symbolic order, at once absorbed by it and struggling to be free.

Joseph's command at the kitchen table that Claire should look into his eyes dramatically formulates this process at an early stage. As she looks into them he asks her what she sees. She sees herself, she replies. He informs her that this means that he likes her, that she is on his mind. As these exchanges take place, the two are in close-shot. At one point he places his hands around her neck, making as if to strangle her. In marked contrast to the Renoir film, where a woman's reflection in another woman's behaviour provided a key to self-discovery, here a woman's self-recognition takes place, doubly displaced, through a child's reflection and entrapment in male desire. The scene brilliantly places in question essentialist notions of femininity, and emphasises at this point—though elsewhere it also stresses the possibility of pre-social motivations—the indocrination of women through the hypnotic, vampiric effects of ideology to accept their place and gender-based roles in the social order. Claire's subjectivity—and, through her, Célestine's and, through both, women's in general—is absorbed by the male, here imaged as the Bad Father who like a Twenties Gallic peasant Saturn (in *Tristana*, it is the Bad Mother, Saturna, who is the child-eating adult) devours the helpless daughter. Reflected in his eye, the daughter temporarily blinds him in turn to any sexual desire that eludes the shapes of virginal innocence bred by his perverted fancy.

The saturnine, vampiric, or hypnotic parallels through which the text terrorizes the audience into shocking awareness of its complicity in such processes of victimization multiply as the film unravels. At night, for instance, dressed in a black cape worthy of Nosferatu's daughter, Célestine finds herself drawn to Joseph's bonfire, preferring to cook her potatoes in the wild—seeking release from the constraints of the social meanings of the house— where she is eventually given a vampire's kiss on the neck by Joseph. A little later on, the kiss on the neck is reversed, as she returns the compliment, only more roughly. Joseph has earlier remarked: 'Je connais vos pensées. Je connais tout ce que se passe dans vos pensées.' ('I know your thoughts. I know everything that goes on in your mind.') Alienated from him, terrified of this monstrous darker side of patriarchy—'J'ai peur de vous' ('I'm afraid of you'), she remarks in his room—Célestine is also helplessly drawn to him, as his female victims are to Dracula, instrument of doom but also exteriorized projection of women's obscurer longings.

Joseph's declared and acknowledged control of Célestine's thoughts and fantasies is no mere boast. He has become another of the film's mirrors of her darkest motivations. And like the vampire's victim, she herself becomes, once bitten—as at the bonfire rituals—addicted to blood. Feeling attraction as well as revulsion, she thrillingly remembers his rape and murder of the little girl Claire, adding a frisson of taboo pleasure to liven up her own seduction by Joseph. In making Célestine, played by an actress as charismatic and popular as Jeanne Moreau, admit to pleasures taken from this most taboo of subjects, the film confronts the audience with its own compromises, collusions, and nightmarish desires, shocking it into an awareness of the monstrous longings, socially created or otherwise, underlying most people's lives.

As Tristana is turned into a monster by the system, mutilated mentally and emotionally as well as physically, so here—without the visually explicit grotesqueness of the later film—Célestine becomes more distanced from positively transgressive ideals of femaleness. Nevertheless, in accepting her feminization, she demands a high price—marriage to the Captain—exacting through social conformity a limited but nevertheless satisfying revenge against the bourgeois order. The irony of this satirical portrait of all too human accommodations with safer options is that

Joseph's undoing and Célestine's passage towards bourgeois respectability hinge on the shoe fetish with which, in a sense, the film begins. Joseph's shoe provides the clue to murder. Célestine removes a piece of metal from the sole of his boot and plants it for the police to discover in the forest. A fetish that above all defines a patriarch (Rabour, whose absurdities are ridiculed in a multitude of ways: his collection of women's boots, Célestine's yawn as he begins to fondle her boots and other parts of her anatomy), it is another symbol, at the end, of her appropriated power. Useful as an ironic revenge on the patriarchal disorder to which she has had to submit, the symbol of the shoe fetish is also, though, the powerful instrument through which Célestine will find, in marriage to the Captain, her own order and comfort, though not, we suspect, the gratification of other, more powerful desires.

4.2. *Belle de jour* and Female Perversion

'a thousand times more subjugated than would be slaves, you must expect naught but humiliation, and obedience is that one virtue whose use I recommend to you.'

Sade, *The 120 Days of Sodom*

PLOT SYNOPSIS: Séverine is married to Pierre. They lead a comfortable bourgeois life but she is troubled by sado-masochistic dreams and reveries. Abused as an 8-year-old child, she finds it difficult to enjoy normal sexual relations with her husband. When she discovers that her friend Henrietta works as a prostitute in a brothel, she decides to follow her example. At Mme Anaïs's brothel, she eventually meets Marcel, the friend of another gangster, Hippolyte the Murcian. Marcel becomes too fond of her, discovers where she lives, and shoots Pierre, leaving him crippled. M. Husson, who has been partially responsible for Séverine's initiation at the brothel, reveals the details of his wife's double life to Pierre. Pierre and Séverine are left alone following M. Husson's departure. Pierre the cripple suddenly rises from his chair and walks lovingly towards Séverine. How much has been a dream or reverie, how much reality?

As Michael Wood points out via Stanley Cavell, Buñuel attempts in *Belle de jour* to imagine a woman's imagination, a 'place of cruel social construction where marriage is safe but dead and desire has taken refuge in the brothel' (Wood 1992: 20). Yet despite wishes or statements to the contrary, the imagination here proves no less compromised than any other realm of human experience, subject like everything else to the laws of neurosis or obsession and the double standards governing daily life. As Wood goes on to say, the only difference between the world of the imagination and all others is that the woman, 'oppressed in her dream of escape, *works* in the brothel while men just visit' (ibid.)

For all Buñuel's disclaimers, *Belle de jour* remains a disturbing and far-reaching enquiry into the motivations of female desire.[9] Though Séverine herself never echoes the first words of Breton's *Nadja* (1928)—'Qui suis-je?' ('Who am I?')—Charlotte, one of the whores *chez* Mme Anaïs (Nin?), formulates the question for her—'Qui êtes-vous?' ('Who are you?')—to help the audience see, however blind Séverine herself remains to her own condition, that this is a narrative exploring the mechanisms of female subjectivity and desire. The film (1967) and the novel (1928) versions of *Belle de jour* were made in times less sensitive to questions related to the eroticization of women's representation, but now any serious discussion of the film cannot proceed without awareness of issues concerning the specularization of the female and the sexual-political implications of women's involvement as participants or spectators in erotica or pornography. For a radical feminist, to whom eroticized female display is regarded as irrevocably linked to male coercion and violence, the film would always be beyond the pale, a further example of women's exploitation through stereotype. For a libertarian feminist, to whom the liberation and exploration of female sexuality are regarded as more important than restraint of the male's, it would probably be seen as having the potential not only for interrogating sexuality in general but also, in, say, Susan Sontag's argument (1982), for exploring extreme situations and behaviour, transgressing realism, and extending the frontiers of consciousness (Sawicki 1991: 35). In the end the film will probably

---

[9] 'Rara vez tomo el punto de vista de la mujer. Reconozco que el mundo de mis películas tiene el tema del deseo, y como no soy homosexual, el deseo toma naturalmente la forma de la mujer. Soy como Robinson cuando ve el espantapájaros vestido con ropas femeninas' (Pérez Turrent and de la Colina 1993: 147). ('I rarely take the woman's point of view. I admit that the world of my films includes the theme of desire, and, as I am not a homosexual, desire naturally takes the form of a woman. I'm like Robinson when he sees the scarecrow dressed in women's clothes.')

frustrate the expectations of both, reflecting in its inconsistencies and prejudices the complexities of Buñuel, Carrière, Joseph Kessel, and everyone else responsible for its final shape and rhythm. Even if some scenes in *Belle de jour* can ultimately be regarded as belonging to a subgenre of pornography, facile dismissals of even the most sado-masochistic fantasies as entirely male created and desired can best be answered through reference to Linda Williams's argument, via Rodowick, Studlar, and others, questioning the puritanism of Laura-Mulvey-inspired theories about the gaze as something exclusively defined through aggression, sadism, and patriarchal power.[10] Negotiating between these two extremes of puritanical rejection of all erotic display in which 'the male fear of castration becomes the cause of an aggressivity that is ultimately a defence against female difference' (Williams 1989: 204) and Studlar's argument about pre-Oedipal pleasures and masochism (1988), Linda Williams favours the more 'bisexual' approach of 'fluid movement on the part of both male and female spectators', alternating between masculine and feminine identifications (Williams 1989: 206).

In *Belle de jour* Séverine is neither the only object of display (Pierre Clementi as the youthful gangster comes into this category as well) nor the only participant in the games and rituals of sado-masochism. The gynaecologist, whose sexual arousal at the brothel can only be achieved through submissiveness, serves as the clearest example of the text's awareness of shared desires and perversions regardless of gender. While Séverine as Belle is often forced to be submissive, she frequently also seeks to be dominated, a sign not necessarily of passivity but also potentially of control. According to Williams, 'these terms are complicated, for in a sense the dominated seeks indirectly to dominate as well' (1989: 196). If this is true of the gynaecologist—inverting the habitual hard-core patterns in which men (not measuring their masculinity by social norms of activity, virility, and so on) are said to be only in gay pornography found in passive, submissive positions—it must also *mutatis mutandis* be true of Séverine.

The least productive approach to the film would be to treat it

---

[10] In an interview with *Cinema Nuovo* given in 1967, Buñuel defined his interest in *Belle de jour* like this: 'En la novela me interesó únicamente el conflicto entre la conciencia de la heroina y su compulsión masoquista' (Buñuel 1985 b: 38). ('In the novel I was only interested in the conflict between the heroine's conscience and her masochistic impulses.')

as part of a general uncontextualized argument about the representation of women, ignoring the various networks through
which the narrative mediates women's desire. Leaving aside for
the moment the erotica/pornography debate, commentary on
whatever use is made of Catherine Deneuve as sexual icon in
Belle de jour must at least refer to her interrelations with all the
other elements of the text contributing to the overall shape and
structure of the film. Catherine Deneuve as Séverine may well
be ultimately a fantasy of male desire—stereotype of the inaccessible, hermetic, ice-cool blonde whose capitulation offers
greater rewards to her eventual sexual conqueror—but there are
various unambiguous strategies in the film designed to explain
her perverse behaviour in terms of complex social and psychological processes. Discussion of her swings between frigidity
towards her husband and sexual uninhibitedness towards her
clients *chez* Mme Anaïs ultimately requires consideration beyond
crude theories about the impossibility of male representation of
female desire, and beyond easy connexions between Buñuel's
self-confessed private fantasies or obsessions and their careful,
detached analysis in film narrative, through reference to serious
writing on sexuality, especially on frigidity. Key texts here include, for instance, those by Freud, Horney, and Kaplan. But
before appeals are made to extraneous material, the interrelationships of form and content within the film itself point to an
awareness of the determinants leading to Séverine's pursuits of
Sadean pleasures. *Mise-en-scène*, costume, character types, chronology, and the thematics of time, as well as the drives of the
narrative itself (above all as regards references to childhood sexual
abuse) are among the film's clearest signposts of its awareness
of Séverine's condition.

Even though her sexual needs drive her out of the arms of her
husband Pierre and into those of the incestuous necrophile Duke
and the bizarre clients at Mme Anaïs's high-class house of
shame,[11] the film never doubts Séverine's desire to remain locked
inside the bourgeois order. Endlessly framed against backgrounds
of expensive lounges, bathrooms, bedrooms, ski-resort bars, or
high-subscription-rate tennis clubs, Séverine seems on the surface totally at ease in a materialistic world. Her appearance—

---

[11] Buñuel's own experiences in brothels are recorded in his autobiography (1982a:
85).

always impeccably coiffeured and dressed in the most chic of bourgeois styles ('Carducci!', exclaims one of the tarts as she hangs up her comrade's coat before settling down to an afternoon's work)—reflects this image of willing confinement or entrapment within the social order. Wherever she goes, Séverine looks more like a timid high-fashion model than a woman bursting for release from a life of crushing boredom and futility. Even though more relaxed at the brothel, she eventually finds the call of the bourgeoisie too powerful to resist, and returns to her life of claustrophobic narcissism.

Séverine seems to bear out Freud's remarks about narcissistic women as attractive to men because of their projection of what the male represses in himself (1984a: 83). Sometimes caught admiring herself in the mirror, Séverine is Buñuel's most fashion-conscious female, smothered in Yves St Laurent creations, a de-moisturized, virtually depersonalized screen of repressed male desire, an often child-like figure ('enfantin', as Marcel says of her behaviour at the end) of inaccessible, hermetic allure, all the more attractive for her enigmatic inscrutability. Though Pierre's mirror image as regards superficial adherence to bourgeois norms, Séverine is also at least on one level a projection of her husband's repressed narcissism, though even here narcissism takes the shape of an ideal of rigid, or 'severe', beauty. More than ever in a Buñuel film, the text is conscious of what Foucault has called the politicization of the body, where 'power relations have an immediate hold upon it; they invest it, mark it, train it, torture it, force it to carry out tasks, to perform ceremonies, to emit signs' (in Rabinow (ed.) 1991: 173). Through fashion Séverine's body becomes a site invested with relations of power and domination, a sign of her willing submission to a social order from which she manages to find only temporary release.

Both in the outer world of social respectability and the underworld of the brothel, Séverine is indeed a pearl, not just in beauty—as Mme Anaïs suggests—but in her confinement, trapped in the shell of the power structures of the bourgeois order. Beautiful but hard, virginal, unyielding, and mysterious, Séverine has become a creation of culture, a cultured pearl, only in her reveries not divested of instinct. A Tanguy-like landscape in which Séverine and Pierre discuss some of the problems of their married life varies the expression of the theme. In an unidentified *mise-en-scène*—the frame mainly composed of sea, sand,

and acres of sky—Séverine rests on a stranded dead tree branch, its splintered wood providing another of the images of lifelessness projecting her inner void, highlighting her entrapment and monotonous life of so-called purity or perfection, more outrageously ridiculed by Buñuel in the obsessively hygienic Mme Monteil in *Le Journal d'une femme de chambre.*

Pierre's talk of perfection in an early scene with Séverine projects an ideal of purity carried most vividly through the film's *mise-en-scène* colour coding. The recurrence of white as a costume colour appropriately reflects the expressionless, glacial features of Catherine Deneuve's Séverine. The whiteness, too, of Pierre's pyjamas, polo-neck sweater, and surgeon's coat, of Séverine's lingerie, tennis clothes, and nightgowns, and of the ski-resort setting itself, is a recurrent sign of an ideology of perfection and order embraced by the couple and parodied by the film. At certain points the blanket use of whiteness as a colour of order often contrasts with others, especially red and black, both ironizing and challenging convention. Séverine's first appearance in the carriage *en route* to her whipping and violation, for instance, dressed in a chic scarlet suit, wittily respects her dream-fantasy identification with a cultural stereotype (the suit is only ever again used by her much later on in the brothel), but elsewhere sombre grey marks her subordination to the bourgeois order. Her first appearance at the brothel sees her in darkly coloured clothes and black sunglasses, both of which—suggestions of authority as well as of bourgeois blindness—associate her with other characters. Sunglasses are also worn, following his accident, by Pierre at the end of the film, by the slavish Sadean butler (Bernard Musson bringing his customarily lugubrious aura to a cameo part) at the Duke's estate, and by M. Husson, all of them figures of authority, or would-be authority.

Of these, Husson epitomizes the darker side of the bourgeois order. Not ultimately the character who sets Séverine on her way to the delights of the *maison de rendez-vous*—since it is actually Renée who first informs her about Henriette's secret career as a working girl—Husson is nevertheless someone whose mission is to spread discontent. He is simultaneously the film's exposure of hypocrisy, unafraid to articulate the repressed desires of the majority, and its representation of consumerist idleness and depravity. To some—Pierre, for instance—the harm done by Husson is only 'drôle' ('amusing'). To the women, he is more threatening: for Séverine, whose knowledge of him is as yet only preliminary and instinctive, he is 'bizarre'; for Renée, who bears his scars on her wrists, he is 'pire que ça' ('worse than that'). In a significant conversation with Renée, Séverine, and Pierre early on in the film at the ski resort, Husson refers to hypnotists, the importance of the remark only becoming clearer a little later in the narrative after his revelation of Mme Anaïs's address to Séverine, which, as it were, leads her on, hypnotizing her into depravity.[12] Husson is a fallen angel, obsessed but also bored by religion (in his first remark he informs his lover that he is not as bored sitting beside her as he would be in a church with only a soul for company), a secular Satan preying on and encouraging the weaknesses of everyone around him.[13] Seizing opportunities to gratify his own guilty pleasures—referring to missed seductions as 'châtiments perdus' ('lost punishments')—Husson takes equal delight in leading others through their own weakness to perdition. In the novel Séverine expresses the disturbing effect that Husson has on her by stressing his general air of coldness and the sinister nature of his voice and eyes:

Il m'est insupportable. . . . Sa voix . . . qui semble toujours chercher en vous quelque chose que l'on ne voudrait pas . . . ses yeux . . . ils ne bougent jamais. . . . Cet air frileux.

(I find him unbearable. . . . His voice . . . always seeming to look for something that one would rather he didn't find . . . his eyes . . . they never move. . . . That cold air.)

In Michel Piccoli's understated playing of the role, the calm matter-of-fact delivery of his voice creates its hypnotic effect precisely through its very reasonableness. Piccoli's eyes, lacking lustre and fire, their unflappability and indifference to suffering serving him well in all his Buñuel roles—especially as the Marquis de Sade in *La Voie lactée*—are most appropriate to the cool or

[12] Hypnotism had a special fascination for Buñuel. He once hypnotized a prostitute to go and knock at the door of a friend in Toledo (Buñuel 1982a: 85). But hypnotism also provided Buñuel with a way of explaining film spectatorship: 'I think the cinema exercises over spectators a certain hypnotic power' (ibid. 83). Husson's hypnotism is therefore another of Buñuel's self-conscious reflexions on audience reception.

[13] As Jean-Claude Carrière points out (Buñuel 1990: 22), one of the reasons why Buñuel lost interest in making the film *Là-bas* was that he preferred to explore the satanic in ordinary human characters rather than through narratives in which Satan himself appears. In *Simón del desierto* and *La Voie lactée*, Satan does, however, appear in person.

'frileux' quality of which Séverine complains in the novel and with which through Catherine Deneuve's icy-maiden playing in the film she herself is so strongly identified. Piccoli's coolness— as when he reacts with unruffled composure to Séverine's refusal to see him at her flat—acquires an occasionally Anglicized aura of Gothic menace. Whereas in the novel Séverine is made to continue the tradition of English Gothic heroines through her English education, here it is Husson who honours that tradition by using the word 'compulsion', caressing the word with leisure on the tongue, savouring the instinct that gives it verbal expression, stressing its linguistic origins, to explain his instinctive lunge towards her at the tennis club, eager for a stolen kiss.

A tall, commanding figure, authoritative both in physical stature and in conversation, Piccoli as Husson is also a character whose importance as a motivating force of ideology is recognized by the camera. After the ski-resort bar conversation with the other three friends, the camera cuts to Husson departing, leaving the others behind, and follows his short journey out of the bar and into the street, catching him put his scarf around his neck, before cutting to the scene days later, in the Paris taxi, in which Renée informs Séverine—with a little help from the taxi driver— about bourgeois ladies supplementing their income at *soignée* houses of ill-repute. Once he leaves the bar, Husson's movements seem in themselves uninteresting and, in a film made by a director not only usually impatient with unnecessary clutter in *mise-en-scène* and narrative, almost self-indulgent. The point is that Husson is regarded as the film's key mechanism of desire. His presence is felt everywhere: in conversation, links between narrative segments, gifts (roses to Séverine), appearances at important moments (such as when he informs Pierre at the end about his wife's infidelities), and so on. His ubiquity is one of the film's most eloquent devices for underlining Séverine's and other characters' loss of control.

Hypnotized, her free will under siege from Husson's insinuations and cajolery, Séverine ultimately surrenders to a process that will not simply release her own sexuality but also, more interestingly, reveal the origins of the neuroses and obsessions by which she is troubled. Through Husson—and his agent Renée (Lola to his *Damn Yankees* devil)—Séverine simultaneously achieves the release of her libido and access to knowledge about her sexual retardment, about her imprisonment in time, endlessly repeating patterns of behaviour associated with her past. The logical conclusion to her helpless surrender to Husson's temptations is employment *chez* Mme Anaïs, but significantly much is made both by her and by Mme Anaïs herself of the restrictions on her working hours, from two to five o'clock. The thematics of time are related to memory, and especially Séverine's experiences in childhood.[14]

Perhaps inspired at this level as well as at many others by an interest in Bergson, or even by mystical writing on the subject, the film fails to respect the priorities of chronology, its narrative shifting, though perhaps not as disjointedly as *Un chien andalou*'s, through various levels of time past (two flashbacks to Séverine as a little girl), to time present, to the future, to hypothesized or frontier-less time-zones of reverie and dream, thus allowing the text's own seemingly chaotic structure to subvert bourgeois obsessions with order. Clocks are frequently heard chiming, church bells tolling, sometimes in ironic commentary on earlier scenes, sometimes giving scenes different perspectives. Perhaps the clearest instance of a scene's ironic shift of perspective through references to time occurs when right at the end of the film Husson arrives at the Sérizy flat to inform Pierre of his wife's involvement at the brothel, while outside the room where these two meet Séverine paces up and down, her hands in close-up nervously touching the marble surfaces of various items of furniture, as the clock strikes five, the magical hour at which like some Sixties Cinderella she always had to be released from her duties *chez* Mme Anaïs.

If at some levels the brothel space is a release from some of the inhibitions of the upper or bourgeois world, at others, as the chiming clock at the end of the film seems ironically to emphasize, it seems only to reflect them. In the upper world not only are clocks heard chiming, but that world's very symbol, M. Husson, also makes a remark about time in the very first words he utters: 'Quelle heure est-il?' ('What time is it?'). Returning to the brothel after a long absence, he finds time standing still, the air *chez* Mme Anaïs continuing to smell of jasmine, the curtains and

---

[14] For further thoughts on time see Víctor Fuentes: 'Sabido es que en el inconsciente —hontanar del imaginario buñueliano—no existe el tiempo y se opera una fusión del espacio interior y del exterior' (Fuentes 1993: 74). ('It is known that in the unconscious—source of the imagination in Buñuel—time does not exist and there is a fusion between interior and exterior space.')

armchair unchanged, the central heating at the same temperature. The *mise-en-scène* of retardment is reflected in the treatment
by Mme Anaïs of her prostitute employees. Although her habitual
term of address to the girls, 'mes enfants' ('my children')—especially when clients demand their attention—implies tenderness
and informality, the relations between brothel madam and
employees reproduce the power structures and patterns of psychological disturbance that characterize the world outside. At
one point, in his final appearance, Husson himself makes the
link on his way to revealing to Pierre the history of his wife's
betrayals. Seeing Séverine in her black dress and white collar,
looking like an Eton schoolboy, he calls her a 'collégienne précoce'
('precocious schoolgirl'), her identification at times in the upper
world with childishness finding its echo in the very place where
she might have expected to lose it, the brothel, where Anaïs refers
to her and the other girls as 'enfants'. She is not alone in being
associated with childishness but, where these links are established, positive as well as negative implications become evident.

In a positive sense, childishness suggests playfulness and an
escape from the laws of the super-ego. In other films the association of childhood with play enables Buñuel to develop
strategies satirizing and challenging the solemnities of the adult
bourgeois order. Buñuel's own weakness for masks and disguises
(for instance, dressing up as a nun with a friend to cruise the
Madrid Metro) is reformulated in the ludic, 'festive' moments
of films like *Le Fantôme de la liberté* and its scenes of monk-
scandalizing bare-bottom spankings, or *La Voie lactée* and its snap-
shots of Christ at home having a shave or sharing a joke.
Moments like these display beyond their graver meditations a
subversion of bourgeois forms of discretion, a schoolboyish taste
for pranks, a creatively regressive, pre-Oedipal streak of comedy. Séverine's involvement at the brothel satisfies some of these
code-breaking urges, and her play-acting finds its most significant parallel in the behaviour of the gynaecologist, an invention
of the film's, not the novel's.

Like her, the dapper little man with bizarre sexual cravings,
some intelligible, like his need for humiliation, some enigmatic,
like his request for an ink-well, seeks release from the burdens
of the super-ego, bringing with him in his Pandora's box of a
medical case not the body-curing equipment used on his patients,
but the flesh-mortifying paraphernalia of a slave to the *vice anglais*.

In his role as the submissive flunkey, ironically named 'Victor', at the mercy of Charlotte the marquise-playing whore, he constructs a theatrical frame not only around himself but also, first, around Séverine and then, after she fails to play the part correctly, around her replacement Charlotte. Though his role is the victim, casting the whore as *dominatrice*, the gynaecologist, serving a profession which *par excellence* exercises control over women's bodies, never loses control and 'breaks frame'—to use Erving Goffman's term (1975)—as soon as the action or dialogue deviates from its decreed course. Removed from the scene, Séverine is made by Mme Anaïs to look through a peep-hole in the wall, her gaze directed not only at Charlotte, whose expertise in the role of *dominatrice* she must emulate, but also at the Professor, voyeuristically responding to the visually enacted drives of a perversion while also recognizing the control of that perversion and of all desire by social as well as natural laws.

The gynaecologist's break of frame is not only a self-conscious conspiratorial gesture to the real spectator, highlighting the text's artifice, offering a reminder of its subordination to conventions and traditions. It also confronts the voyeur, here represented by Séverine, with a mirror image of herself. Her first glimpse through the peep-hole at the self-inflicted degradations of the gynaecologist ends with an expression of disgust and withdrawal. But her detachment is temporary. Among the various impulses that compel her to return her eye to the peep-hole must be not only an uncontrollable desire to satisfy a natural curiosity about deviant forms of sexuality, but also fascination with the spectacle of someone from her own social background admitting to desires outlawed in the outside world to which they both belong. That moment of recognition, both caught in the grip of perversion, parallels through identification with Séverine the real spectator's voyeurism, highlighting the extent to which, like the gynaecologist—now defined as her double, to whose actions her attention is drawn—Séverine is even here controlled by introjected social laws.

Regarded by Séverine as a refuge from time, from the social determinants and priorities of the world outside, the brothel is in fact a freeze-frame of time.[15] This is in some ways a positive

---

[15] On the significance of the brothel, Andrew Sarris takes a different view: 'It is Buñuel himself who is the most devoted patron of *chez* Madame Anaïs, and the most pathetic admirer of Catherine Deneuve's Séverine-Belle de Jour. Never before has

image, having what Mircea Eliade calls in another context (1979) the aura of a 'sacred place', the licence of a place apart, reserved for celebration and ritual, for communication with (diabolical) deities and concentration on weightier matters, all beyond the normal constraints of time and place. So, if in the bourgeois world Séverine's libido has frozen over, it enjoys here a momentary thaw. If in her normal life with Pierre her carnality is regimented or imprisoned—as her military-style clothes sometimes suggest—in the shady modiste world (the front for prostitution) of Mme Anaïs alternative modes of dress and undress free the body and the spirit from various inhibitions. If friends and acquaintances are uniformly French and bourgeois in her usual social world, here they come from exotic backgrounds (Hippolyte the Murcian, the Korean), as well as from tacky ones (Adolphe the confectioner), and from different classes (Marcel the gangster, the whores Matilde and Charlotte). The bourgeois world is not, however, without its representatives: Séverine herself and another victim of its various repressions, the masochistic gynaecologist, member of a profession to which, after all, her husband belongs.

Less positively, though, as the gynaecologist's break of frame and inability or refusal to lose control suggest, the brothel remains in some ways a distorted reflection of the outside world. The film's explorations of Séverine's masochistic desires at this level move beyond exclusively biological determinants to an analysis of the social laws that often govern them. Satisfied that his slaps succeed in making Séverine docile, M. Adolphe remarks that she seems to like rough play, almost exactly echoing Mme Anaïs's earlier comment about Séverine's evident need for a firm hand. As if acting like a schoolgirl in these scenes with M. Adolphe and Mme Anaïs, Séverine responds to their rough treatment with pleasure, in her reflex obedience to sternness welcoming an opportunity for release from responsibility, surrendering her will to the hazards and authority of a world in which she can apparently be free, above all to act out a key incident from her past, one that blocks her sexual behaviour in the adult world outside. Other characters may also be suffering

Buñuel's view of the spectacle seemed so obliquely Ophulsian in its shy gaze from behind curtains, windows and even peepholes. Buñuel's love of Séverine is greater than Kessel's, simply because Buñuel sees Belle de Jour as Séverine's liberator' (Sarris 1971: 24).

from childhood traumas. Marcel, above all, perhaps comes into this category—the minor detail in close-up of his undarned sock stressing the point—a waif-like youth, partly drawn to Séverine as a mother-surrogate, significantly concentrating like a suckling child on her breasts (where the unchildish Korean is exclusively attracted to her lower regions), remarking that he likes them so much he wishes there were more than two. While partly recalling Buñuel's approval of Gómez de la Serna's brand of humour, exemplified in this context especially by his treatise on female breasts, *Senos* (1968), Marcel's admiration for her 'senos de francesita' ('little French girl's breasts') also invokes the tradition of the witch as devil's mistress, described in the *Malleus Maleficarum* as possessing a third nipple for the exclusive gratification of Satan himself. His gangster friend Hippolyte treats him, as the latter confirms, like a son, while Hippolyte's own name carries ironic references to a famous son outraging his father through a suspected relationship with his stepmother. Even the crossword puzzle that Charlotte is doing at the brothel involves a clue concerning the father–son relationship between Aeneas and Anchises. But none of these characters has suffered from a childhood incident like Séverine's leading to such serious emotional retardment.

The key incident and root cause of her spellbound condition, from which the film develops all sorts of subsidiary interests, is the moment of sexual abuse at the age of 8. In the novel this incident acts as a sort of prologue, detached from the rest of the narrative. In the film it is recorded in flashback, introduced only after the first reverie, in which Séverine is flogged and then raped by the coachmen, and the holiday scenes at the ski resort. Following her return to her sumptuous Paris apartment, Séverine, by now familiarized with the story of Henriette's secret life of prostitution, becomes agitated and knocks over first a vase of red roses sent her by Husson, and then a bottle of perfume in the bathroom. As she sits on a stool, facing the camera, the film cuts to a flashback scene in which, sitting in roughly the same position as the adult Séverine, the child is sexually abused by a workman (the novel describes him as a plumber), kneeling beside her at the left hand side of the frame, clutching a phallic tool in his right, priapically raised just beyond the girl's face at the right. In the flashback, Séverine is not in the bathroom but in some other room with a much tawdrier *mise-en-scène*. Memories of sexual abuse return naturally in the bathroom, exteriorized projection of her desire ever since to purge herself of the unwelcome attention of the plumber.

Husson's presence in her life—his insinuating words generally and directly addressed to her at the ski resort, and now his gift of carnally red roses—finally prompts Séverine to confront the reality of her sexual neurosis, even though the cure she takes proves ultimately unreliable. The memory of sexual abuse is followed directly through a cut to a conversation at night with Pierre, in which Buñuel stresses through camera movement the tight grip on her behaviour, especially sexual behaviour, by those troubling memories. Often referring disparagingly to his own interest in the form of his work, Buñuel nevertheless concedes that his late films are all characterized by a discreetly roving camera style, something that in general terms, especially as exemplified by the thematics of *Le Journal d'une femme de chambre*, reflects preoccupation with exploration and enquiry, but which in *Belle de jour* stresses the entrapment of a character by the forces of male desire.

From the bathroom's austere, spotlessly clean *mise-en-scène*, seemingly not of bodily self-indulgence but of denial, the camera cuts to a study scene, the clock again significantly striking the hour, once more stressing Séverine's time-locked neurosis. In relaxed domesticity Pierre sits at a desk, attending to some paperwork. Séverine, in a pink dressing-gown (a colour not only flattering to Deneuve's placid beauty, but also further stressing the character's little girl aura), approaches Pierre, troubled by recent events and memories, and begins to question him on the existence and practices of brothels. As the shot begins, it shows Pierre at the left-hand side of the frame, in profile, with Séverine at the right, facing the camera directly. As soon as Pierre begins to answer her questions about brothels, lifting his head from his papers, straightening up at his desk, the camera begins to track almost imperceptibly around him in a semi-circle from left to right, so that by the time he has said, somewhat lewdly and triumphantly, but, as ever, in the subdued, well-mannered tones of a *comme il faut* husband, 'semen retentum venenum est', he is at the centre of the frame, facing the camera, while she is now in profile at the right, poised to rise in anger and to exit from the frame. Eventually, Séverine calms down, but asks Pierre to remain beside her in the bedroom until she falls asleep, a request that prompts Pierre to ask her, lovingly and protectively, like a father soothing his anxious child, whether she will ever grow up.

Pierre's centrality in the frame—power having shifted through camera movement from wife to husband—together with the full force of the Latin quotation's unqualified sexual content, emphasize the reality of the power structures in which Séverine is trapped. Her experiences as a child and her adult life as a bourgeois housewife are sources both of gratification and revulsion. The camera movement and framing stress subordination and entrapment, paralleling her remarks to Pierre to remain beside her not as a lover but as a father, keeping her in a childlike state. The experiences of childhood have retarded her in a way that, additionally, forces her to seek sexual fulfilment not through the mild-mannered, civilized approaches of a husband like Pierre, but in the form she has ever since that moment in childhood identified with roughness, brutality, and proletarian modes and contexts of behaviour. Significantly, even though camera and framing endorse Pierre's authority, other drives pull in a different direction to undermine it. Pierre's authority and desire are expressed in Latin, not in plain French; they are given a discourse that, as well as highlighting his middle-class education and surgeon's familiarity with Latin, also stresses his class-based refusal or inability to address questions of sexuality directly. The timid Boy Scout's sexual approach to his wife eventually drives Séverine to find its manly alternative in the Sadean ambience of the brothel. The novel puts this very clearly: 'Elle voulait servir Pierre et c'etait lui qui, sans cesse, se mettait à son service' (Kessel 1980: 37). ('She wanted to serve Pierre, and it was he who incessantly put himself at her service.')

Loving Pierre as a husband, companion, and fellow bourgeois is incompatible with a desire for him to act brutishly, like M. Adolphe or Marcel or, from another film, the primitive muscleman Pedro in *El bruto*. At Mme Anaïs's Sadean or perhaps even Genet-inspired fashion-house of debauchery, the clients eventually realize that the route to her cooperation lies through discipline (Sarris 1971: 26). Even the Korean arouses Séverine's interest through authority not kindness. With her clients she can become, as the novel puts it, sweet, submissive, and fearful (Kessel 1980: 51), using what Mme Anaïs calls her gentle and fresh schoolgirl looks, in an ambience perfectly suited to her search for powerlessness and submissiveness. Séverine clearly regards her twin desires of bourgeois respectability and sexual fulfilment as incompatible, a feeling that ultimately leads to frigidity in her relations with her husband and a failure not just to enjoy the physical sensations of love-making but to respond to his sexual advances at all.

Her inability to enjoy a conventional sexual relationship with Pierre leads to yet more reasons for rejecting him, an unconscious horror prompted by the feeling that taking the initiative in sexual relations with her husband would eventually undermine the very status and authority that another part of her, the socialized bourgeoise, also needs. Freud's definition of frigidity in 'The Taboo of Virginity' (1981*d*: 261–84) as a condition arising from defloration is relevant to this discussion. Although Freud's focus is mainly anthropological, related specifically to the defloration of brides on wedding nights, the argument can be given a wider application, one, moreover, not exclusively dealing with the absence of physical sensations during intercourse itself, but to a general hostility felt by the wife towards the whole idea of sexual relations with her husband. Freud's main insight is to see a clash between the physical pleasures of the woman in the act of love-making and other impulses apparently in conflict with such sensations: 'The first act of intercourse activates in a woman other impulses of long standing as well as those already described, and these are in complete opposition to her womanly role and function' (1981*d*: 278).

No longer by now, we assume, actually a virgin, Séverine is nevertheless at one level another of what might loosely be called Buñuel's virginal women (others include Viridiana or Tristana), the equivalent of those anguished and menaced heroines of nineteenth-century Gothic fiction, here also perhaps sharing— even though she is not raven haired—some of the inner sexual drives and mystery which Poe, whom Breton(1988: 329) called 'Surréaliste dans l'aventure' ('Surrealist in adventure'), attributes to one of his most forceful heroines of desire, Ligeia: her 'luxurious surface and smoothness' masks the torrid passions of a woman who, outwardly calm, 'was the most violently a prey to the tumultuous vultures of stern passion' (Poe 1965: 152–3). Overall, the Buñuel and Poe texts have much in common, especially their predilection for blurred, overlapping frontiers between reverie, dream, and reality, introjected or externalized phantasmagoria, conditioned by an ambience of claustrophobic bourgeois grandeur. As regards characterization, too, Séverine and Ligeia are both split between glacial impassivity and voracious sexual appetite.

The conflict raging within Séverine between desires for sexual gratification and conformism to bourgeois standards of behaviour appropriate to a married woman may not be related consciously to questions of penis envy, in the narrow psychological sense described in 'The Taboo of Virginity'. But Freud's remarks and Lacan's subsequent elaborations through stress on the association of the phallus with the Symbolic leave the way open for a reading of Séverine's disturbed behaviour in terms of anxieties about threats to the hegemony of the male through uninhibited role-reversing patterns of sexual behaviour. Freud's argument emphasizes the primordial origins of frigidity:

Behind this envy for the penis, there comes to light the woman's hostile bitterness against the man, which never completely disappears in the relations between the sexes, and which is clearly indicated in the strivings and in the literary productions of 'emancipated' women. In a paleo-biological speculation, Ferenczi has traced back this hostility of women . . . to the period in time when the sexes became differentiated. At first, in his opinion, copulation took place between two similar individuals, one of which, however, developed into the stronger and forced the weaker one to submit to sexual union. (1981*d*: 279)

This argument prefaces further remarks about beheading as a symbolic substitute for castration, the ultimate revenge against defloration—something exacted not on the husband but on a husband substitute, as in Judith's assault on Holofernes—a motivation that has a direct relevance to *Tristana*, especially in view of Buñuel's changes to the original Galdós narrative, where now a tragic ending replaces the original's happy one, and where Tristana dreams of her guardian/husband Don Lope's severed head. The implications of Freud's views on frigidity are picked up via Karen Horney in a feminist reworking by Louise J. Kaplan, who defines the condition's characteristics as 'strategies that both conceal and reveal sadistic wishes toward the opposite sex' (1993: 180). Frigidity in a woman becomes, moreover, 'a virtuous submissiveness that assures everyone she is just a passive, clean little girl without any nasty, active, clitoral excitements that might invite parental retaliations' (ibid. 180)

In other words, beyond unlocking deeply buried resentments

connected with penis envy, frigidity, or the castration complex, is a sign of unease at the prospect of revealing a desire for sexual activity in a world where for a woman to take sexual initiatives and to seem to find pleasure in polymorphous types of sexuality are considered threatening. Kaplan's argument includes an approving reference to Karl Abraham's associations between frigidity and prostitution in 'Manifestations of the Female Castration Complex':

By taking the active, dominating role and appearing to care about sex as much or even more than a man, the prostitute, who typically is frigid despite her outward appearance of active, sexual interest, is making conscious what is unconscious in her proper, middle-class sisters—the wish to be *more* than a man and more sexually potent than any man. (ibid.)

These remarks come very close to Karen Horney's emphasis on frigidity as a 'determined rejection of the female role' (1967: 74). Significantly, for an understanding of the psychodynamics of *Belle de jour*, Horney not only lists among a number of side-effects of frigidity an overvaluation of housework (Séverine's flat looks as spotless and orderly as a sterilized operating theatre), but also warns against 'equating frigidity with the rejection of sex' (ibid. 73, 74). For Horney, as for Freud and Kaplan, frigidity —'the masculinity complex of woman'—is to a large extent conditioned by a 'more or less intensive wish for, or fantasies of, masculinity' (ibid. 74), which in Séverine's case is entirely at odds with a desire to accept her submissive role in the bourgeois order.[16]

The parallels with Séverine are clear. For various reasons, including above all the trauma caused by sexual abuse in childhood, Séverine has become sexually retarded, unable to engage in sexual activity in a way that does not reproduce the power relations of that incident. Her marriage to a member of the *haute bourgeoisie*, identified through his behaviour, apartment, and the clothes his money buys, prohibits any form of sexual activity initiated by her that will either scandalize him or transgress the laws and conventions to which she willingly submits. Overwhelmed by sexual desires which cannot be released

---

[16] Taking a different view of the relationship between Pierre and Séverine, Virginia Higginbotham makes interesting connections between the film and the fairy-tale about Beauty and the Beast (1979: 129–38).

in her normal social and private worlds, Séverine indulges these in a brothel, a place which, as Kaplan and Abraham argue, legitimates, however temporarily, female sexual potency and initiatives (Séverine reverses the conventions at one point by making Marcel the prostitute, herself the client, by waiving her fee), but also in which that childhood trauma is endlessly replayed. Here Séverine releases her desires; but here also she endlessly plays the little girl submissively yielding to the plumber-father-surrogates among her clients, colluding in attitudes that both liberate and further entrap her subjectivity.[17] In so far as she submits herself to male authority, the prostitute is also someone, as Estela Welldon defines her, who 'colludes' with her clients in a 'vengeful and denigrating action against mother' (1992: 116) and by extension against her own sex (1988: 128). The brothel becomes a place where in anonymity the prostitute can liberate self-denigrating desires, considered in this case by Séverine too vile for expression in normal bourgeois life with Pierre.

The brothel's liberations, though, should not be underestimated even if ultimately *chez* Mme Anaïs also proves to be an ideological cul-de-sac. Classically a woman's realm, it does truly offer, at some levels, reversals of patriarchal power, even if the actual traffic in sexuality is paid for and controlled by men. In some limited ways it does manage to become for Séverine a place not exclusively associated with men. Although it has the primary importance of helping her develop, through an awareness of her own sexuality, her relations with her husband and other men, it is also a place where, however faintly, more intimate, more natural relations with women are allowed to develop. Once Séverine becomes an accepted member of the all-female family, she is soon relaxing and playing cards with the girls. On some occasions, too, this world of polymorphous and perverse pleasures reveals an underlying potential of lesbianism, something established almost immediately when, during only their second encounter, Mme Anaïs plays with Séverine's fingers, lightly touching their tips, kissing her gently on her pale, as yet unsexualized lips. Mme Anaïs's kiss acts as a sort of customs

---

[17] Gwynne Edwards (1982: 205) takes a different view, both as regards the therapeutic function of the brothel and the function of the Marcel character: 'in agreeing to work for her from two until five each afternoon she begins to free herself from the constraints of her past existence'. Later on, he suggests that 'She has found both her ideal lover and her true self' (ibid. 212).

officer's seal of approval, allowing entry into a foreign world of desire. By the end it is Séverine who takes the initiative in kissing Anaïs, though in the latter's gesture of denial, as she turns her lips away, by now angered at Séverine's decision to resign from prostitution, there is a clear sign of sorrow as well as bitterness at the prospect of never again seeing a woman on whom she has perhaps developed a crush. The possible undercurrent of a desired lesbian relationship with Séverine has the further effect here of highlighting the eroticization of Catherine Deneuve and the other prostitutes, especially in their various states of undress, for the pleasure of lesbian as well as straight audiences. Buñuel's comments about the gratification of his own heterosexual desires through the use of beautiful women does not of course preclude their appreciation by audiences whose orientations differ from his own.[18]

On a less highly charged erotic lesbian level, though, the all-female relationships at Mme Anaïs's—aside from those with the male clients—bear out feminist intuitions about Western culture's creation of a more favourable atmosphere for the potential of greater intimacy among women. Nancy Chodorow's remarks as representative of a certain tendency in feminist writing stressing the supportive, nurturing nature of friendships between women, often developed as a way of coping with difficulties encountered in some heterosexual relationships, seem highly relevant to this discussion:

While they are likely to become and remain erotically heterosexual, they are encouraged both by men's difficulties with love and by their own relational history with their mothers to look elsewhere for love and emotional gratification. One way that women fulfill their needs is through the creation and maintenance of important personal relations with other women. (1984: 200)

The relations struck up by Séverine with other women in the outside world can be judged on the basis of her contact with Renée, someone with whom she does share a private moment (as in the taxi ride), a friendship, though, ultimately defined by her involvement with Husson. In their own female world the women here find time for greater relaxation and intimacy in one another's company, being able at the very least to share experiences of their own and their clients' desires.

[18] On female erotica, see Myers (1987: 189–202).

And yet, of course, these moments of informality in a place defined at some levels as a sanctuary are fleeting, their transferences of the working girls to an alternative social world only provisional. The brothel may be owned and run by a woman, but her sponsors and clients remain men, who for the price of a trick can dictate the various shapes of their fancy. The *bonhomie* of M. Adolphe, the submissiveness of the gynaecologist, the childishness of Marcel, and the exoticism of the Korean are all eventually overshadowed by an assertiveness tolerating no compromises of its urgent needs. All exercise power over their chosen *poule*, some, like Marcel and Adolphe, not hesitating to use violence against failures of complaisance.

As the ambiguous ending proves, the brothel has probably not cured Séverine's perversion.[19] No one who has ever written on *Belle de jour* has failed to be perplexed by the ending, but perplexity only arises if one is looking there for an answer to the question of Séverine's perversion. If instead the ending is simply taken as another reformulation of her conflicts between libidinal and social desires, a further expression of the time-locked, libido-releasing function of the brothel, no other conclusion is possible, and Buñuel's own remarks—even though their customary dismissiveness is not to be taken too seriously—about a double ending should make this clear.[20] Séverine will always be divided between instincts for social conformity and forms of sexual expression conditioned by childhood trauma. As such, she is one of Buñuel's most vivid portrayals of the constitution of the sexualized subject in culture and history as much as in biology.[21] *Le hasard* has condemned Séverine to a life of psychological trauma

[19] A view shared by Raymond Durgnat: 'Thus the film reveals its true bitterness. It is a circle of near liberations by Séverine, by Pierre, by Marcel, by Husson, none of which can be completed, all of which frustrate one another' (1968: 145).

[20] See Buñuel's views on the ending: 'No hay dos finales, sino un final ambiguo. Yo no lo entiendo. Esto indica falta de certidumbre mía. Es el momento en que no sé qué hacer, tengo varias soluciones y no me decido por ninguna. Entonces, en el final, he puesto mi propia incertidumbre. Ya me ha pasado otras veces. Sólo puedo decir que en la vida hay situaciones que no terminan, que no tienen solución' (Pérez Turrent and de la Colina 1993: 147). ('There aren't two endings but one ambiguous one. I don't understand it. This shows a lack of certainty on my part. It is a moment where I'm unsure about what to do. I have various solutions and don't decide on any one. So, at the end I have reflected my own uncertainty. It's happened before. I can only say that in life there are situations without resolutions, that don't have an ending.')

[21] Elliot Stein refers to the ending as a 'decent neutrality which condemns no one' (1971: 20).

in which sexual abuse in childhood, together with the contradictory impulses of a bourgeois background, have led to inner confusions from which there seems no final release. But at least the laws of chance have spared her from an untimely death. When one of the other whores reads out aloud from the *New York Herald Tribune* brought in by Hippolyte the Murcian, the action —in a scene highly reminiscent of *A bout de souffle*—seems more than simply an indirect gesture of solidarity with Godard's New Wave aesthetics. The headline she reads out in her painfully slow Gallic English is: 'A-b-e-r-f-a-n: I-n-q-u-i-r-y A-c-c-u-s-e-d'. The detail gives a documentary feel to the film, grounding it in up-to-the-minute international news, while simultaneously drawing attention to an aleatory law to which all are vulnerable, here causing, through a landslide, the tragic premature deaths of children in a South Walian valley, elsewhere, through the chance meeting between a child and a male abuser, the psychological havoc that provokes a wife, perhaps vainly, to seek sexual therapy in a brothel.

Conclusion

THIS discussion of one of the great figures of world cinema has set out to draw Buñuel's films into some of the more lively theoretical and critical debates in film studies, especially those related to sexual theory, of the last decade or so. The analysis has also been governed to a large extent by a refusal to engage in theory at the expense of careful, detailed description of the films themselves and the contexts in which they were made. This has meant seriously addressing not only Buñuel's conscious choices of form and content—e.g. narrative strategies, visual style, acceptance or subversion of generic conventions—but also his unconscious assimilation of accepted norms and practices. The approach has been unapologetically eclectic. Balancing provision of empirical data with constructions of theoretical frameworks in order to distance the book from much previously unproblematized writing, this study has sacrificed neither historical nor biographical data to the finer nuances of abstract theory only loosely connected to commentary on the films themselves.

No approach can ever be ultimately wholly objective or innocent. But whatever its faults and weaknesses, this one has sought to allow the films, as far as possible, to speak for themselves, an aim that takes as axiomatic the dependence of sensible use of film theory, cultural theory, or gender theory on the accurate description and cataloguing of textual data.

Since so much has been written about Buñuel's very early career and its origins in the Surrealist movement, I have advanced fairly rapidly towards discussion of his Mexican period before eventually moving on to the great 'international' films of maturity, not by any means neglecting the early films, but allowing them to inform rather than to dictate the shape of the book's various priorities. This has meant reserving more space for the Mexican films. These, especially the commercial melodramas, have been undeservedly overlooked, above all in writing in English on Buñuel. Their significance has been stressed here in order precisely to highlight the interaction of popular and auteurist tendencies. Comparison of these complementary strains has usefully opened up questions of authorship, and this has perhaps led towards a sounder understanding of Buñuel's over-all achievement, his compromises as well as his subversiveness.

To a very considerable extent Buñuel's films have retained their provocative, disturbing force. Taking their audiences to the limits of experience, they have lost none of the impact of their enduringly shocking contempt for sanctimoniousness, triumphalism, and various other powerful delusions that turn individuals into the victims or 'subjects' of discourse. In Buñuel's films subjectivity is given access only to illusory forms of free-dom. More complicatedly, though, his explorations of desire—usually heterosexual desire, but with some interesting, somewhat hesitant excursions into homosexuality in e.g. *Un chien andalou*, *El*, and *Ensayo de un crimen*—seem now, in the light of twenty years or so of intensive gender theorizing, more problematic. Buñuel's films characteristically dramatize the often irresistible force of sexual desire, but *amour fou* here—unlike its appearances in the texts of the French Surrealists—has a much more jaun-diced expression. His characters, male as well as female, express their sexual orientations through the prejudices of social and cultural constructions. But, however profound their diagnosis of desire's frenzied release or repression, Buñuel's films can be accused of sometimes failing to interrogate traditional assump-tions about male-orientated notions of gender and sexuality. Nevertheless, in female-centred as well as in male-centred narratives, men are as often as women the victims of the social order. Questions about the power of the look, pleasure, or posi-tionality cannot be discussed in Buñuel's films as if they were merely elements of a hermetically sealed phallocentric system never disrupted by dissident voices.

In *Cet obscur objet du désir*, a male-centred film in the sense that male desire is its primary interest, the female rebels, humiliates her suitor, returns the gaze, and exposes to ridicule the outworn over-simplifications of essentialist views of femininity. The hu-miliation of the male may well perpetuate the stereotype of the *belle dame sans merci*, but no one could fail to notice in Conchita's persecution of Mateo approval as well as disapproval of the conventional male's painful sentimental education. In *Belle de jour*, a female-centred film, exploring polymorphously perverse female desires, Buñuel brilliantly keeps in focus questions relating simultaneously to the quasi-demonic urges of human sexuality, the enigmatic eroticism of Catherine Deneuve, the pursuit through sexuality of the self's powerlessness and, even, its dissolution, and the deconstruction, as Séverine is made to watch through the peep-hole the gynaecologist's self-inflicted humiliations, of the power structures that enable men to exercise control over women. The film can be accused of gratifying the voyeuristic, fetishistic pleasures of the male, but it cannot be accused either of failing to interrogate the origins of male constructions of femininity or of disavowing the wilder forms of female desire.

While Buñuel's films cannot be said to promote a political correctness ahead of its time, they cannot be charged either with neglecting to investigate the processes of representation that make of both men and women the victims of ideology. With a few significant exceptions—*Los olvidados, Abismos de pasión, Una mujer sin amor*—where the representation of these matters is given a relentlessly bleak formulation, Buñuel's films reflect in their expression of the turmoil of sexual desire the tolerance and humour of a genius projecting through his long-suffering characters—female as much as male—his own uncomprehending victimization by the laws of desire:

depuis l'âge de quatorze ans jusqu'à ces dernières années, je peux dire que le désir sexuel ne m'a pas quitté. Un désir puissant, quotidien, plus exigeant même que la faim, souvent plus difficile à satisfaire. A peine connaissais-je un moment de repos, a peine m'asseyais-je par exemple dans un compartiment de chemin de fer, que des images érotiques m'enveloppaient. Impossible de résister a ce désir, de le surmonter, de l'oublier, je ne pouvais que lui céder ... (Buñuel 1982a: 180)

(from the age of 14 until recently, I can say that sexual desire has not abandoned me. A powerful desire, afflicting me daily, more urgent even than hunger, often more difficult to satisfy. No sooner would I be granted a moment's peace, no sooner would I have found myself a seat in a train compartment, than I'd be assailed by erotic images. Useless to resist this desire, to overcome it, to forget it. I would have no option other than to surrender to it ...)

A Buñuel Filmography

Abismos de pasión (*The Abyss of Passion*), 1953

Production Company: Producciones Tepeyac
Producers: Oscar Dancigers and Abelardo L. Rodríguez
Executive Producer: Federico Amérigo
Script: Luis Buñuel, Julio Alejandro, and Arduino Mairui (based on
 Emily Brontë's *Wuthering Heights*)
Photography: Agustín Jiménez
Décor: Edward Fitzgerald
Music: Raúl Lavista (based on melodies from *Tristan and Isolde* by
 Wagner)
Editor: Carlos Savage
Assistant Director: Ignacio Villarreal
Chief of Production: Alberto A. Ferrer
Sound: Eduardo Arjona and Caldino Samperio
Costume: Armando Valdés Peza
Make-up: Felisa Ladrón de Guevara
Actors: Irasema Dilián (Catalina), Jorge Mistral (Alejandro), Lilia
 Prado (Isabel), Ernesto Alonso (Eduardo), Luis Aceves Castañeda
 (Ricardo)
Duration: 91 minutes

Âge d'or, L' (*The Golden Age*), 1930

Producer: Viscount of Noailles
Script: Luis Buñuel and Salvador Dalí
Photography: Albert Duverger
Décor: Pierre Schilzneck
Music: Georges Van Parys and fragments by Mendelssohn, Mozart,
 Beethoven, Debussy, and Wagner
Editor: Luis Buñuel
Assistant Directors: Jacques Bernard Brunius and Claude Heymann
Sound: Peter-Paul Brauer
Actors: Gaston Modot (the lover), Lya Lys (the daughter of the Mar-
 quise), Caridad de Lamberdesque (the woman), Pierre Prévert (the
 bandit), Max Ernst (leader of the bandits), Paul Éluard
Duration: 63 minutes

Angel exterminador, El (The Exterminating Angel), 1962

Production Company: Producciones Alatriste, Uninci, Films 59
Producer: Gustavo Alatriste
Executive Producer: Antonio de Salazar
Script: Luis Buñuel and Luis Alcoriza
Photography: Gabriel Figueroa
Décor: Jesús Bracho
Music: Raúl Lavista, based on pieces from Beethoven, Chopin, Scarlatti, Gregorian Plainsong, and several *Te Deums*
Editor: Carlos Savage
Assistant Director: Ignacio Villarreal
Chief of Production: Fidel Pizarro
Sound: José B. Carles
Costume: Georgette Somohano
Actors: Silvia Pinal (Leticia), Enrique Rambal (Edmundo Nobile), Jacqueline Andere (Alicia de Roc), José Baviera (Leandro Gómez), Augusto Benedicto (Doctor Carlos Conde), Claudio Brook (Julio)
Duration: 93 minutes

Belle de jour (Beauty of the Day), 1966

Production Company: Paris Films Production, Five Films
Producers: Robert and Raymond Hakim
Executive Producer: Robert Demollière
Script: Luis Buñuel and Jean-Claude Carrière
Photography: Sacha Vierny, in eastmancolor
Décor: Robert Clavel
Editor: Louisette Taverna-Hautecœur
Assistant Director: Pierre Lary and Jacques Fraenkel
Chief of Production: Henri Baum
Sound: René Longuet
Costume: Hélène Nourry and Yves Saint-Laurent
Make-up: Janine Jarreau
Actors: Catherine Deneuve (Séverine), Jean Sorel (Pierre), Michel Piccoli (M. Husson), Geneviève Page (Mme Anaïs), Francisco Rabal (Hippolyte), Pierre Clementi (Marcel), Georges Marchal (the Duke), Françoise Fabian (Charlotte), Marie Latour (Mathilde), Francis Blanche (M. Adolphe), Macha Meril (Renée), Iska Khan (the Asiatic client), François Maistre (the gynaecologist), and Muni (Pallas)
Duration: 100 minutes

Bruto, El (The Brute), 1952

Production Company: Internacional Cinematográfica, for Columbia
Producer: Sergio Kogan
Executive Producer: Gabriel Castro
Script: Luis Buñuel and Luis Alcoriza

Photography: Agustín Jiménez
Décor: Gunther Gerszo, assisted by Roberto Silva
Music: Raúl Lavista
Editor: Jorge Bustos
Assistant Director: Ignacio Villarreal
Chief of Production: Fidel Pizarro
Sound: Javier Mateos and Galdino Samperio
Make-up: Ana Guerrero
Actors: Pedro Armendáriz (Pedro), Katy Jurado (Paloma), Rosita
    Arenas (Meche), Andrés Cabrera (Andrés Soler), Roberto Meyer
    (Carmelo González), Paco Martínez (Don Pepe)
Duration: 83 minutes

Cela s'appelle l'aurore (*The Break of Dawn*), 1955

Production Company: Les Films Marceau, Laetitia Films
Script: Luis Buñuel and Jean Ferry (based on the novel by Emmanuel
    Robles)
Photography: Robert Lefebvre
Décor: Maz Douy
Music: Joseph Kosma
Editor: Marguerite Renoir
Assistant Directors: Marcel Camus and Jacques Deray
Chief of Production: André Cultet
Sound: Antoine Petitjean
Actors: Georges Marchal (Doctor Valerio), Lucía Bosé (Clara), Nelly
    Borgeaud (Angela), Gianni Espósito (Sandro Galli), Julien Bertheau
    (chief of police)
Duration: 102 minutes

Cet obscur objet du désir (*That Obscure Object of Desire*), 1977

Production Company: Greenwich Film Production, Les Films Galazie,
    In Cine
Producer: Serge Silberman
Script: Luis Buñuel and Jean-Claude Carrière (based on Pierre Louÿs's
    La Femme et le pantin)
Photography: Edmond Richard, in eastmancolor
Décor: Pierre Guffroy and Pierre Bartlet
Music: Fragments from Wagner's *Walkiria* and from flamenco music
Editor: Hélène Plemiannikov
Assistant Directors: Pierre Lary and Juan Luis Buñuel
Chief of Production: Ully Pickard
Sound: Guy Villette
Costume: Sylvia de Segonzac
Make-up: Odette Berroyer

Actors: Fernando Rey (Mathieu), Angela Molina (Conchita), Carole Bouquet (Conchita), Julien Bertheau (Édouard), André Weber (Martin), Bernard Musson (police inspector), María Asquerino (Conchita's mother), Muni (concierge)
Duration: 103 minutes

Charme discret de la bourgeoisie, Le (*The Discreet Charm of the Bourgeoisie*), 1972

Production Company: Greenwich Film Production
Producer: Serge Silberman
Script: Luis Buñuel and Jean-Claude Carrière
Photography: Edmond Richard, in eastmancolor
Décor: Pierre Guffroy
Editor: Hélène Pleniannikov
Assistant Director: Pierre Lary
Chief of Production: Ully Pickard
Sound: Guy Villette
Actors: Fernando Rey (Rafael), Jean-Pierre Cassel (Sénéchal), Stéphane Audran (Alice), Paul Frankeur (Thévenot), Delphine Seyrig (Simone), Bulle Ogier (Florence), Julien Bertheau (bishop), Muni (peasant woman), Michel Piccoli (minister), Bernard Musson (waiter), François Maistre (police inspector)
Duration: 100 minutes

Chien andalou, Un (*An Andalusian Dog*), 1928

Producer: Luis Buñuel
Script: Luis Buñuel and Salvador Dalí
Photography: Albert Duverger
Décor: Pierre Schilzneck
Music: Fragments from Wagner's *Tristan and Isolde*, Beethoven, and tangos chosen by Buñuel
Editor: Luis Buñuel
Actors: Pierre Batcheff, Simone Mareuil, Jaume Miravitlles, Salvador Dalí, and Luis Buñuel
Duration: 17 minutes

El (*He*), 1952
Production Company: Ultramar Films
Producer: Oscar Dancigers
Executive Producer: Federico Amérigo
Script: Luis Buñuel and Luis Alcoriza (based on the novel by Mercedes Pinto)
Photography: Gabriel Figueroa
Décor: Edward Fitzgerald and Pablo Galván
Music: Luis Hernández Bretón

Editor: Carlos Savage
Assistant Director: Ignacio Villarreal
Chief of Production: Fidel Pizarro
Sound: José D. Pérez and Jesús González Gancy
Make-up: Armando Meyer
Actors: Arturo de Córdova (Francisco), Delia Garcés (Gloria), Luis Beristáin (Raúl), Aurora Walker (Esperanza), Carlos Martínez Baena (Padre Velasco), Manuel Dondé (manservant)
Duration: 91 minutes

Ensayo de un crimen / La vida criminal de Archibaldo de la Cruz
  (*The Criminal Life of Archibaldo de la Cruz*), 1955

Production Company: Alianza Cinematográfica
Producer: Alfonso Patiño Gómez
Executive Producer: Roberto Figueroa
Script: Luis Buñuel and Eduardo Ugarte (based on the novel by Rodolfo Usigli)
Photography: Agustín Jiménez
Décor: Jesús Bracho
Music: Jorge Pérez Herrera
Editor: Jorge Bustos
Assistant Director: Luis Abadíe
Chief of Production: Armando Espinosa
Sound: Rodolfo Benítez, Enrique Rodríguez, and Ernesto Caballero
Make-up: Sara Mateos
Actors: Ernesto Alonso (Archibaldo), Miroslava Stern (Lavinia), Rita Macedo (Patricia), Ariadna Welter (Carlota), José María Linares Rivas (Willy), Rodolfo Landa (Alejandro), Andrea Palma (Sra Cervantes), Eva Calvo and Enrique Díaz Indiano (Archibaldo's parents)
Duration: 89 minutes

Fantôme de la liberté, Le (*The Phantom of Liberty*), 1974

Production Company: Greenwich Film Production
Producer: Serge Silberman
Script: Luis Buñuel and Jean-Claude Carrière
Photography: Edmond Richard, in eastmancolor
Décor: Pierre Guffroy
Music: Galaxie Musique
Editor: Hélène Plemiannikov
Assistant Directors: Pierre Lary and Jacques Fraenkel
Chief of Production: Ully Pickard
Sound: Guy Villette
Costume: Jacqueline Guyot
Make-up: Monique Archambault

Actors: Adriana Asti (woman in black), Julien Bertheau (prefect), Jean-Claude Brialy (Foucauld), Adolfo Celi (doctor), Paul Frankeur (owner of the inn), François Maistre (instructor), Monica Vitti (Mme Foucauld), Muni (maid), Bernard Musson (monk), Hélène Perdrière (aged aunt), Pierre Maguelon (Gérard)
Duration: 104 minutes

Fièvre monte à El Pao, La / Los ambiciosos (*The Temperature Rises in El Pao*), 1959

Production Company: Filmex, Films Borderie, Groupe des Quatre, Cité Films, Cormoran Films, Indus Films, Terra Films
Producers: Gregorio Walerstein and Raymond Borderie
Associate Producer: Oscar Dancigers
Executive Producer: Vicente Fernández
Script: Luis Buñuel, Luis Alcoriza, Louis Sapin, Charles Dorat, Henri Castillou, and José Luis González de León (based on the novel by Henri Castillou)
Photography: Gabriel Figueroa
Décor: Jorge Fernández and Pablo Galván
Music: Paul Misraki
Editor: James Cuenet (French version) and Rafael Caballos (Mexican version)
Assistant Director: Ignacio Villarreal
Chief of Production: Manuel Rodríguez
Sound: William-Robert Sivel (French version); Rodolfo Benítez and Roberto Camacho (Mexican version)
Costume: Ana María Jones and Armando Valdés Peza
Make-up: Armando Meyer
Actors: Gérard Phillipe (Vázquez), María Félix (Inés), Jean Servais (Alejandro), Víctor Junco (Indarte), Roberto Cañedo (Olivares)
Duration: 97 minutes

Gran calavera, El (*The Great Carouser*), 1949

Production Company: Ultramar Films
Producers: Fernando Soler and Oscar Dancigers
Executive Producer: Federico Amérigo
Associate Producer: Antonio de Salazar
Script: Luis Alcoriza and Raquel Rojas (based on the comedy by Adolfo Torrado)
Photography: Ezequiel Carrasco
Décor: Luis Moya and Darío Cabañas
Music: Manuel Esperón
Editor: Carlos Savage
Assistant Director: Moisés M. Delgado
Chief of Production: Alberto A. Ferrer

Sound: Rafael Ruiz Esparza and Jesús González Gancy
Make-up: Ana Guerrero
Actors: Fernando Soler (Ramiro), Rosario Granados (Virginia), Andrés
    Soler (Ladislao), Rubén Rojo (Pablo), Gustavo Rojo (Eduardo)
Duration: 90 minutes

Gran Casino (Gran Casino), 1946

Production Company: Películas Anahuac
Producer: Oscar Dancigers
Executive Producer: Federico Amérigo
Script: Mauricio Magdaleno, based on a novel by Michel Weber
Photography: Jack Draper
Décor: Javier Torres Rorija
Music: Manuel Esperón (songs by Francisco Canario, Mariano Mores,
    A. G. Villoldo, Francisco Alonso, and F. Vigil)
Editor: Gloria Schoemann
Assistant Director: Moisés M. Delgado
Chief of Production: José Luis Busto
Sound: Javier Mateos and José de Pérez
Make-up: Armando Meyer
Actors: Libertad Lamarque (Mercedes), Jorge Negrete (Gerardo),
    Mercedes Barba (Camelia), Agustín Isunza (Heriberto), Julio
    Villarreal (Demetrio)
Duration: 85 minutes

Hija del engaño, La / Don Quintín el amargao (Daughter of Deceit), 1951

Production Company: Ultramar Films
Producer: Oscar Dancigers
Executive Producer: Federico Amérigo
Script: Luis Alcoriza and Raquel Rojas (based on a play by Carlos
    Arniches and José Estremera)
Photography: José Ortiz Ramos
Décor: Edward Fitzgerald and Pablo Galván
Music: Manuel Esperón
Editor: Carlos Savage
Assistant Director: Mario Llorca
Chief of Production: Fidel Pizarro
Sound: Eduardo Arjona and Jesús González Gancy
Make-up: Ana Guerrero
Actors: Fernando Soler (Quintín), Alicia Caro (Mara), Rubén Rojo
    (Paco), Fernando Soto 'Mantequilla' (Angelito), Nacho Contla
    (Jonrón)
Duration: 80 minutes

Hurdes, Las / Tierra sin pan (*Land Without Bread*), 1932
Producer: Ramón Acín
Script: Luis Buñuel, Pierre Unik, and Julio Acín
Photography: Eli Lotar
Music: Fragments from Brahms's 4th Symphony
Editor: Luis Buñuel
Assistant Directors: Pierre Unik and Rafael Sánchez Ventura
Sound: Charles Goldblatt and Pierre Braunberger
Actors: Abel Jacquin (narrator)
Duration: 27 minutes

Ilusión viaja en tranvía, La (*A Tram-Ride of Dreams*), 1953
Production Company: Clasa Films Mundiales
Producer: Armando Orive Alba
Executive Producer: José Ramón Aguirre
Script: Mauricio de la Serna, José Revueltas, Luis Alcoriza, and Juan de la Cabada
Photography: Raúl Martínez Solares
Décor: Edward Fitzgerald
Music: Luis Hernández Bretón
Editor: Jorge Bustos
Assistant Director: Ignacio Villarreal
Chief of Production: Fidel Pizarro
Sound: José D. Pérez and Rafael Ruiz Esparza
Make-up: Elda Loza
Actors: Lilia Prado (Lupita), Carlos Navarro (Juan), Fernando Soto 'Mantequilla' (Tarrajas), Agustín Isunza (Papá Pinillos), Miguel Manzano (Don Manuel)
Duration: 82 minutes

Journal d'une femme de chambre, Le (*The Diary of a Chambermaid*), 1964
Production Company: Speva Films, Ciné Alliances Filmsonor, Dear Films
Producers: Serge Silberman and Michel Safra
Script: Luis Buñuel and Jean-Claude Carrière (based on Octave Mirbeau's novel)
Photography: Roger Fellous, in franscope
Décor: Georges Wakhevitch
Editor: Louisette Taverna-Hautecœur
Assistant Directors: Juan Luis Buñuel and Pierre Lary
Chief of Production: Henri Baum
Sound: Antoine Petitjean
Costume: Jacqueline Moreau
Actors: Jeanne Moreau (Célestine), Michel Piccoli (Monteil), Georges Géret (Joseph), Françoise Lugagne (Mme Monteil), Daniel Ivertiel

(the Captain), Jean Ozenne (Rabour), Gilbert Geniat (Rose), Jean-Claude Carrière (the priest), Bernard Musson (the sacristan), Muni (Marianne), Dominique Sauvage (Claire)

Duration: 98 minutes

Mort en ce jardin, La (*Garden of Death*), 1956

Production Company: Producciones Tepeyac, Films Dismage
Producers: Oscar Dancigers and David Mage
Executive Producers: Léon Caré and Antonio de Salazar
Script: Luis Buñuel, Luis Alcoriza, Raymond Queneau, and Gabriel Arout (based on the novel by José-André Lacour)
Photography: Jorge Stahl Jr., in eastmancolor
Décor: Edward Fitzgerald
Music: Paul Misraki
Editor: Marguerite Renoir
Assistant Directors: Ignacio Villarreal and Dossia Mage
Chief of Production: Alberto A. Ferrer
Sound: José D. Pérez and Galdino Samperio
Actors: Simone Signoret (Djinn), Georges Marchal (Shark), Charles Vanel (Castin), Michel Piccoli (Father Lisardi), Tito Junco (Chenko), Michèle Girardon (Maria)
Duration: 97 minutes

Mujer sin amor, Una (*A Loveless Woman*), 1951

Production Company: Internacional Cinematográfica, for Columbia
Producer: Sergio Kogan
Script: Jaime Salvador (based on *Pierre et Jean*, by Guy de Maupassant)
Photography: Raúl Martínez Solares
Décor: Gunther Gerszo
Music: Raúl Lavista
Assistant Director: Mario Llorca
Chief of Production: José Luis Busto
Sound: Rodolfo Benítez
Make-up: Ana Guerrero
Actors: Rosario Granados (Rosario), Tito Junco (Julio), Julio Villarreal (Don Carlos), Jaime Calpe (Carlitos), Joaquín Cordero (Carlos), Xavier Loyá (Miguel), Elda Peralta (Luisa), Eva Calvo, and Miguel Manzano
Duration: 90 minutes

Nazarín (*Nazarin*), 1958

Production Company: Producciones Barbáchano Ponce
Producer: Manuel Barbáchano Ponce
Executive Producer: Federico Amérigo
Script: Luis Buñuel and Julio Alejandro

Photography: Gabriel Figueroa
Décor: Edward Fitzgerald
Music: Macedonio Alcalá
Editor: Carlos Savage
Assistant Director: Ignacio Villarreal
Chief of Production: Carlos Velo
Sound: José D. Pérez and Galdino Samperio
Costume: Georgette Somohano
Actors: Francisco Rabal (Nazarín), Marga López (Beatriz), Rita Macedo (Andara), Jesús Fernández (the dwarf), Ignacio López Tarso (the blasphemer), Ofelia Guilmáin (Chanfa)
Duration: 97 minutes

Olvidados, Los (*The Dispossessed*), 1950

Production Company: Ultramar Films
Producers: Oscar Dancigers and Jaime Menasce
Executive Producer: Federico Amérigo
Script: Luis Buñuel and Luis Alcoriza, with the help of Max Aub and Pedro de Urdimalas
Photography: Gabriel Figueroa
Décor: Edward Fitzgerald
Music: Rodolfo Halffter, based on pieces by Gustavo Pittaluga
Editor: Carlos Savage
Assistant Director: Ignacio Villarreal
Chief of Production: Fidel Pizarro
Sound: José B. Carles and Jesús González Ganci
Make-up: Armando Meyer
Actors: Alfonso Mejía (Pedro), Roberto Cobo (Jaibo), Stella Inda (Pedro's mother), Miguel Inclán (Carmelo), Alma Delia Fuentes (Meche), Mario Ramírez (Ojitos)
Duration: 88 minutes

Río y la muerte, El (*River of Death*), 1954

Production Company: Clasa Films Mundiales
Producer: Armando Orive Alba
Executive Producer: José Ramón Aguirre
Script: Luis Buñuel and Luis Alcoriza (based on a novel by Manuel Alvarez Acosta)
Photography: Raúl Martínez Solares
Décor: Gunther Gerszo
Music: Raúl Lavista
Editor: Jorge Bustos
Assistant Director: Ignacio Villarreal
Chief of Production: José Alcalde Gámiz
Sound: José D. Pérez and Rafael Ruiz Esparza

Make-up: Margarita Ortega
Actors: Columba Domínguez (Mercedes), Miguel Torruco (Felipe Anguiano), Joaquín Cordero (Gerardo), Jaime Fernández (Rómulo), Víctor Alcocer (Polo)
Duration: 93 minutes

Robinson Crusoe (Robinson Crusoe), 1952

Production Company: Ultramar Films and OLMEC, for United Artists
Producers: Oscar Dancigers and Henry F. Ehrlich
Script: Luis Buñuel and Phillip Ansell Roll (based on the novel by Daniel Defoe)
Photography: Alex Phillips, in Pathecolor
Décor: Edward Fitzgerald
Music: Luis Hernández Bretón and Anthony Collins
Editor: Carlos Savage and Alberto Valenzuela
Assistant Director: Ignacio Villarreal
Chief of Production: Federico Amérigo
Sound: Javier Mateos
Make-up: Armando Meyer
Actors: Dan O'Herlihy (Robinson), Jaime Fernández (Friday), Felipe de Alba (Captain), Chel López (Bosun), José Chávez and Emilio Garibay (mutineers)
Duration: 89 minutes

Simón del desierto (Simon of the Desert), 1965

Production Company: Producciones Alatriste
Producer: Gustavo Alatriste
Script: Luis Buñuel and Julio Alejandro
Photography: Gabriel Figueroa
Music: Raúl Lavista, *saetas* and drums for Holy Week rituals in Calanda
Editor: Carlos Savage
Assistant Director: Ignacio Villarreal
Chief of Production: Armando Espinosa
Sound: James L. Fields and Luis Fernández
Make-up: Armando Meyer
Actors: Claudio Brook (Simón), Silvia Pinal (Devil), Hortensia Santoveña (Simón's mother), Jesús Fernández (dwarf), Luis Acedes Castañeda (Trifón)
Duration: 42 minutes

Subida al cielo (Stairway to Heaven), 1951

Production Company: Producciones Isla
Producers: Manuel Altolaguirre and María Luisa Gómez Mena
Script: Luis Buñuel, Manuel Altolaguirre, Juan de la Cabada, and Lilia Solano Galeana

Photography: Alex Phillips
Décor: José Rodríguez Granada
Music: Gustavo Pittaluga
Editor: Rafael Portillo
Assistant Director: Jorge López Portillo
Chief of Production: Fidel Pizarro
Sound: Eduardo Arjona and Jesús González Gancy
Costume: Georgette Somohano
Actors: Lilia Prado (Raquel), Carmen González (Albina), Esteban Márquez (Oliverio), Luis Aceves Castañeda (Silvestre), Roberto Cobo (Juan)
Duration: 85 minutes

Susana / Demonio y carne (*The Devil and the Flesh*), 1950

Production Company: Internacional Cinematográfica, for Columbia
Script: Luis Buñuel, Jaime Salvador, and Rodolfo Usigli
Photography: José Ortiz Ramos
Décor: Gunther Gerszo
Music: Raúl Lavista
Editor: Jorge Bustos
Assistant Director: Ignacio Villareal
Chief of Production: Fidel Pizarro
Sound: Nicolás de la Rosa
Make-up: Ana Guerrero
Actors: Fernando Soler (Guadalupe), Rosita Quintana (Susana), Víctor Manuel Mendoza (Jesús), Matilde Palou (Carmen), María Gentil Arcos (Felisa), and Luis López Somoza (Alberto)
Duration: 80 minutes

Tristana (*Tristana*), 1970

Production Company: Epoca Films, Talía Films, Selenia Cinematográfica, and Les Films Corona
Executive Producers: Joaquín Gurruchaga and Eduardo Ducay
Script: Luis Buñuel and Julio Alejandro (based on the novel by Benito Pérez Galdós)
Photography: José F. Aguayo
Décor: Enrique Alarcón
Editor: Pedro del Rey
Assistant Director: José Puyol
Chief of Production: Juan Estelrich
Sound: José Nogueira and Dino Fronzetti
Make-up: Julián Ruiz
Actors: Catherine Deneuve (Tristana), Fernando Rey (Lope), Franco Nero (Horacio), Lola Gaos (Saturna), Jesús Fernández (Saturno)
Duration: 96 minutes

Viridiana (Viridiana), 1961

Production Company: Producciones Alatriste, Uninci, Films 59
Producers: Gustavo Alatriste, Pere Portabella
Executive Producer: Ricardo Muñoz Suay
Script: Luis Buñuel and Julio Alejandro
Photography: José F. Aguayo
Décor: Francisco Canet
Music: Fragments from Handel's *Messiah*, from Mozart's *Requiem*, and from Beethoven, arranged by Gustavo Pittaluga
Editor: Pedro del Rey
Assistant Directors: Juan Luis Buñuel and José Puyol
Chief of Production: Gustavo Quintana
Actors: Silvia Pinal (Viridiana), Francisco Rabal (Jorge), Fernando Rey (Jaime), Margarita Lozano (Ramona), Victoria Zinny (Lucía), Teresa Rabal (Rita), Lola Gaos (Enedina)
Duration: 90 minutes

Voie lactée, La (The Milky Way), 1969

Production Company: Greenwich Film Production, Fraia Film
Producer: Serge Silberman
Associate Producer: Ully Pickard
Script: Luis Buñuel and Jean-Claude Carrière
Photography: Christian Matras, in eastmancolor
Décor: Pierre Guffroy
Music: Luis Buñuel
Editor: Louisette Taverna-Hautecœur
Assistant Director: Pierre Lary
Chief of Production: Ully Pickard
Sound: Jacques Gallois
Costume: Jacqueline Guyot
Actors: Paul Frankeur (Pierre), Laurent Terzieff (Jean), Alain Cuny (man in cape), Edith Scob (María), Bernard Berley (Jesus), François Maistre (mad priest), Julien Bertheau (Richard), Muni (Jansenist nun), Michel Piccoli (Marquis de Sade), Pierre Clementi (Devil), Georges Marchal (Jesuit), Claudio Brook (bishop), Jean-Claude Carrière (Priscillian), Delphine Seyrig (prostitute)
Duration: 98 minutes

Young One, The, 1960

Production Company: Producciones OLMEC, for Columbia Pictures
Producer: George P. Werker
Script: Luis Buñuel and H. B. Addis (based on Peter Mathiessen's *Travelin' Man*)
Photography: Gabriel Figueroa
Décor: Jesús Bracho

Music: Chucho Zarzosa (song by Leon Bibb)
Editor: Carlos Savage
Assistant Directors: Ignacio Villarreal and Juan Luis Buñuel
Chief of Production: Manuel Rodríguez
Sound: James L. Fields, José B. Carles, and Galdino Samperio
Make-up: Armando Meyer
Actors: Zachary Scott (Miller), Bernie Hamilton (Travers), Kay Meersman (Evie), Graham Denton (Jackson), and Claudio Brook (Reverend Fleetwood)
Duration: 96 minutes

AS ASSISTANT DIRECTOR

Chute de la Maison Usher (The Fall of the House of Usher), 1928. Director: Jean Epstein
Mauprat (Mauprat), 1926. Director: Jean Epstein
Sirène de Tropiques, La (Tropical Siren), 1927. Directors: Henri Etievant and Marius Nalpas

AS EXECUTIVE PRODUCER (AT FILMOFONO)

¡Centinela Alerta! (Sentinel Alert!), 1936. Director: Jean Grémillon
Don Quintín el amargao (The Bitterness of Don Quintin), 1935. Director: Luis Marquina
Hija de Juan Simón, La (Juan Simon's Daughter), 1935. Director: José Luis Sáenz de Heredia
¿Quién me quiere a mí? (Who's In Love With Me?), 1936. Director: José Luis Sáenz de Heredia

Bibliography

ALEJANDRO, JULIO (1980), 'Colaborar con Buñuel' (interview by Francesc Llinás and Javier Vega), *Contracampo*, 16 Oct–Nov.), 40–5.

ALTHUSSER, LOUIS (1977), *Lenin and Philosophy and Other Essays*, trans. Ben Brewster. London: N.L.B. (First pub. 1971.)

ARANDA, FRANCISCO (1975), *Luis Buñuel: A Critical Biography*. London: Secker & Warburg.

Arena, BBC, 11 Feb. 1984, 'The Life and Times of Don Luis Buñuel'. Produced by Alan Yentob and directed by Anthony Wall.

AUB, MAX (1985), *Conversaciones con Buñuel*. Madrid: Aguilar. (First pub. 1984.)

BABINGTON, BRUCE, and EVANS, PETER W. (1985), 'The Life of the Interior: Dreams in the Films of Luis Buñuel', *Critical Quarterly*, 27/ 4, pp. 5–20.

—— —— (1989), *Affairs to Remember: The Hollywood Comedy of the Sexes*. Manchester and New York: Manchester University Press.

—— —— (1990), 'All that Heaven Allowed: Another Look at Sirkian Irony', *Movie*, 34–5 (Winter), 48–58.

—— —— (1993), *Biblical Epics: Sacred Narrative in the Hollywood Cinema*. Manchester and New York: Manchester University Press.

BAKHTIN, MIKHAIL (1968), *Rabelais and his World*, trans. Helen Iswolsky. Cambridge, Mass.: MIT Press.

BARBÁCHANO, CARLOS (1986), *Buñuel* (Biblioteca Salvat de Grandes Bibliografías). Barcelona: Salvat.

BARR, CHARLES (1974), 'Cinemascope: Before and After', in Gerald Mast Marshall and Cohen (eds.), *Film Theory and Criticism: Introductory Readings*. New York, London, and Toronto: Oxford University Press, 120–50. (First pub. 1963.)

BARTHES, ROLAND (1973), *Le Plaisir du texte*. Paris: Seuil.

BEAUVOIR, SIMONE DE (1969), *The Second Sex*, trans. H. M. Parshley. London: New English Library. (First pub. 1949.)

BEHAR, RUTH (1989), 'Sexual Witchcraft, Colonialism, and Women's Powers: Views from the Mexican Inquisition', in Lavrin (ed.), 178–206. (First pub. 1984.)

BENJAMIN, JESSICA (1990), *The Bonds of Love: Psychoanalysis, Feminism, and the Problem of Domination*. London: Virago Press. (First pub. 1988.)

BERGSON, HENRI (1956), 'Laughter', in Henri Bergson and George Meredith, *Comedy* (Introduction and appendix by Wylie Sypher). Garden City, NY: Doubleday, 61–190. (First pub. 1900.)

BETTELHEIM, BRUNO (1988), *The Uses of Enchantment: The Meaning and Importance of Fairy Tales.* Harmondsworth: Penguin Books. (First pub. 1976.)

BORDWELL, DAVID (1979), 'The Art Cinema as a Mode of Film Practice', *Film Criticism,* 4/1.

BORGES, JORGE LUIS (1979), 'Borges y yo', in *El Hacedor.* Madrid: Alianza Editorial, 69–70. (First pub. 1960.)

BOURDIEU, PIERRE (1984), *Distinction: A Social Critique of the Judgement of Taste,* trans. Richard Nice. Cambridge, Mass.: Harvard University Press. (First pub. 1979.)

BRETON, ANDRÉ (1977), *L'Amour fou.* Paris: Gallimard. (First pub. 1937.)

—— (1988), 'Manifeste du surréalisme', in *Œuvre complète.* Paris: Gallimard, 309–46. (First pub. 1924.)

BROOKS, PETER (1984), *The Melodramatic Imagination: Balzac, Henry James, Melodrama, and the Mode of Excess.* New York: Columbia University Press. (First pub. 1976.)

BUACHE, FREDDY (1973), *The Cinema of Luis Buñuel,* trans. Peter Graham. London: Tantivy Press. (First pub. 1970.)

BUÑUEL, LUIS (1971*a*), *Belle de jour,* English trans. and description of action by Robert Adkinson (Modern Film Scripts). London: Lorrimer Publishing.

—— (1971*b*), *Le Journal d'une femme de chambre.* Paris: Seuil.

—— (1982*a*), *Mon dernier soupir.* Paris: Éditions Robert Laffont.

—— (1982*b*), *Obra literaria,* ed. Agustín Sánchez Vidal. Zaragoza: Ediciones del Heraldo de Aragón.

—— (1985*a*), 'Pesimismo', *Andalán,* 435–6, pp. 31–6.

—— (1985*b*), 'Preguntas a Luis Buñuel para la revista de Milán *Cinema Nuovo,* hechas en Venecia en Septiembre de 1967', *Andalán,* 435–6, pp. 37–8.

—— (1990), *Là-bas.* Teruel: Instituto de Estudios Turolenses.

—— (1992), *Goya.* Teruel: Instituto de Estudios Turolenses.

BUTLER FLORA, CORNELIA (1979), 'The Passive Female and Social Change: A Cross-Cultural Comparison of Women's Magazine Fiction', in Pescatello (ed.), 59–85.

BYARS, JACKIE (1991), *All that Hollywood Allows: Re-Reading Gender in 1950s Melodrama.* London: Routledge.

CANOVAS, JOAQUIN T. (ed.) (1992), *Francisco Rabal.* Murcia: Filmoteca Regional de Murcia.

CAPLAN, PAT (1991), 'Introduction', in Caplan (ed.), 1–30.

—— (ed.) (1991), *The Cultural Construction of Sexuality.* London and New York: Routledge. (First pub. 1987.)

CARRIÈRE, JEAN-CLAUDE (1978), 'The Buñuel Mystery', in Mellen (ed.), 90–102. (First pub. 1970.)

CHODOROW, NANCY (1984), *The Reproduction of Mothering: Psychoanalysis and the Sociology of Gender*. Berkeley and Los Angeles: University of California Press. (First pub. 1978.)

COOK, PAM, (ed.) (1985), *The Cinema Book*. London: British Film Institute.

CREED, BARBARA (1993), *The Monstrous-Feminine: Film, Feminism, Psychoanalysis*. London and New York: Routledge.

DELEUZE, GILLES (1971), *Masochism: An Interpretation of Coldness and Cruelty*. New York: George Braziller.

DERRIDA, JACQUES (1987), *L'Écriture et la différance*. Paris: Seuil.

DÍAZ TORRES, DANIEL, and COLINA, ENRIQUE (1972), 'El melodrama en la obra de Luis Buñuel', *Cine Cubano*, 78–80, pp. 156–64.

DOANE, MARY ANN (1988), *The Desire to Desire: The Woman's Film of the 1940s*. London: Macmillan. (First pub. 1987.)

DURGNAT, RAYMOND (1968), *Luis Buñuel*. London: Studio Vista. (First pub. 1967.)

—— (1978), '*The Discreet Charm of the Bourgeoisie*', in Mellen (ed.), 373–96. (First pub. 1975.)

DYER, RICHARD (1979), *Stars*. London: British Film Institute.

—— (1982), 'Don't Look Now—the Male Pin-Up', *Screen*, 23/3–4, pp. 61–87.

EDWARDS, GWYNNE (1982), *The Discreet Art of Luis Buñuel: A Reading of His Films*. London and Boston: Marion Boyars.

—— (1983), 'On Buñuel's Diary of a Chambermaid', in Margaret Rees (ed.), *Luis Buñuel: A Symposium*. Leeds: Trinity and All Saints' College, 27–58.

ÉLIADE, MIRCEA (1979), *Patterns in Comparative Religion*. London: Sheed and Ward. (First pub. 1958.)

ÉLUARD, PAUL (1939), *Donner à voir*. Paris: Gallimard.

FIDDIAN, ROBIN W., and EVANS, PETER W. (1988), *Challenges to Authority: Fiction and Film in Contemporary Spain*. London: Tamesis Books.

FISCHER, LUCY (1989), *Shot/Countershot: Film Tradition and Women's Cinema*. London: British Film Institute.

FOUCAULT, MICHEL (1984), *The History of Sexuality: An Introduction*. Harmondsworth: Penguin Books. (First pub. 1976.)

FOWLIE, WALLACE (1963), *Age of Surrealism*. Bloomington: Indiana University Press. (First pub. 1950.)

FREUD, SIGMUND (1979), 'Some Neurotic Mechanisms in Jealousy, Paranoia and Homosexuality', in *On Psychopathology* (Pelican Freud Library, vol. 10). Harmondsworth: Penguin Books, 195–208. (First pub. 1922.)

—— (1981*a*), 'Family Romances', in *On Sexuality* (Pelican Freud Library, vol. 7). Harmondsworth: Penguin Books, 217–26. (First pub. 1909.)

—— (1981*b*), 'Female Sexuality', in *On Sexuality* (Pelican Freud Library, vol. 7). Harmondsworth: Penguin Books, 367–92. (First pub. 1931.)

—— (1981*c*), 'Fetishism', in *On Sexuality* (Pelican Freud Library, vol. 7). Harmondsworth: Penguin Books, 345–58. (First pub. 1927.)

—— (1981*d*), 'The Taboo of Virginity (Contributions to the Psychology of Love III)', in *On Sexuality* (Pelican Freud Library, vol. 7). Harmondsworth: Penguin Books, 261–84. (First pub. 1918.)

—— (1982), *The Interpretation of Dreams* (Pelican Freud Library, vol. 4). Harmondsworth: Penguin Books. (First pub. 1900.)

—— (1983), *Jokes and their Relation to the Unconscious* (Pelican Freud Library, vol. 6). Harmondsworth: Penguin Books. (First pub. 1905.)

—— (1984*a*), 'On Narcissism: An Introduction', in *On Metapsychology* (Pelican Freud Library, vol. 11). Harmondsworth: Penguin Books, 65–97. (First pub. 1914.)

—— (1984*b*), 'The Economic Problem of Masochism', in *On Metapsychology* (Pelican Freud Library, vol. 11). Harmondsworth: Penguin Books, 409–26. (First pub. 1924.)

—— (1985), 'Group Psychology and the Analysis of the Ego', in *Civilization, Society and Religion* (Pelican Freud Library, vol. 12). Harmondsworth: Penguin Books, 91–178. (First pub. 1921.)

—— (1990), 'The "Uncanny" ', in *Art and Literature* (Penguin Freud Library, vol. 14). Harmondsworth: Penguin Books, pp. 339–76. (First pub. 1919.)

FROMM, ERICH (1968), *The Art of Loving*. London: George Allen & Unwin (First pub. 1957.)

FUENTES, CARLOS (1978), 'The Discreet Charm of Luis Buñuel', in Mellen (ed.), 51–71.

FUENTES, VÍCTOR (1993), *Buñuel en México: Iluminaciones sobre una pantalla pobre*. Teruel: Instituto de Estudios Turolenses.

GILBERT, SANDRA, and GUBAR, SUSAN (1979), *The Madwoman in the Attic: The Woman Writer and the Nineteenth-Century Literary Imagination*. New Haven: Yale University Press.

GIRARD, RENÉ (1969), *Deceit, Desire and the Novel: Self and Other in Literary Structure*, trans. Yvonne Freccero. Baltimore and London: Johns Hopkins University Press.

GLEDHILL, CHRISTINE (ed.) (1987), *Home Is Where the Heart Is: Studies in Melodrama and the Woman's Film*. London: British Film Institute.

—— (1988), 'Pleasurable Negotiations', in E. Deidre Pribram (ed.), *Female Spectators: Looking at Film and Television*. London and New York: Verso, 64–89.

—— (ed.) (1991), *Stardom: Industry of Desire*. London and New York: Routledge.

GOFFMAN, ERVING (1975), *Frame Analysis. An Essay on the Organisation of Experience*. Harmondsworth: Penguin Books. (First pub. 1974.)

HASKELL, MOLLY (1987), *From Reverence to Rape: The Treatment of Women in the Movies*. Chicago and London: University of Chicago Press.

HAYMAN, RONALD (1984), *Fassbinder: Film Maker*. London: Weidenfeld & Nicolson.

HIGGINBOTHAM, VIRGINIA (1979), *Luis Buñuel*. Boston: Twayne Publishers.

HORNEY, KAREN (1967), *Feminine Psychology*, ed. with introd. by Harold Kelman. London: Routledge & Kegan Paul.

HORTON, ANDREW (1991), 'Introduction', in Andrew Horton (ed.), *Comedy / Cinema / Theory*. Berkeley, Los Angeles, Oxford: University of California Press, 1–21.

HUTCHINGS, PETER (1993), 'Masculinity and the Horror Film', in Pat Kirkham and Janet Thumim (eds.), *You Tarzan: Masculinity, Movies and Men*. London: Lawrence & Wishart, 84–94.

IRIGARAY, LUCE (1974), *Spéculum de l'autre femme*. Paris: Minuit.

JACKSON, ROSEMARY (1981), *Fantasy: The Literature of Subversion*. London and New York: Methuen.

JUNG, CARL G. (1959), *Collected Works*. Princeton: Princeton University Press.

KAPLAN, E. ANN (1992), *Motherhood and Representation: The Mother in Popular Culture and Melodrama*. London and New York: Routledge.

KAPLAN, LOUISE J. (1993), *Female Perversions: The Temptations of Madame Bovary*. Harmondsworth: Penguin Books. (First pub. 1991.)

KESSEL, JOSEPH (1980), *Belle de jour*. Paris: Gallimard. (First pub. 1928.)

KINDER, MARSHA (1993), *Blood Cinema: The Reconstruction of National Identity in Spain*. Berkeley, Los Angeles, and London: University of California Press.

KING, JOHN (1990), *Magical Reels*. London and New York: Verso.

KLEIN, MELANIE, and RIVIERE, JOAN (1964), *Love, Hate and Reparation*. New York: W. W. Norton & Company.

KOFMAN, SARA (1985), *The Enigma of Woman*, trans. Catherine Porter. Ithaca: Cornell University Press.

KRISTEVA, JULIA (1982), *Powers of Horror: An Essay on Abjection*. New York: Columbia University Press.

KRUTNIK, FRANK (1991), *In a Lonely Street: Film Noir, Genre, Masculinity*. London: Routledge.

LACAN, JACQUES (1970), *Écrits I*. Paris: Éditions du Seuil.

LAVRIN, ASUNCIÓN (1989), 'Sexuality in Colonial Mexico: A Church Dilemma', in Lavrin (ed.), 47–95.

—— (ed.) (1989), *Sexuality and Marriage in Colonial Latin America*. Lincoln, Neb.: University of Nebraska Press.

LOUŸS, PIERRE (1981), *La Femme et le pantin*. Paris: Albin Michel. (First pub. 1898.)

LOVELL, TERRY (1980), *Pictures of Reality: Aesthetics, Politics and Pleasure*. London: British Film Institute.

LUIS DE LEÓN, Fray (1963), *La perfecta casada*. Madrid: Espasa Calpe. (First pub. 1583.)

MACÍAS, ANA (1978), 'Felipe Carrillo Puerto and Women's Liberation in Mexico', in Asunción Lavrin (ed.), *Latin American Women: Historical Perspectives*. Westport, Connecticut, and London: Greenwood Press, 286–301.

MAUPASSANT, GUY DE (1981), *Pierre et Jean*. Paris: Albin Michel. (First pub. 1888.)

MELLEN, JOAN (1977), *Big Bad Wolves: Masculinity in the American Film*. New York: Pantheon.

—— (ed.) (1978), *The World of Luis Buñuel: Essays and Criticism*. New York: Oxford University Press.

MIDDLETON, PETER (1992), *The Inward Gaze: Masculinity and Subjectivity in Modern Culture*. London: Routledge.

MILNE, TOM (1978), 'The Two Chambermaids', in Mellen (ed.), 257–69.

MIRBEAU, OCTAVE (1968), *Le Journal d'une femme de chambre*. Paris: Fasquelle.

MITCHELL, JULIET (1982), *Psychoanalysis and Feminism*. Harmondsworth: Penguin Books. (First pub. 1974.)

MODLESKI, TANIA (1988), *The Women Who Knew Too Much: Hitchcock and Feminist Theory*. London and New York: Methuen.

MOI, TORIL (1985), *Sexual/Textual Politics: Feminist Literary Theory*. London: Methuen.

MOIX, TERENCI (1983), 'Con Buñuel en su casa mexicana', *Fotogramas* (Sept.), 14–15.

MONEGAL, ANTONIO (1993), *Luis Buñuel: de la literatura al cine. Una poética del objeto*. Barcelona: Anthropos.

MORA, CARL J. (1989), *Mexican Cinema: Reflections of a Society 1896–1988*, rev. edn. Berkeley, Los Angeles, London: University of California Press. (First pub. 1982.)

MORIN, EDGAR (1960), *The Stars*. New York: Grove Press.

MORRIS, C. B. (1980), *This Loving Darkness: The Cinema and Spanish Writers, 1920–1936*. Oxford, London: University of Hull.

MYERS, KATHY (1987), 'Towards a Feminist Erotica', in Rosemary Betterton (ed.), *Looking On: Images of Femininity in the Visual Arts and Media*. London and New York: Pandora, 189–202.

NEALE, STEVE (1983), 'Masculinity as Spectacle', *Screen*, 24/6, pp. 2–12.

NIEDERGANG, MARCEL (1971), *The Twenty Latin Americas 1*, trans. Rosemary Sheed (Pelican Latin American Library). Harmondsworth: Penguin Books. (First pub. 1962.)

NOWELL-SMITH, GEOFFREY (1987), 'Minnelli and Melodrama', in Gledhill (ed.), 170–4.

OMS, MARCEL (1987), 'Une problématique de l'enfance', *Co-textes*, 12 (May), 111–20.

ORTEGA Y GASSET, JOSÉ (1976), *La deshumanización del arte y otros ensayos de estética*. Madrid: Ediciones de la Revista de Occidente. (First pub. 1925.)

PAZ, OCTAVIO (1949), *Libertad bajo palabra*. Mexico, Madrid, Buenos Aires: Fondo de Cultura Económica.

—— (1991), *El laberinto de la soledad*. México, Madrid, Buenos Aires: Fondo de Cultura Económica. (First pub. 1950.)

PÉREZ TURRENT, TOMÁS, and DE LA COLINA, JOSÉ (1993), *Buñuel por Buñuel*. Madrid: Plot.

PERISTIANY, J. G. (ed.) (1965), *Honour and Shame: The Values of Mediterranean Society*. London: Weidenfeld & Nicolson.

PESCATELLO, ANN (ed.) (1979), *Female and Male in Latin America*. London: Pittsburgh University Press.

POE, EDGAR ALLAN (1965), *Tales of Mystery and Imagination*. London: Pan Books. (First pub. 1960.)

PUNTER, DAVID (1980), *The Literature of Terror*. London: Longman.

RABINOW, PAUL (ed.) (1991), *The Foucault Reader: An Introduction to Foucault's Thought*. Harmondsworth: Penguin Books. (First pub. 1984.)

REQUENA, JESÚS G. (1980), 'Dios, Familia, Propiedad', *Contracampo*, 16 (Oct.–Nov.), 16–21.

RICH, ADRIENNE (1981), *Of Woman Born: Motherhood as Experience and Institution*. London: Virago. (First pub. 1976.)

RODOWICK, D. N. (1991), *The Difficulty of Difference: Psychoanalysis, Sexual Difference and Film Theory*. New York: Routledge.

ROUGEMONT, DENIS DE (1956), *Passion and Society*, trans. Montgomery Belgion. London: Faber and Faber. (First pub. 1940.)

RUBIO BARCIA, JOSÉ (1992), *Con Luis Buñuel en Hollywood y después*. Sada, A Coruña: Ediciós do Castro.

RUCAR DE BUÑUEL, JEANNE (1991), *Memorias de una mujer sin piano* (written by Marisol Martín del Campo). Madrid: Alianza Editorial. (First pub. 1990.)

RULFO, JUAN (1973), *Pedro Páramo*. Mexico: Fondo de Cultura Económica. (First pub. 1955.)

RUTHERFORD, JONATHAN (1992), *Men's Silences: Predicaments in Masculinity*. London and New York: Routledge.

SAID, EDWARD W. (1987), *Orientalism*. Harmondsworth: Penguin Books. (First pub. 1978.)

SÁNCHEZ VIDAL, AGUSTÍN (1984), *Luis Buñuel: obra cinematográfica*. Madrid: Ediciones J. C.

—— (1988), *Buñuel, Lorca, Dalí: el enigma sin fin*. Barcelona: Planeta.

SANDRO, PAUL (1987), *Diversions of Pleasure: Luis Buñuel and the Crises of Desire*. Columbus: Ohio State University Press.

SARRIS, ANDREW (1971), 'Belle de Jour', in Buñuel, (1971*a*), 21–8.

SAURA, CARLOS (1993) 'Voces lejanas', *El Mundo, Cinelandia*, Año I, no. 11 (24 July), 1.

SAWICKI, JANA (1991), *Displacing Foucault: Feminism, Power, and the Body*. New York and London: Routledge.

SEDGWICK, EVE KOSOFSKY (1985), *Between Men: English Literature and Male Homosocial Desire*. New York: Columbia University Press.

SEIDLER, VICTOR J. (1991), 'Reason, Desire, and Male Sexuality', in Caplan (ed.), 82–112.

—— (1994), *Unreasonable Men: Masculinity and Social Theory*. London and New York: Routledge.

SONTAG, SUSAN (1982), 'The Pornographic Imagination', in Georges Bataille, *Story of the Eye*. Harmondsworth: Penguin Books, 83–118. (First pub. 1967.)

STEIN, ELLIOT (1971), 'Buñuel's Golden Bowl', in Buñuel (1971 *a*), 12–20. (First pub. 1968.)

STEVENS, EVELYN P. (1979), ' "Marianismo": The Other Face of "Machismo" in Latin America', in Pescatello (ed.), 89–101. (First pub. 1973.)

STUDLAR, GAYLYN (1988), *In the Realm of Pleasure: Von Sternberg, Dietrich, and the Masochistic Aesthetic*. Urbana, Chicago: University of Illinois Press.

TAMBLING, JEREMY (1990), *Confession, Sexuality, Sin, the Subject*. Manchester and New York: Manchester University Press.

TANNER, TONY (1981), *Adultery in the Novel: Contract and Transgression*. Baltimore and London: Johns Hopkins University Press. (First pub. 1979.)

TARANGER, MARIE-CLAUDE (1990), *Luis Buñuel: Le Jeu et la loi*. Saint-Denis: Presses Universitaires de Vincennes.

TURIM, M. (1989), *Flashback in Film*. London: Routledge.

VEBLEN, THORSTEIN (1970), *The Theory of the Leisure Class: An Economic Study of Institutions*. London: Unwin Books. (First pub. 1899.)

VINCENDEAU, GINETTE (1993), 'Fire and Ice', *Sight and Sound*, 3/4 (April), 20–2.

VIVES, JUAN LUIS (1944), *Instrucción de la mujer cristiana*. Buenos Aires, Mexico: Espasa Calpe.

WARNER, MARINA (1983), *Joan of Arc: The Image of Female Heroism*. Harmondsworth: Penguin Books. (First pub. 1981.)

WELLDON, ESTELA V. (1992), *Mother, Madonna, Whore: The Idealization and Denigration of Motherhood*. London and New York: Guilford Press. (First pub. 1988.)

WILLIAMS, LINDA (1987), ' "Something Else Besides a Mother": *Stella Dallas* and the Maternal Melodrama', in Gledhill (ed.), 339–49.

—— (1989), *Hard Core: Power, Pleasure, and the 'Frenzy of the Visible'*. Berkeley, Los Angeles: University of California Press.

—— (1992), *Figures of Desire: A Theory and Analysis of Surrealist Film*. Berkeley, Los Angeles, Oxford: University of California Press. (First pub. 1981.)

WOOD, MICHAEL (1981), 'The Corruption of Accidents', in Andrew S. Horton and Joan Magretta (eds.), *Modern European Filmmakers and the Art of Adaptation*. New York: Frederick Ungar Publishing, 329–43.

—— (1992), 'Double Lives', *Sight and Sound*, 1/9 (Jan.), 20–3.

ZARETSKY, ELI (1976), *Capitalism, the Family and Personal Life*. London: Pluto Press.

Index of films, directors, authors, actors, and sources